The New Mutualism in Public Policy

Recently, a new word has entered the English vocabulary – demutualisation. Building societies and mutual insurers are being dissolved so their members can get at the assets and make a 'windfall' profit. At the same time, 'new mutualism' has been proposed as the next big idea for the UK New Labour government; locally-owned credit banks, mutual leisure trusts, housing co-ops, community associations, are promoted for their capacity to include people who are socially and economically excluded. This book asks whether demutualisation matters, and whether the new mutualist rhetoric has any substance.

A mutual is a type of business that is owned and – in the theory at least – controlled by its customer members rather than by investors. Is it an alternative to global capitalism, or merely the tail end of an old institution that has outlasted its usefulness? To answer this question the authors introduce the established types of mutual – building societies, credit unions, housing co-ops, consumer co-ops, mutual insurance, farmer co-ops – and examine their strengths and weaknesses. They argue that, given a fair chance, mutuals can run public services better than local authorities and privatized utilities better than investors-owned companies, and can create local economies that counteract the drift towards globalisation. However, they can only do so if they take seriously their nature as member-owned businesses, putting first the interest of key stakeholders such as workers and consumers. They must become in practice what they are in principle – a blend of business and democracy.

The book will be useful to anyone concerned with stakeholding, corporate governance, business ethics, social exclusion, government regulation of markets, public service management, local economic development, the design of complex organisations, and participatory democracy.

Johnston Birchall is a Senior Lecturer in Social Policy at Stirling University, Scotland. His publications include *Building Communities: The Co-operative Way* (1988), *Co-op: The People's Business* (1994) and *The International Co-operative Movement* (1997).

Routledge Studies in Business Organizations and Networks

1 **Democracy and Efficiency in the Economic Enterprise**
   Edited by Ugo Pagano and Robert Rowthorn

2 **Towards a Competence Theory of the Firm**
   Edited by Nicolai J. Foss and Christian Knudsen

3 **Uncertainty and Economic Evolution**
   Essays in honour of Armen A. Alchian
   Edited by John R. Lott Jr

4 **The End of the Professions?**
   The restructuring of professional work
   Edited by Jane Broadbent, Michael Dietrich and Jennifer Roberts

5 **Shopfloor Matters**
   Labor-management relations in twentieth-century American manufacturing
   David Fairris

6 **The Organisation of the Firm**
   International business perspectives
   Edited by Ram Mudambi and Martin Ricketts

7 **Organizing Industrial Activities Across Firm Boundaries**
   Anna Dubois

8 **Economic Organisation, Capabilities and Coordination**
   Edited by Nicolai Foss and Brian J. Loasby

9 **The Changing Boundaries of the Firm**
   Explaining evolving inter-firm relations
   Edited by Massimo G. Colombo

10 **Authority and Control in Modern Industry**
   Theoretical and empirical perspectives
   Edited by Paul L. Robertson

11 **Interfirm Networks**
   Organization and industrial competitiveness
   Edited by Anna Grandori

12 **Privatization and Supply Chain Management**
   Andrew Cox, Lisa Harris and David Parker

13 **The Governance of Large Technical Systems**
   Edited by Olivier Coutard

14 **Stability and Change in High-Tech Enterprises**
   Organisational practices and routines
   Neil Costello

15 **The New Mutualism in Public Policy**
   Edited by Johnston Birchall

16 **An Econometric Analysis of the Real Estate Market and Investment**
   Edited by Peijie Wang

The New Mutualism in Public Policy

Edited by
Johnston Birchall

London and New York

First published 2001
by Routledge
11 New Fetter Lane, London EC4P 4EE

Simultaneously published in the USA and Canada
by Routledge
29 West 35th Street, New York, NY 10001

Routledge is an imprint of the Taylor & Francis Group

Typeset in by Keyword Publishing Services Ltd
Printed and bound in Great Britain by St Edmundsbury Press, Bury St Edmunds, Suffolk

British Library Cataloguing in Publication Data
A catalogue record for this book is available from the British Library

Library of Congress Cataloging in Publication Data

Birchall, Johnston
   The new mutualism in public policy / Johnston Birchall.
      p. cm – (Routledge studies in business organizations and networks; 15)
      Includes bibiliographical references and index.
      1. Mutualism – Great Britain. 2. Mutualism. 3. Cooperative societies – Great Britain. 4. Cooperative societies. I. Title. II. Routledge studies in business organization and networks; 15

HD3485.A4 B57 2001
334'.0941–dc21   00-065331

ISBN 0-415-24130-8

Contents

List of figures   vii
List of tables   viii
Notes on the contributors   ix

Introduction   1
JOHNSTON BIRCHALL

1 **The economics of mutuality: a perpective on
   UK building societies**   14
   LEIGH DRAKE AND DAVID T. LLEWELLYN

2 **Mutuality through credit unions:
   a cross-national approach**   41
   OLIVE McCARTHY, ROBERT BRISCOE AND MICHAEL WARD

3 **Housing co-operatives and social exclusion**   60
   DAVID RODGERS

4 **Consumer co-operatives in retrospect and prospect**   72
   JOHNSTON BIRCHALL

5 **Mutuality and public services: lessons from
   the 'new leisure trusts'**   95
   RICHARD SIMMONS

6 **Mutuality in insurance and social security: retrospect
   and prospect**   118
   DEBORAH MABBETT

7 **Farmer co-operatives: organisational models and their
   business environment**   132
   JERKER NILSSON

8 **Mutuals in regional economic development: Mondragon and Desjardins**   155
RACE MATHEWS

9 **The competitive advantages of stakeholder mutuals**   171
SHANN TURNBULL

10 **Member participation in mutuals: a theoretical model**   202
JOHNSTON BIRCHALL AND RICHARD SIMMONS

11 **The new mutualism and Labour's Third Way**   226
STEPHEN YEO

Conclusion: the future of mutuality   243
JOHNSTON BIRCHALL

Index   251

List of figures

1.1   Relationship between annual growth rate of a financial mutual
     and required rate of return on assets   20
5.1   A downward service spiral   108
9.1   Anglo unitary control compared with
     Japanese distributed control   178
9.2   Information and control architecture
     of Mondragon Co-operatives   184
9.3   Stakeholder mutual information and
     control architecture   189
10.1 A hierarchy of member involvement   206
10.2 Preconditions for participation   208
10.3 Individualistic variables affecting participation   210
10.4 Mutualistic variables affecting participation   213
10.5 Feedback between mutualistic variables and
     participation, and synergy between each other   217
10.6 Individual attitudes to participation   219
10.7 A four-stage model of mobilisation of members   220

List of tables

1.1	Required ROA for mutual building societies	22
1.2	Required ROA for banks	23
2.1	Some features of the typology of credit union development (1)	43
2.2	Some features of the typology of credit union development (2)	44
5.1	Types of public sector reform	97
7.1	Main structural characteristics of EU agricultural co-operatives	135
7.2	Characteristics of agricultural co-operative models	138
7.3	Different co-operative organisational models' suitability for different strategic choice	144
7.4	Property rights and agency theoretical problems in traditional co-operatives with different business strategies	146
9.1	Typology of firms discussed	172
9.2	Examples of the different types of firms discussed	173
9.3	Corrupting powers of a unitary board	175
9.4	Human constraints in transacting bytes	180

Notes on the contributors

Johnston Birchall is a senior lecturer in Social Policy at Stirling University. Editor of the Journal of Co-operative Studies, consultant to the International Labour Office and others on co-operative development, his publications include *Building Communities, the Co-operative Way* (1988), *Co-op: the People's Business* (1994), and *The International Co-operative Movement* (1997).

Robert Briscoe lectures and researches in the areas of co-operative management and organisational development. He is currently Programme Director at the Centre for Co-operative Studies, University College Cork, and senior lecturer in the Department of Food Business and Development.

Leigh Drake is Professor of Monetary Economics at Loughborough University. He has published widely in academic and professional journals, and is the author of the book *The Building Society Industry in Transition* (1989). He has provided consultancy services to a number of banks and building societies. In 1997 he was commissioned, jointly with Professor David Llewellyn, to write a series of papers for the Building Societies Association on the subject of mutuality and the future of building societies.

David T. Llewellyn is Professor of Money and Banking at Loughborough University. He has recently been a Public Interest Director of the Personal Investment Authority and is a member of the International Advisory Boards of the NCR Corporation and the Italian Bankers Association. He has researched in the area of mutuality and has been a consultant to several banks and building societies in various countries.

Deborah Mabbett is a lecturer in the Department of Government at Brunel University. Her main research interest is the comparative cross-national study of social security, with a particular focus on institutional issues.

Olive McCarthy is a doctoral candidate and lecturer in the Department of Food Business and Development at University College Cork and researcher with the Centre for Co-operative Studies. Her main research and publication interests lie in the area of credit unions and other forms of co-operatives. She is also actively involved in the Irish credit union movement.

Race Mathews is a senior research fellow in the Business and Economics faculty at Monash University, Australia, and a former federal MP, state MP and minister, municipal councillor, and board member and chairman of the Waverley Credit Union Co-operative. His publications include *Australia's First Fabians: Middle-Class Radicals, Labour Activists and the Early Labour Movement* (1994) and *Jobs of Our Own: Building a Stakeholder Society* (1999).

Jerker Nilsson is Professor of Business Administration at the Swedish University of Agricultural Sciences. He has edited *Strategies and Structures in the Agro-Food Industries* (1997), and contributed to *Agricultural Co-operatives in the European Union* (1997). His research concerns the market adaptation of farmer co-operatives.

David Rodgers is Executive Director of CDS Co-operatives, represents the co-operative housing sector nationally and internationally, and acts as administrator for the All Party Parliamentary Group on Housing Co-operatives in the UK Parliament. Publications include *Co-operative Housing: realising the potential* (1998) and *New Mutualism: the third estate* (1999).

Richard Simmons is a research fellow at Stirling University, working on an Economic and Social Research Council-funded project, 'A theoretical model of what motivates public service users to participate'. His research interests in the governance and delivery of public services derive from lengthy prior experience as a senior public service manager.

Shann Turnbull is a founding member and past President of the Australian Employee Ownership Association and a pioneer in the study and teaching of corporate governance. His publications include *Democratising the wealth of nations* (1975), Australian *Parliamentary Papers on Aboriginal Development in the Northern Territory* (1977/8), *New Economics for a New World Democracy* (1994), and *Building Sustainable Communities* (co-author, 1989).

Michael Ward is a lecturer in Co-operative Business in the Department of Food Business and Development at University College Cork and Acting Director of the Centre for Co-operative Studies. He is academic director of programmes in co-operative business at undergraduate and postgraduate levels, including distance learning. He has researched and published in a number of areas including agricultural co-operatives, community co-operatives and credit unions.

Stephen Yeo is a Visiting Professor at the Centre for Civil Society at the London School of Economics. He chairs the Management Board of the Co-operative College and is chair of Co-operative Futures. He was Principal of Ruskin College from 1989–1997, and before that a social historian at the University of Sussex. He edited *New Views of Co-operation* (1988), and re-interpreted the life and work of a co-operative pioneer '*Who Was JTW Mitchell?*' (1995).

Introduction

Johnston Birchall

This book arises out of an attempt to understand two contradictions and a paradox. The *first contradiction* is that in the last few years in the UK the New Labour government has become more and more sympathetic to the idea of mutuality, while doing almost nothing to prevent the erosion of the mutual business sector through demutualisation. In a pamphlet published by the Co-operative Party, a well-known journalist and political commentator, Peter Kellner, suggests that New Labour should drop the word 'socialism' in favour of a new label, 'mutualism'. The prime minister, Tony Blair, had talked about a 'third way', and Kellner argues persuasively that 'new mutualism' encapsulates what the third way really means. Although he talks broadly of corporate responsibility and business ethics, he expressly argues that 'a thriving financial industry needs mutual building societies and insurance companies owned by their members' (1998, p15). Tony Blair has written a foreword to the pamphlet. Similarly, in the second pamphlet in the same series, another well-known journalist, Ian Hargreaves, analyses the rhetoric of New Labour's 'third way' and concludes that 'the interface between this civic liberalism and the co-operative tradition could hardly be clearer' (1999, p14).

Blair himself has recognised in one of his speeches that 'The Labour Party at times forgot its own roots in self-help, friendly societies, co-operatives and voluntary organisations' (quoted in Hargreaves, 1999, p12). Yet when it comes to supporting the existing mutual and co-operative sectors, the record has fallen far short of the rhetoric. When the government was elected in 1997, the UK Co-operative Council (the umbrella organisation for all co-operative sectors) prepared a Co-operatives Bill that modernises co-operative law and provides a much clearer set of criteria for what constitutes a co-operative. The government has consistently failed to find time for the bill in its legislative programme. Even more seriously, very little has been done to stem the tide of demutualisations, other than a raising of the threshold needed by building society members to force a vote; carpetbaggers have got round this restriction by opening websites on which members can sign up in large numbers. The rhetoric of mutuality does not seem to extend into any real commitment towards existing mutuals.

There are two possible explanations for this contradiction. One is that when the government first came to power the intellectual climate even among its own advisers was prejudiced against mutuals. There was a feeling, cultivated in the City, that they were an outdated form that ought to be superseded by the more modern joint stock company. Then, when the ensuing debate led to a reappraisal of the strengths and weaknesses of the mutual form, the argument became fashionable that organisational form is no longer important, and that competition and regulation are the main guarantees of organisational performance. It has taken a long time for advocates of mutuality to challenge and begin to change this intellectual climate, and in the meantime most of the large mutuals have been converted.

The second explanation is that the image of mutuals is a poor one, because they have failed to demonstrate that they are more efficient or ethically superior to their competitors. Mutual insurers are implicated in the pensions 'mis-selling' scandal of the early 1990s, in which hundreds of thousands of people were persuaded to get out of occupational pensions in favour of personal pensions that were less productive. Building societies were criticised for being ruthless in evicting mortgage-defaulters during the downturn in the property market that followed the boom of the late 1980s; for the first few years of the 1990s around 50,000 households were losing their homes each year. A further criticism was that the societies were selling the properties at auction for low prices, using insurance cover to indemnify themselves but leaving the mortgage-holders with even more debts. In the aftermath of these practices, it is no wonder that ethical appeals to vote for mutuality have sounded hollow.

The *second contradiction* is that, when mutual building societies and mutual insurers are under siege from 'carpetbaggers' who want to force a vote to demutualise and make windfall gains, they have to try to persuade their member-owners to vote against their immediate interest and preserve the mutual nature of the business. Yet these mutuals, in common with mutuals the world over, long ago lost touch with their members as members, treating them merely as customers and playing down their democratic rights to be involved. They have a large credibility gap that cannot be filled in time to influence a vote. Even when they try to reach out to their members through publicity campaigns, the message tends to be garbled. Boards do not want to say boldly that members are the owners and ultimate controllers of the business, and that the board holds its mandate from the members. Over the years they have argued successfully that the members can leave the running of the business to them, with only a poorly attended annual meeting to ratify their appointments. Their attempts to communicate the meaning of mutuality have demonstrated some equivocation, timidity and confusion.

The *paradox* is that mutuals and co-operatives are rediscovering the benefits of mutuality, not from first principles or from their own experience, but from the strategies of their competitors. Investor-owned businesses, openly envious of the advantages that having a membership base might bring, have been trying to capture these advantages by inviting their customers to join a club. Airlines and retail chains in particular have been developing memberships that reinforce brand identities, reward customers' repeat business with discounts and special services, and attempt to engender a feeling of loyalty; all without giving away any ownership or control rights. The best example is the loyalty cards issued by retail chains. In the 1970s, consumer co-operatives, both in the UK and in several other European countries, abandoned the paying of dividends to members and began a policy of downplaying membership in favour of treating everyone as a customer. When electronic cards became available they could have reinstated the dividend, but chose not to do so until all their major competitors had issued their own loyalty cards, by which time they had lost all competitive advantage from being a mutual (Birchall, 1987). In the book, several of our authors will, directly or indirectly, be examining the two contradictions and the paradox outlined above.

The meaning of mutuality

So what do we mean by mutuality? There are three meanings that are also levels of analysis. At the top level we have a particular way of understanding political values; a 'doctrine that individual and collective well-being is obtainable only by mutual dependence' (Kellner, 1998, p7). Here, mutuality connects up with some familiar communitarian arguments about society being organic, individual potential being dependent on connection to a community, rights being balanced by duties, and so on. The particular contribution that mutuality might make has yet to be worked out. Kellner suggests that it mediates between the three basic principles of liberty, equality and fraternity: they 'can be achieved only if we develop a culture of mutual responsibility' (1998, p9). More exactly, it might be used as a (gender neutral) synonym for fraternity. We could then take up an idea suggested by Halsey, that mutuality is the sense of common citizenship that leads people not to press too far their claims for personal liberty (in particular the liberty to hold very unequal wealth) and to agree on a certain amount of basic equality of condition among citizens (Halsey, 1978). It is a kind of honest broker between the claims of liberty and equality, supplying the goodwill needed to secure people's assent to political decisions that are not in their individual short-term interest. We might see mutuality as a value that, if held by enough people, overcomes the 'collective goods' problem specified by rational choice theorists. It is essentially a sociological or social psychological concept that measures something essential to the long-run stability and cohesion of modern societies. In this book we shall not be exploring this high level usage of the term, but will be keeping it in mind as a set of powerful arguments that could be used to value – and evaluate the performance of – mutual businesses.

At the middle level, mutuality refers to a particular way of solving the 'agency problem' faced by all complex organisations. Given that there are a number of stakeholder interests in any business or association, the question is, which of these will have primacy in the goals the organisation pursues, and how will the benefits and costs of the organisation's activities be shared out? A related problem concerns how the organisation will be regulated by government, in order to protect the interests of weaker stakeholders and the public interest. Mutuals eliminate one important stakeholder – the investor-owner – in favour of one of the other stakeholders, usually the customer, who becomes both user and joint owner of the business. Some commentators stretch this term 'user' to include workers, and call worker co-operatives mutuals. This goes beyond most people's understanding of the term, but it raises an interesting issue for the future. New types of co-operative are being developed in which both customers and workers are involved: Swedish child care co-ops, and the Eroski retail chain in the Mondragon group are good examples. Mutuality may be redefined not as customer ownership but as stakeholder ownership by any of those who are beneficiaries *other than* a separate group of investors. In this book, most authors will be taking the narrow definition, but Turnbull's discussion of 'stakeholder mutuals' will be exploring this new, wider meaning.

Several of our authors will be exploring the agency and regulation issues that arise when there is no separate group of investors. Ideally, mutuals that are controlled by their users to meet their own needs should cut down the agency costs, because they do not have a separate group of investors with different priorities, and they can exercise indirect democratic control over their managers. This should give their business a strong sense of direction and incentives to succeed. Also, ideally, because the aims of the business and of the main beneficiaries are in line, there should be less need for government regulation; mutuals will be largely self-regulating. As we shall see, the divergences from this ideal model are considerable, and our authors will be analysing the ways in which established mutual sectors have 'fallen from grace'. In the conclusion, we shall be asking whether the potential offered by the ideal model of mutuality can ever be realised in practice.

The third definition is at the base level, where actual businesses that call themselves mutuals operate. Here, we are interested in identifying the characteristics of mutual sectors, the history of their development, their current extent in different countries, their legislative and regulatory frameworks, and so on. At this level, we want to identify the strengths and weaknesses of individual businesses, the blocks to further development of the form, the competitive conditions under which they operate, their managerial cultures, the extent of participation of members, and so on.

Some of our authors provide this kind of analysis, but to do it properly we need a book dedicated to describing each particular form in detail, and with a good deal of cross-national comparative analysis. This author's book on co-operatives is a good example of this genre, but it is limited to those kinds of mutual that regard themselves as part of the co-operative movement (Birchall, 1997). A more comprehensive text is needed.

Such a book would require tight control by the editor, with authors working to a schedule that promotes maximum comparability between the chapters. However, the subject is a new one, and too much editorial control at this stage would be inappropriate; after all, we are only just beginning to define what the subject is about. This book does two things well. First, it identifies and provides an introduction to the main forms of mutual business. Chapter 1 covers financial service mutuals and in particular building societies; Chapter 2, credit unions; Chapter 3, housing co-operatives; Chapter 4, consumer co-ops; Chapter 5, mutual providers of public services; Chapter 6, friendly societies and insurance mutuals; and Chapter 7, agricultural co-operatives. Chapter 8 focuses on regional clusters of different types of mutual that are agents of regional economic development. Chapter 9 considers multi-stakeholder mutuals and brings in the interests of workers. Second, the book explores most of the key themes concerning the survival of mutuals, their comparative advantages and disadvantages in their markets, ethical arguments concerning their desirability as member-owned businesses, and their future vulnerability to demutualisation and potential for growth.

Taking the subject matter of the book as a whole, would it be claiming too much to see the outlines of a new, multi-disciplinary field of study, that we might label 'mutuality studies'? This is a question we shall return to in the conclusion.

Synopsis of the book

The first chapter is provided jointly by Leigh Drake and David Llewellyn, who begin by charting the trend towards demutualisation of building societies and mutual insurance companies in the UK. They consider the main alleged weakness of mutuals: that their agency costs are higher because customer-owners have less influence on managers than do plc shareholders (there is greater scope for managers to seek rewards for themselves than for their owners). To answer this question, they provide a useful summary of the literature on agency costs, showing that, if we conceive of a firm as a set of contracts between stakeholders, all firms face such problems. They suggest that financial service mutuals are better able to address these than are their non-financial counterparts. They have the advantage that the residual claims in mutuals are redeemable on demand; owner-customers can discipline the managers by withdrawing their funds or switching mortgages to a different company.

They cite American evidence that stock companies may solve the agency problem more effectively than do mutuals, but that they face another, even greater, problem concerning conflicts of interest between debt and equity holders. Another control mechanism in financial mutuals is that, because they do not have access to external equity finance, they are more reliant on retained profits to fund their growth. Managers have an incentive to aim for growth, so they have an interest in maximising profits. We might question whether this was always true. In the days before deregulation, in the absence of strong competitive pressures, building society managers had a relatively easy life. There is an old joke about managers following the 'rule of three'; they borrowed at 1 per cent, lent at 2 per cent and were 'on the golf course by three'. The authors show how increased competition eliminates managerial complacency.

They take this argument further, going so far as to declare 'the degree of competition in a market is more important than organisational or corporate form in terms of influencing firms' objectives and strategy'. This is an uncomfortable truth for those who wish to argue that mutuals are inherently superior to 'capitalist' businesses. Later in this book, other authors who are considering mutuals in different sectors reach similar conclusions. There is even a technical term – 'isomorphism' – for the process by which, under competitive pressures, consumer co-ops become almost indistinguishable from other retailers (see Birchall in Chapter 4).

There are some more positive arguments for mutuals. Financial mutuals have a particular advantage: the absence of external shareholders can be deemed to be an inherent efficiency advantage. In a closely argued analysis, they find that the 'margin advantage' means that mutual building societies do have the potential to remain a powerful competitive force, provided that the sector remains large enough. The problem is that this margin advantage leads, in a not very competitive market, to their being able to build up large reserves of spare cash. This was what happened in the UK in the 1980s before deregulation; they explain that, 'As reserves were built up, the implicit or embedded value to the owners was being steadily increased even if they were unaware of it'.

This is the 'Achilles heel', or fatal weakness, of the mutual model. Because the company's shares are not traded, large reserves can be built up without this being reflected in the market value of the business. There *are* ways of releasing this built-up value without dissolving the business: increase margins by lowering interest rates to borrowers and increasing them to savers, or give members an annual loyalty bonus. Yet building societies did not do this, and so some members looked to conversion as another way of releasing this embedded value to owners. Put this way, conversion appears to be logical, but the authors raise the important ethical question of who owns the reserves. They conclude that the current generation of owners is appropriating value built up over many years by previous generations of owners. This is, in fact, the main ethical case for opposing demutualisation.

Drake and Llewellyn explain that, by the time some societies began to use their reserves more creatively, it was too late for over 70 per cent of the sector that had already demutualised. This is an important issue for other types of mutual as well, and we shall be returning to it with a fuller discussion in the book's Conclusion. One of the advantages of mutuals is that they tend to adopt a lower risk profile than their competitors, the major banks. They are not subject to the asset substitution agency problem, and are therefore not subject to the 'herd instinct' that compels banks to enter risky markets all at the same time. This leads the authors to recommend that the financial system should be 'characterised by a mixed array of corporate structures', because this will be inherently more stable than one composed of only investor-owned banks. (Recent evidence bears this out: borrowers who have received windfall payments from the demutualisation of their societies have, in increasing numbers, been switching their mortgages to one of the remaining mutuals, because it is thought to be safer.) They come close to suggesting that the less risky the business the more appropriate is the mutual form, and vice versa. However, we might also propose that demutualisation will continue to occur, not because this leads to a more appropriate form of organisation for a particular kind of business but because of the short-term opportunism of current owner-members.

The second chapter is by Olive McCarthy, Robert Briscoe and Michael Ward, who provide a worldwide perspective on the credit union movement, a significant and rapidly growing form of mutual business. After providing an introduction to the subject, they use two 'stages of growth' typologies suggested by experts in the field to describe the movement in Ireland, Britain, the USA, Canada and developing countries. These stages are 'nascent, transitional and mature' and 'formative, national and international'. From the case studies of different countries they derive some thought-provoking lessons that credit union leaders must learn if they are to meet the challenges of intensified competition with conventional banks. The national movements must become more cohesive, the right kind of legislative framework is needed, a good relationship with government must be fostered, development should be as much as possible from the bottom up, imbalances in the distribution of membership should be examined, and so on.

Demutualisation has not yet become an issue (though this author is aware of one or two attempts to demutualise Australian credit unions), but safeguards against demutualisation of credit unions should be put in place. One lesson that will also be emphasised in later chapters, by authors dealing with other types of mutual, is that they need to be differentiated from conventional financial institutions if they are to succeed, and 'project themselves as a movement'. Last, they raise the perennial problem of member participation, and say volunteerism should be encouraged. (In a later chapter, Birchall and Simmons suggest how this might be achieved.)

Chapter 3 is provided by David Rodgers, who argues that co-operatives are an essential means in the New Labour government's policy of combating social exclusion. He provides examples of successful schemes, and reviews the by now quite substantial amount of evidence on the benefits of co-operatives. The conclusion is that 'applying the principles of mutuality in housing through the positive promotion of housing co-operatives and other community-led housing providers unlocks the potential of socially excluded communities in a way that is of benefit to the whole of society'. The significance of co-ops is that they go beyond the conventional benefits of improved management and maintenance of housing estates. They also provide the individual benefits of learning new skills and developing latent talents among tenants, and social benefits created by co-operatives that foster informal social support networks that previously did not exist. They build up social capital, provide opportunities for informal learning, and strengthen democracy.

Chapter 4, by Johnston Birchall, explores the subject of consumer co-operatives. He begins by outlining their origins in attempts by consumers to protect themselves against monopolies and adulteration of food, and shows how the 'Rochdale system' spread all round the world. After tracing the growth of the co-operative movement, he shows how it declined in the postwar period almost everywhere under pressure from intensified competition. Noting the exceptions to this (Japan in particular), he then evaluates the performance of co-ops externally in relation to their competitors, and internally in relation to co-operative principles. A short case study is then provided of the attempted demutualisation of the largest consumer co-operative, the Co-operative Wholesale Society (CWS), and its aftermath in attempts to shore up the sector in the UK. From the literature, three types of argument for the continued existence of consumer co-ops are identified: derived from ideologies; from co-operative principles; and from theories of market failure. The conclusion is that, while reforms have been significant, they have not gone far enough to ensure the loyalty of members in the event of further attempts at demutualisation.

Richard Simmons analyses in Chapter 5 the current wave of devolution of local authority services in Britain to independent provider agencies. He begins by describing the process of public-sector reform that has been common to most Western European countries since the 1980s. It is a process by which public services have been reorganised and restructured away from the previous provider-dominated bureaucratic form of admin-istration towards more flexible forms of organisation. Devolution of services to independent provider agencies has become possible, and with this, new opportunities for the growth of co-operative and mutual structures in the provision of public services.

Housing co-operatives are one beneficiary of this change, along with child care co-ops, and various kinds of health and social service provider co-ops. Another example has been the transfer of public sector leisure services in Britain to trusts, some of which are constituted as charities, and others as stakeholder co-ops in which the worker interest predominates. By analysing the nature of the pressures on local authorities, Simmons shows how devolution to these new agencies has secured some financial and managerial advantages and has led to improved performance. For instance, the quality of management has benefited from the 'single-issue focus' that transfer has provided. Financial results have been so good that local authorities have been able to reduce their annual grants, while trusts have been able to resist commercialisation and remain committed to the pursuit of social objectives.

It is too early to say whether the co-operative form of trust is better than the charitable form. However, he identifies a need for greater clarity in accountability between the authority and the trust, the need for 'trust relationships' (in the sense of trusting one another without becoming complacent), and a need to develop the fuller involvement and participation of service users and their local communities. There are opportunities here for the unique advantages provided by multi-stakeholder organisations, and in particular those that can draw on co-operative principles for their organisational culture. The discussion of multi-stakeholding leads into some theorising about agency and regulation problems that could usefully be referred back to Drake and Llewellyn's work on building societies.

Deborah Mabbett, in Chapter 6, considers the past history and future prospects of insurance mutuals. Insurance against life's risks can be provided in three ways: by mutuals; by commercial companies; and by the state. She recounts how the mutual sector, which had been predominant in the provision of sickness benefits, was from 1911 onwards brought more and more under state control, until in the post-1945 system it was excluded altogether from social security provision. (This explains why the friendly society sector is only a shadow of its former self. From more than 18,000 they have reduced to less than 300 societies.) Her analysis shows that the societies had the disadvantage (from the state's point of view) of having an incentive to exclude the most risky customers, compared to the large, commercial insurers. Their advantages were that they were able to top up benefits from their surpluses, and they were genuine working-class institutions that fostered social solidarity and participatory democracy. However, under state subsidy and regulation, they began to lose their convivial character, and when they were finally excluded from state welfare provision the argument had been lost.

Switching to the present day, Mabbett considers the current relationship between mutuals, investor-owned providers and government pensions policy. Like Drake and Llewellyn, she examines the agency costs and corporate governance problems of mutuals compared to plcs, concluding that both forms experience these problems, hence both were implicated in the pensions mis-selling scandal of the early 1990s. When the government wanted to introduce 'stakeholder pensions' to encourage low earners to top up state pensions with a private pension, two different options emerged. The Treasury wanted the industry to be regulated to promote the provision of simple, transparent pension products, while the Department of Social Security supported the idea of mutual pensions based on 'affinity organisations' (a similar idea to the 'common bond' in credit unions). It looks as if the first of these will win out over the mutual alternative.

Mabbett goes on to explain that in both cases, the postwar takeover by the state, and the current preference for competition over mutuality, the fate of mutual financial institutions is the product of two sets of processes:

> On one side, competition and the emphasis on consumer choice undermines the salience of mechanisms to give contributors a voice in the management of financial service providers. On the other side, 'statism' in British public policy means that mutual associations do not have a significant role in policy formulation, despite the importance of government policy decisions for the protection of contributors' interests.

The thought-provoking conclusion is that competition and 'statism' are two sides of the same coin. Mutuals have been pulled out of shape by forces that have proved stronger than they.

Jerker Nilsson explains another puzzling aspect of mutuality in Chapter 7. Agricultural co-operatives have always been mutual, in the sense that they are owned solely by their farmer-members. Working along co-operative principles, they capitalise the business but have one person, one vote regardless of shareholding and do not generally remunerate shares with profits (though they do pay fixed rates of interest or link bonuses to the amount of business transacted). Recently, under the pressure of competition and the need to extend their interest down the food chain towards 'value-added' processing, many co-operatives have compromised these principles. They have demutualised into plcs, or gone into partnerships with investor-owned companies, or asked their members for more significant shareholdings (rewarding these variably within a more or less restricted market for shares), and so on. It is extremely difficult to track these developments and make sense of which form of organisation is best suited to which type of business.

Nilsson begins by analysing changes in the business environment of farmer-owned businesses. He shows that the form of organisation has developed directly in response to changes in this environment. He identifies five types: traditional co-op; participation share co-op; co-op with subsidiary; proportional tradable share co-op; and plc co-op. The last four are then divided into external-investor and member-investor types. This shows that some versions of what others have seen as demutualisation are really just changes in the way the farmer-owners raise and remunerate their own capital. Like Leigh and Llewellyn, and Mabbett, Nilsson is concerned with the agency problems of his type of mutual. The application of the theory shows that the traditional type of co-operative is, under the circumstances, still right for the job it is doing. It is one among several strategic choices that face the industry urgently. The characteristics of the five models are identified, and shown to match their trading conditions; Nilsson is therefore able to predict with some confidence what type of co-operative will be chosen in the future, to meet which set of market conditions.

Should these new forms of co-operative be seen as adaptations of a mutual form, or as deformations from mutuality, or even as a kind of demutualisation? They certainly depart from strict co-operative principles, but Nilsson argues they are still mutual as long as they remain essentially for the benefit of and largely under the control of farmers.

In Chapter 8, Race Mathews is concerned with the impact of globalisation on regional economies, and identifies the credit union movement as a potential agency for the development of locally-owned businesses that, unlike international capital, will not migrate in search of a quick profit. There is substance in his view, because the agencies that are so successful in stimulating the local economy in Quebec are underpinned by the '*caisses* Desjardins', and in Mondragon by a co-operative credit bank. Not surprisingly, Mathews provides a detailed case study of these, applying the lessons learned to the Australian credit union movement, and asking whether it too could be an agent for regional development.

The problem is that credit unions are under attack from demutualisers; the conversion of one union has shown how corporate greed on the part of managers, and indifference on the part of government, can lead to the stripping of those very assets that are necessary to launch economic developments. The underlying argument is that credit unions cannot afford to stand still; they must reinvent their structures constantly, as both Desjardins and Mondragon have been doing, in order to meet the needs of their communities. Government has, on the one hand, to protect credit unions from demutualisation, and on the other to get out of their way and allow them to develop their potential without excessive regulation.

Shann Turnbull in Chapter 9 explores the radical new concept of multi-stakeholding, which he defines as ownership and control of a firm by its employees, customers and suppliers. The advantage of such an arrangement is that it creates *distributed* ownership among *diversified* stakeholders. Each stakeholder constituency elects its own board, which is a component of a 'compound board' that introduces *distributed* control but not necessarily with *diversified* control. The argument is that firms work much better when the agency problems associated with the different interests and time horizons of stakeholders are recognised and built into the governance and decision-making structure.

The analysis of the shortcomings of existing firms with centralised control is devastating; the potential for inefficiency, self-seeking and corruption among managers and unitary boards is too great. The Japanese *keiretsu* and the Mondragon systems are explored as alternatives, examples of multi-stakeholding in action, as are some experiments the author has himself designed for worker-owner firms in Australia. The idea is applied to privatisation of public-sector industries, and to the mutualisation of existing firms. Here, Turnbull combines the stakeholding principle with a strategy for gradual buyout of the existing investors in a firm. The idea could not be more radical, but here it is backed up by relevant cases, and a wide range of other empirical evidence.

In Chapter 10, Johnston Birchall and Richard Simmons are concerned with the problem of member participation in mutuals. In the past, when mutuals were small and locally based, participation was not seen as a problem. Now that many of them are very large indeed, and regionally, or even nationally, based, how can they make member participation meaningful? Also, when they face increasing competition it is hard to see how mutuals can afford to give members any real say in decision-making that is largely conditioned by the market. The question is given urgency by the need to defend mutuals against 'carpetbaggers' intent on windfall gains from conversion. Boards who want to defend against demutualisation are suddenly faced with the problem of communicating with members whom they had for many years treated as customers. If it is not possible, for structural reasons, to make membership meaningful, then mutuals may as well accept demutualisation.

The authors present a comprehensive model of what motivates people to participate. This has an individualistic and a mutualistic set of propositions, derived from social psychological theories. They apply these to the situation of large-scale mutuals, and conclude that while motivation of members will not be easy, it can be achieved. They suggest a staged mobilisation strategy that includes the provision of individual benefits such as loyalty payments, and the development of group incentives such as a sense of community, shared values and a common sense of purpose.

Finally, in Chapter 11, Stephen Yeo brings a historian's eye to the 'new mutualism' that is claimed by the current UK government. He delves deep into the history of the Labour Party and the mutual and co-operative sectors, and analyses the relationship between the two. He distinguishes between 'old Labour', which was statist and emphasised parliamentary politics and nationalised industries, and 'old old Labour', which was associationist and emphasised the primacy of the social over the political. The new Labour project has to rediscover its roots in 'old old Labour' and foresake the statist assumptions of 'old Labour'. Coining the term 'co-operative and mutual enterprises' – CMEs for short – Yeo challenges the government to support the sector, and foster the deep values and traditions on which the 'new mutualism' can draw.

References

Birchall, J. (1987) *Save Our Shop: the fall and rise of the small co-operative store*, Manchester: Holyoake Press.
—— (1997) *The International Co-operative Movement*, Manchester: Manchester University Press.
Halsey, A. H. (1978) *Change in British Society*, Oxford: Oxford University Press.
Hargreaves, I. (1999) *New Mutualism: In from the Cold*, London: Co-operative Party.
Kellner, P. (1998) *New Mutualism: The Third Way*, London: Co-operative Party.

1 The economics of mutuality

A perspective on UK building societies

Leigh Drake and David T. Llewellyn

The mutual corporate form is very prevalent in financial services but much less common in other non-financial business areas. Mutual institutions have generally dominated housing finance and life assurance markets, both in the UK and in many other developed economies such as the USA. This has been particularly true in the UK housing market, where mutual building societies have traditionally dominated the mortgage market, even after the intensification of competition that followed deregulation and the entry of banks and wholesale-funded lending institutions in the early 1980s. Not only have mutual institutions tended to dominate certain segments of the financial services market, but they have also tended to enjoy a superior public image over their joint stock company or plc counterparts and to compare very favourably in terms of performance measures such as relative profitability and cost/income ratios. This is especially true in respect of the contrast between UK building societies and banks.

A powerful trend has emerged in recent years, however, towards demutualisation; that is, mutual financial institutions converting to plc status. This trend has been particularly evident in the housing finance and savings bank sectors of many 'Anglo-Saxon' economies such as the USA, Australia, New Zealand and South Africa. The UK had seemed to be largely immune from this general trend prior to 1995, with only the Abbey National building society taking advantage (in 1989) of the conversion option introduced under the 1986 Building Society Act. However, the mid-1990s witnessed a wave of plc conversions by UK building societies. The Cheltenham and Gloucester building society was acquired by Lloyds Bank, and a number of other building societies, such as the Halifax (which merged with the Leeds Permanent in 1995), Woolwich, Alliance and Leicester, and Northern Rock, all converted to plc status during 1996/97. These conversions amounted to a very significant demutualisation, with over 65 per cent of the sector's assets being transferred to the plc sector.

More recently, the boards of other UK building societies, such as the Nationwide and Bradford and Bingley, have been forced to hold votes on plc conversion motions following pressure from members. In the case of the Bradford and Bingley, this pressure forced the board to change from a pro-mutual to a pro-plc stance, and in July 2000, the members voted overwhelmingly for conversion: 94.5 per cent of saving members and 89.5 per cent of borrowers supported the conversion option. This vote leaves the Nationwide as the sole remaining large mutual building society. There is also evidence that a similar trend is emerging in the life assurance sector, with the Norwich Union and Scottish Widows being the latest and most significant mutuals to announce a plc conversion. In the case of Scottish Widows, this conversion is via an acquisition by Lloyds TSB. Furthermore, the board of Standard Life, the UK's largest mutual life assurance company, only narrowly fought off a conversion challenge mounted by a member.

This apparent trend towards demutualisation in the UK has, not surprisingly, brought the 'mutual versus plc' debate sharply into focus. A key element in this debate typically centres around the differences in ownership structure and the often alleged greater scope for managers of financial mutuals to engage in rent seeking or expense preference behaviour. In other words, it is typically asserted that agency costs are more serious in mutuals than in plcs because the owners (investors and borrowers) of the former have less influence on managers than do their equity shareholding counterparts. The purpose of this chapter, therefore, is to draw on the vast literature relating to property rights, corporate ownership structure and agency costs in order to cast an objective light on these issues in respect of financial services and, in particular, UK building societies. Aside from providing insights into the recent pressures inducing mutuals to convert to plc status and addressing the economic and welfare issues relating to this trend, this literature should also provide insights into why mutuals have traditionally dominated certain sectors of the financial services marketplace and have competed very successfully alongside plcs in these areas for many years.

The purpose of this chapter is not to make a case for one form of corporate structure over another. There are good reasons why different corporate forms may coexist within the same marketplace (and indeed there may be clear advantages in such a diversity of corporate form), and there are clear economic rationales for the predominance of certain corporate forms, such as mutuals, in cases where institutions are relatively narrowly focused on providing long-term financial products such as mortgages and life assurance. Similarly, the literature on property rights and ownership structure can help to explain why relatively risky and highly diversified activities, such as commercial banking, tend to be dominated by plc or stock corporate forms.

The theory of the firm

A useful starting point in the analysis of the economics of mutuality is to recognise that mutuals are economic firms, organisations that use resources to add value in the creation of goods and services. In this regard, a mutual is one among many types of economic firm: sole proprietors, closed companies, partnerships, plcs, co-operatives, state owned agencies, etc. Different types of firm often compete with each other in the same markets. Mutuals are therefore one of many forms for organising economic activity. Each type of economic firm has its own strengths and weaknesses, which is why different organisational forms are able to co-exist, and sometimes in direct competition with each other.

A particular problem relating to the economic analysis of mutuals, however, is that they are typically contrasted against inappropriate or unrealistic benchmark corporate forms. Boxall and Gallacher (1997), for example, in their analysis of mutuality, elect to use the model of a profit-maximising firm as 'the obvious standard of comparison for an economist' (p2). If we refer back to the traditional or classical theory of the firm, however, this tended to focus on the role of the entrepreneur, or owner-manager, and it was they who were presumed to operate the firm so as to maximise profits. As Jensen and Meckling (1976) point out, however, the classical theory of the firm really relates to the theory of markets (perfect competition, monopoly, etc.) in which firms are important actors. As they put it, 'the firm is a "black box" operated so as to meet the relevant marginal conditions with respect to inputs and outputs, thereby maximising profits, or more accurately, present value' (p306).

It is clear that, in practice, modern large corporations bear little resemblance to the classical entrepreneur, and this has spawned a wealth of literature dating back to Adam Smith (1776) and Berle and Means (1932) concerned with the incentive problems that can arise when firms are run by managers who are not the owners or security holders of the firm. This is the so-called 'agency problem' in firms which is generally characterised as a problem emanating from the separation of ownership and control. More precisely, Fama and Jensen (1983) argue that agency problems can arise in any organisation in which there is a separation of decision-making and risk-bearing functions such that important decision agents do not bear a substantial share of the wealth effects of their decisions.

Potential conflicts of interest (between managers and owners) arise because contracts are necessarily incomplete: it is not feasible to set down in advance a set of complete contracts that specify courses of action for each stakeholder in all conceivable future circumstances. There necessarily must be discretion, but the discretion of managers can be abused. Hart (1995) notes that corporate governance issues arise when: (1) agency problems (conflicts of interest) arise within a firm; and (2) transactions costs are such that the problem cannot be dealt with through explicit contracts. Also in this context, Fama and Jensen argue that agency problems arise because contracts are not costlessly written and enforced. Agency costs include the costs of structuring, monitoring and bonding a set of contracts among agents with conflicting interests. Agency costs also include the value of any outputs lost through the fact that the costs of full enforcement of contracts are greater than the benefits. Clearly, therefore, agency problems can arise in both plc banks and mutual financial institutions such as building societies.

The initial response to these perceived agency problems was to abandon the notion of the classical entrepreneur and of profit maximisation, and to focus on the motivations of managers who run, but do not own, firms. This resulted in the development of managerial theories of the firm (Baumol, 1959; Cyert and March, 1963; and Williamson, 1964) which fostered the notion that agency problems may manifest themselves in costs associated with managers' rent-seeking behaviour. Such expense preference behaviour is usually argued to take the form of non-salary perquisites such as 'excessive' office expenditure, business lunches, travel expenses, etc. Not surprisingly, this strand of literature has spawned a wealth of empirical research investigating the degree of expense preference behaviour in financial institutions. A particularly active strand of this literature involves contrasting the relative extent of expense preference behaviour in regulated and deregulated industries, and in cases where different corporate forms co-exist in large numbers in the same market place. Examples of the latter include the numerous investigations into expense preference behaviour in mutual and stock (plc) Savings Banks and Savings and Loan Associations (S & Ls) in the USA.

A more recent development in theory of the firm literature, however, rejects the classical model of the profit-maximising firm in favour of models that emphasise classical forms of maximising behaviour on the part of the various agents making up the firm (Alchian and Dempsetz, 1972; Jensen and Meckling, 1976; Fama, 1980; and Fama and Jensen, 1983). Because of the emphasis on the importance of rights established by contracts within an organisation, this literature is often described under the rubric 'property rights'. This emphasis on property rights and contracts is very evident in the definition of a firm (organisation) offered by Fama and Jensen (1983):

> An organisation is the nexus of contracts, written and unwritten, among owners of factors of production and customers. These controls or internal 'rules of the game' specify the rights of each agent in the organisation, performance criteria on which agents are evaluated and the payoff functions they face. The contract structure combines with available production technologies and external legal constraints to determine the cost function for delivering an output with a particular form of organisation. The form of organisation that delivers the output demanded by customers at the lowest price while covering costs survives. (p302)

Fama and Jensen also point out that agency problems occur whenever the separation of decision-making and risk-bearing functions is observed, and hence are common to large corporations, large professional partnerships, financial mutuals and non-profit organisations. Clearly, the prevalence of the separation of decision-making and risk-bearing functions in large institutions can readily be explained by the benefits of specialisation (specialised managers, security holders, etc.). If the agency costs that allegedly follow from this separation are to be squared with the assertion that only low-cost producers survive in the long run, however, then these institutions must find a common approach to controlling such agency problems. This is particularly pertinent in respect of financial mutuals, such as UK building societies, since it is often asserted that agency problems are more severe in mutuals than in plcs. According to Fama and Jensen (1983), this common approach 'is that the contract structures of all of these organisations separate the ratification and monitoring of decisions from initiation and implementation of decisions' (p302).

Drawing on the structure and theoretical insights provided by the property rights literature, therefore, the remainder of this chapter attempts to answer some key questions central to the current mutuality versus plc debate in respect of UK building societies. First, given that low-cost producers can be expected to survive in the longer run, and that agency costs are allegedly more severe in financial mutuals, how do we explain the prevalence of mutuals in the financial sector and particularly in certain sub-sectors such as the mortgage and life assurance sectors? In other words, are there features of the mutual corporate structure which make them particularly suited to these types of product markets? Second, given that agency problems potentially affect both plc and mutual financial institutions, how do they compare across the two corporate forms, and what are the 'common approaches' adopted by these institutions in order to curb the associated agency costs? A further related issue is to examine the relative levels of expense preference behaviour across financial mutuals and plcs, and the extent to which this is influenced by other factors such as the degree of competition in the market place. Clearly, the extent of any measured residual agency costs (such as expense preference behaviour) evident in each corporate form will be the net outcome of the gravity of the underlying relative agency problems and the effectiveness of any control measures adopted. Finally, this chapter will attempt to identify specific factors that have influenced the current trend towards demutualisation in UK building societies, and provide some tentative insights into possible future trends in the industry.

Mutuals in the financial services sector

Within the 'nexus of contracts' paradigm established under the property rights literature, any firm is simply a set of contracts among the various factors of production, agents or 'stakeholders' within the organisation. Clearly, within this paradigm there are many alternative ways in which these sets of contracts can be structured and the mutual form is simply one among many possible corporate forms. That being said, the prevalence (and long history) of mutuals in the financial sectors of many economies, together with their relative scarcity in non-financial sectors, is suggestive of the fact that mutuality may be particularly suited to the provision of financial services, and particularly those relating to longer-term contractual relationships such as mortgages and life assurance. This may be a result of: an inherent efficiency advantage in this area; or the greater ability of financial, as opposed to non-financial mutuals, to address any inherent agency problems; or some combination of the two. With respect to the former, Llewellyn (1997) points out that:

> there are two fundamental differences between firms in say the manufacturing sector of the economy, and those providing financial intermediation services:
>
> 1. One of the major inputs of the financial intermediary is money which is the same commodity that companies require as capital;
> 2. In the case of the financial intermediary, its customers provide money and stand at both ends of the value process: customers provide the basic input (money) but also demand the service being supplied.
>
> Put another way, the key difference is that in the mutual the customers are themselves the owners of the firm whereas there is a separation of the two in the case of the plc. For these basic reasons there is no *necessity* to have a specialist supplier of capital independently of the customers.

Since external suppliers of capital to plc institutions need to be remunerated (in the form of a required rate of return on equity), the absence of external shareholders in mutuals can be deemed to be an inherent efficiency advantage of financial mutuals in the sense that, other things being equal, they should be able to operate on lower margins in respect of the financial intermediation process. Miles (1991), for example, has suggested that this inherent efficiency advantage amounts to a potential reduction in the margin between deposit and lending rates of at least 0.42 per cent for UK building societies, although more recent estimates suggest that this figure may be as high as 0.75 per cent.

The potential efficiency advantages of mutuals

There are three potential sources of competitive advantage for a mutual: the absence of external capital that needs to be serviced; the existence of free reserves which generate a rate of return; and frequently lower costs, although it is recognised that comparisons of cost ratios between plcs and mutuals are complicated by their different business structures.

The fundamental economics of the mutual firm (the 'margin advantage', caused partly by the absence of external capital that needs to be remunerated) are favourable to building societies (and life assurance offices). However, the margin advantage is complex, as it depends upon the rate of growth of the building society. In order to maintain a constant capital ratio, and in the absence of external injections of capital, it can be shown that the required surplus (as measured by the rate of return on assets) rises as the growth rate of the society rises. This is because, leaving aside debt capital, the only source of capital to a mutual is its profits. On the other hand, a plc can in principle finance high growth rates through external injections of capital.

The relationship between the annual growth rate (g) of a financial mutual (such as a building society) and the required rate of return on assets (RROA) is given in Equation 1.1 below, on the assumption that the mutual holds no capital in excess of the minimum prudential capital to assets ratio (r).

$$RROA = (g.r)/(100 + 0.5g) \tag{1.1}$$

This relationship between the required ROA and the annual growth rate of assets is illustrated in Figure 1.1 as the line ORS. It might be thought that the same relationship would apply to a plc, on the assumption that all capital was generated internally. This view is incorrect in two respects,

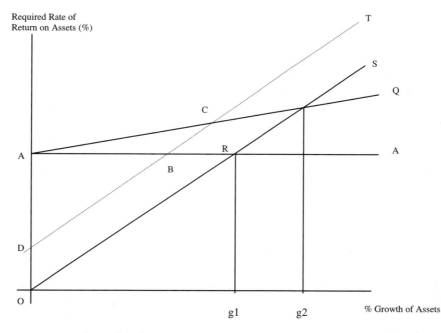

Figure 1.1 Relationship between annual growth rate of a financial mutual and required rate of return on assets

however. First, unlike mutuals, plc institutions pay dividends out of net profits, which are therefore not available to add to reserves (capital). Hence, for any given growth rate, a positive dividend policy would inevitably imply a higher required rate of return on assets than that of a mutual. The plc relationship would therefore be drawn as the line DBCT in Figure 1.1, rather than the line ORS, which is applicable for a mutual.

The second distinction emanates from the fact that the plc's shareholders are the owners of all the equity capital, whether it be internally generated reserves or externally generated share capital. Hence, shareholders will have a required rate of return on this equity capital, and assuming a given minimum equity to assets ratio and no excess capital, this implies an exogenously determined required rate of return on assets. This is typically calculated using a model such as the Capital Asset Pricing Model (CAPM), whereby shareholders will require a premium over a risk-free return (such as a Treasury Bill), with the size of the premium being related to the specific risk on the equities (typically measured by the covariance of the equity return with the market return commonly known as Beta) and the excess of the market return over the risk-free rate. This is illustrated in Equation (1.2).

$$\text{RROE} = Rf + \text{Beta}\,(Rm - Rf), \tag{1.2}$$

where RROE is the required rate of return on equity, Rf is the risk free rate, Rm is the equity market return and Beta is as defined above.

Assuming that this required return on equity (and assets) is exogenously given, this implies that the relationship between the ROA and growth with internally generated capital is given by ABCT, where the distance OA indicates the exogenously determined rate of return on assets. Clearly, in the case where all capital is generated externally, the relationship would expressed by the line AA, on the assumption that plc institutions such as banks could raise any amount of capital they desired at an exogenously fixed required return on equity (and assets). This latter assumption is probably unrealistic, however, as faster annual growth rates are unlikely to be achievable without raising the specific risk profile of the plc institution (via riskier lending, for example). This would imply a relationship something like ACQ for plc banks with external capital (although the relationship may be non-linear), and ACT for internally generated capital.

In summary, Figure 1.1 produces powerful implications. First, in the case of internally generated capital (for plcs), the required rate of return on assets for a plc would exceed that of a mutual at any growth rate. Clearly, this implies a margin advantage in the sense that the mutual could operate with a lower interest margin than a plc in the same market, such as the mortgage market, for example. Second, in the case where the plc raised all capital externally (in itself an extreme assumption), the mutual would still enjoy a margin advantage at growth rates of either less than $g1$ (on the most favourable assumption for plcs) or less than $g2$. In order to gain some insight as to the critical growth rate implied by $g1$ we have undertaken some simulations. Table 1.1 provides a simulation matrix of required ROAs versus growth rates for mutuals on the basis of Equation (1.1) and an assumed minimum and binding capital ratio of 4 per cent. Since we are assuming that plc banks raise all capital externally (i.e. along line AA in Figure 1.1), Table 1.2 translates a range of required ROEs into implied required ROAs, again assuming a required minimum equity to assets ratio of 4 per cent (which would be appropriate for the mortgage market).

Clearly, in order to identify the critical growth rate $g1$ in Figure 1.1 we need some estimate of the cost of capital (required rate of return on equity) for plc banks. We do this using Equation (1.2) and quarterly data over the recent period 1991–96. Using quarterly data on the FT All Share Price Index, and the FT All Share Dividend Yield, the average annualised total market return over this period was 16.1 per cent and the average premium over the risk-free rate (proxied by the 3-month Treasury Bill rate) was 9.1 per cent. Estimates of Betas for UK banks in recent years have tended to be at or slightly above unity. Hence, with the risk-free rate averaging 6.99 per cent over the period, Equation (1.2) produces a rough proxy of the cost of capital for a plc bank of 16.1 per cent. As can be seen from Table 1.2, this translates into a required ROA of around 0.64 per cent. Hence, if we contrast this with the figures in Table 1.1, it is clear that mutual building societies would face a margin advantage *vis-à-vis* plc banks at all growth rates up to 18 per cent per annum.

Over the period 1991–95, the average annual growth rates of the remaining top ten mutual building societies ranged from 2 per cent for the Nationwide to 10.6 per cent for the Yorkshire. Furthermore, even during 1996, which was a period of relatively rapid growth in both market shares

Table 1.1 Required ROA for mutual building societies ($r = 4$)

g	ROA
0	0.000
2	0.079
4	0.157
6	0.233
8	0.308
10	0.381
12	0.453
14	0.523
16	0.593
18	0.661
20	0.727
22	0.793
24	0.857

Table 1.2 Required ROA for banks ($r = 4$)

ROE (per cent)	ROA (per cent)
2	0.080
4	0.160
6	0.240
8	0.320
10	0.400
12	0.480
14	0.560
16	0.640
18	0.720
20	0.800
22	0.880
24	0.960

and assets following the earlier significant reductions in interest margins, growth rates still ranged from only 1.4 per cent for the Leeds and Holbeck to a maximum of 15.7 per cent for the Chelsea. For the mutual building society sector as a whole, total assets expanded by only 8.7 per cent during 1996. Clearly, these figures are well below the critical growth rate ($g1$) of 18 per cent, and it is therefore not surprising that mutual building societies were able to reduce margins aggressively in the mortgage market in the mid- to late 1990s and gain market share relative to the banks and, in particular, the recently converted 'mortgage banks'. Indeed, the potential 'margin advantage' of mutuals versus plcs in the mortgage market is understated by the above analysis to the extent that building societies had built up substantial excess capital during the 1980s and early 1990s and hence did not face a binding capital constraint as assumed in Equation (1.1). This implies that mutual building societies could operate with lower ROAs (and hence lower interest margins) than implied by Table 1.1 if they permitted a gradual reduction in excess capital levels.

Finally, although the cost of bank capital may be overstated somewhat because of the buoyancy of the stock market in the early 1990s, it should be recognised that in Tables 1.1 and 1.2 we make the most favourable assumption for plc banks (i.e. that they can raise unlimited amounts of capital at an exogenously fixed cost of capital). We also make the equally unrealistic assumption that building societies face a binding capital constraint. In reality, building societies have typically held large amounts of excess capital, as alluded to above, while banks raise the vast majority of their capital internally. Hence, as we have already demonstrated, building societies will always have a margin advantage over plc banks when capital is raised internally, so it seems highly probable in practice that mutual building societies will tend to have an 'inherent margin advantage' over plc banks.

The efficiency advantage and pressures for plc conversion

If there is such an 'inherent margin advantage', building societies can adopt one of three broad strategies:

1   Maintain a wider margin than is necessary and build up reserves through high profits; or
2   Maintain a wide margin but distribute some of the profits at the end of the year; or
3   Maintain a low (but sustainable) margin and increase market share.

With respect to the final strategy, some UK building societies in the late 1990s began instigating reductions in their margins in the mortgage and deposit markets precisely to demonstrate the alleged benefits of mutuality to their customers. Some building societies, however, chose to demonstrate the virtues of mutuality via the second strategy; i.e. by paying their members an annual 'mutual dividend', a bonus payment paid out of net profits that would otherwise be added to reserves.

On the face of it, it would seem logical for a mutual to adopt these latter strategies. However, there are advantages to building up reserves (security, credit-rating effects, enhanced strategic options, etc.) and during the 1980s and early 1990s this was the chosen strategy. This was feasible, as building societies operated with a margin that was excessive for them but not for their bank competitors. Building societies chose to price their business on the basis of banks' costs, even though their own were lower. The result is that reserves were augmented and profits were buoyant, often at a time when the opposite was the case for their bank competitors. However, this in itself, though it was unknown at the time, made eventual conversion an attractive option. The reserves (net worth) belong to the members in the same way as the equity capital belongs to banks' shareholders. But there are three major differences between the two:

1   In the case of a plc, the shares have a market value that is immediately observable and known to all; and there is a continuous revaluation of the company. This is not the case with a mutual;
2   With a plc, the ownership rights are tradable and immediately realisable at any time; the owner can liquidate the ownership claim by selling it at a known price on the stock market. Again, this is not the case with a mutual; and
3   With a mutual the owners are also the customers and there is no specialist supplier of risk capital.

As reserves were built up (because building societies were maintaining a margin wider than was necessary) the implicit or embedded value to the owners was being increased steadily even if they were unaware of it. And yet the value could not be released. Conversion is one way that embedded value can be released to owners (in the absence of a secondary market in ownership stakes in mutuals). It is perhaps to be expected therefore that, at some point, and as the value of the unrealisable stake is increased, there would be a demand to unlock it. In effect, the demand to unlock value can be viewed as an *ex post* payment to members as an alternative to an *ex ante* payment in the form of a lower mortgage interest rate or higher interest rate on deposits. It was therefore, perhaps inevitable that, at some point, the payment would be demanded. An alternative interpretation is that, because of the excess margin, building societies were imposing forced savings on their members. Again, it is perhaps to be expected that, at some stage, members would want their forced savings released.

However, this picture is not quite accurate, and in one important respect. The two images presented above (*ex post* liquidation, and the element of forced saving) both presuppose that those who gain from the conversion (current members) are the same as those who, over many years, contributed to the reserves (net value) of the society, and who were forced to save in this form. Neither of these is in fact the case. This means that the current generation of owners can appropriate value built up over many years and decades by previous generations of owners. In effect, there is an inter-generation financial transfer. However, for the future, the potential 'margin advantage' means that building societies as mutuals do have the potential to remain a powerful competitive force in the financial system, provided the sector remains large enough.

The resolution of agency problems

In addition to their inherent efficiency advantage, it can also be argued that mutual financial institutions are better able to address agency problems than are their non-financial counterparts. This advantage relates to the unique nature of the residual claims in mutuals. Specifically, that they are redeemable on demand: building society shareholders (investors) can simply withdraw their deposits. Fama and Jensen (1983), for example, point out that:

> The decision of the claim holder to withdraw resources is a form of partial take-over or liquidation which deprives management of control over assets. This control right can be exercised independently by each claim holder. It does not require a proxy fight, a tender offer, or any other concerted take-over bid. In contrast, customer decisions in open non-financial corporations and the repricing of the corporation's securities in the capital market provide signals about the performance of its decision agents. Without further action, however, either internal or from the market for take-overs, the judgement of customers and of the capital market leave the assets of the open non-financial corporation under the control of the managers. (p318)

Thus, if equity stakeholders in a plc sell their ownership stake on the stock market, this does not remove assets from the control of the management of the company.

This greater ability to address agency issues explains why mutuals are common in financial organisations but not in non-financial organisations. Similarly, the inherent efficiency advantage of mutual financial institutions explains why they have been able to compete very effectively with plc institutions over a very long period of time, and in many countries, in spite of their allegedly greater agency problems. Indeed, it can be argued that the presence of external shareholders in plc financial institutions can add a further dimension to the agency problem by virtue of the potential conflict between the owners (equity shareholders) and depositors/customers. For example, equity shareholders may prefer a higher risk profile for the institution than would depositors, because of the formers' limited liability. This implies that shareholders can benefit from potentially significant 'upside gains' while being exposed to only limited downside potential. In contrast, depositors do not share this upside potential and would implicitly be subject to greater risk given the limited scope of deposit insurance. Clearly, in financial mutuals, this particular aspect of the agency problem is absent, because owners and customers are one and the same.

Moreover, it can be argued that, while mutuals have an inherent efficiency advantage in respect of financial intermediation, they have a particular advantage when long-term customer relationships are involved rather than 'spot' transactions. Kay (1991), for example, argues that:

> The special value of mutuality rests in its capacity to establish and sustain relational contract structures. These are exemplified in the most successful mutual organisations, which have built a culture and an ethos among their employees and customers, which even the best of plc structures find difficult to emulate.

This clearly helps to explain the relative dominance of mutuals in areas such as mortgage finance and life assurance, which involve long-term relationships with customers. Within the financial sector, however, it is often alleged that mutuals are more prone to agency problems and costs than their plc counterparts. While these greater agency costs may be offset by the inherent efficiency advantage of mutuals, the argument that mutuals experience more significant agency problems is itself a controversial argument. We consider this issue further in the next section.

Agency problems in financial institutions: insights from the property rights literature

The traditional view of agency problems in financial institutions has tended to focus on the direct control (or lack of control) exerted by owners (risk bearers) on managers/decision-takers. This form of control is typically observed to be *potentially* strong in plcs because voting rights are proportional to the value of shareholdings and hence institutional share-holders can, in principle, exert a powerful influence on plcs. It is also typically argued that the fact that shares are tradable gives rise to a potentially powerful market for corporate control. In turn, this can be argued to exert a powerful influence on poor management as the threat of a take-over is faced. In contrast, neither of these mechanisms is present in mutuals. Hence, this contrast has fostered the view that agency problems will tend to be more severe in mutuals.

According to the property rights literature, however, this is tantamount to viewing the issue of agency problems from the perspective of a plc institution. The fact that mutual owners have no effective means of directly influencing decision-takers does not mean that agency problems are not addressed, but rather that they may be addressed effectively via alternative control mechanisms. The key to whether agency issues are being dealt with both effectively in financial institutions is therefore not the specific mechanism adopted, but rather the ability of the institution to deliver the products demanded by customers both efficiently and cost effectively, and thereby to survive in the longer term in a competitive marketplace.

Fama and Jensen (1983) maintain that the different forms of large organisations typically afflicted by agency problems will tend to handle them in different specific ways (appropriate to their corporate structure) but will tend to have a common, effective approach revolving around the separation of decision implementation and decision monitoring. In the case of the plc organisation, this clearly revolves around the monitoring role of shareholders and the threat of a take-over. Fama (1980), however, raises serious question marks over the ability (or willingness) of shareholders to solve agency problems in plcs, and emphasises instead the role of the managerial labour market:

> since he holds the securities of many firms precisely to avoid having his wealth depend too much on any one firm, an individual security holder generally has no special interest in personally overseeing the detailed activities of any firm. In short, efficient allocation of risk bearing seems to imply a large degree of separation of security ownership from control of a firm ... On the other hand, the managers of a firm rent a substantial lump of wealth—their human capital—to the firm and the rental rates for their human capital signalled by the managerial labour market are likely to depend on the success or failure of the firm.

The important contribution of the property rights literature, therefore, is to emphasise, not the ability of stakeholders to influence firm performance, but their motivation and willingness to do so. Managers clearly have the ability to influence their own firm's performance, as well as having the motivation provided by the workings of the managerial labour market. That is, future alternative employment prospects, promotion prospects and future remuneration are all likely to be influenced by the recent performance of the firm. The latter will be especially true in cases where formal profit-related pay schemes are in operation, and where management are allocated shares and/or option contracts. While such schemes are common in plcs, it is interesting to note that performance-related pay has become increasingly popular in UK building societies in recent years.

In contrast, while shareholders do have the ability to monitor the firm's decisions, limited liability and portfolio diversification suggest that they may have little incentive to do so. We must also bear in mind that monitoring is a costly activity and hence there must be a sufficiently strong incentive (potential reward) for shareholders to incur these costs. This question mark over the motivation of shareholders to monitor, actively and adequately, the decisions of firm managers prompts the property rights literature to emphasise the role of substitute or delegated monitoring. The most obvious example of this form of delegated monitoring is the role of the boards of directors in large organisations, and particularly the role of non-executive directors on those boards. Indeed, the presence of boards of directors in all plcs comprised partly of non-executives is itself indicative of the extremely imperfect monitoring afforded by shareholders in these forms of firm. This point has been emphasised recently in the Cadbury Report. While boards of directors are also clearly important in mutuals, Fama and Jensen (1983) point out that the nature and structure of financial mutuals make them less crucial than in their plc counterparts:

> Like other organisations characterised by substantial separation between decision managers and residual risk bearing, the top level decision control device in financial mutuals is a board of directors. Because of the strong form of diffuse decision control inherent in the redeemable residual claims of financial mutuals, however, their boards are less important in the control process than the boards of open non-financial corporations.

Hence, the property rights literature suggests that the usual emphasis on factors such as: limited voting rights; poor attendance at AGMs; lack of owner-members on the board of directors, etc., in respect of mutuals is misplaced. In practice, as potential depositor/member withdrawals imply a partial liquidation in a mutual organisation this should generate a strong incentive to supply financial services on competitive terms and to provide a high quality of service (especially in a highly competitive environment). In this context, Fama and Jensen's argument can be seen as an extension of the Hirschman (1970) *exit-voice* dichotomy. In mutual organisations, depositors/owners typically exhibit little member *voice* (for the reasons outlined previously) but rather can exercise the easy and costless option of *exit*. In other words, it is easier and less costly for a member simply to (almost costlessly) withdraw business (e.g. a deposit) and transfer it to a competitor than to seek to change the behaviour of the firm. This is a powerful discipline and is in some senses a more direct threat to the managers since, as was emphasised in an earlier section, when a depositor withdraws funds, the capacity of the mutual is immediately reduced, whereas the sale of an equity stake in a plc does not immediately influence the capacity of the firms though the share price might fall. Hence, shareholders in plcs can use the *exit* option but could find it disproportionately expensive if other shareholders do likewise, thereby deflating capital values. Accordingly, shareholders might opt for *voice* rather than *exit*, although there are doubts over the effectiveness of the latter in practice.

A further obvious control mechanism in financial mutuals is that mutual organisations traditionally do not have access to external equity finance and this makes them more reliant on retained profits for growth. If managers have growth maximisation as a primary objective (there is empirical evidence of links between growth and management remuneration; see Ingham and Thompson, 1995) this will therefore be consistent with profit maximisation (or at least with a strong profit motive), providing that capital adequacy ratios are potentially binding.

It should also be recognised that the ability of different corporate forms to operate with very different objectives is, in large part, a function of the degree of competition, or lack of competition, between the different sets of institutions. Drake and Llewellyn (1988), for example, argue that the degree of competition in a market is more important than organisational or corporate form in terms of influencing firms' objectives and strategy. A good example of this is the behaviour of UK building societies in the mortgage market. Prior to the early 1980s building societies had a virtual monopoly in the mortgage market, and banks in particular were not active participants in this market. This lack of competition, combined with their mutual status, enabled UK building societies to eschew a strong profit motive and to operate an interest rate cartel designed to serve the interests of both borrowing and investing members, and to sustain less efficient societies. In other words, the absence of competition meant that building societies had a choice over their strategies.

This type of behaviour did not survive the entry of banks into the mortgage market in the early 1980s, however. Building societies became much more overtly concerned with profitability as an objective during the 1980s, and the interest rate cartel was formally abandoned in 1983. This entailed a general rise in the structure of building society interest rates relative to market rates, a tendency for building society rates to adjust more frequently and rapidly in line with market rates and, consequently, the elimination of mortgage rationing, which had been a feature of the market during the 1970s. It is also the case that building societies began to raise significant amounts of funds from the wholesale money and capital markets during the 1980s, which brought them for the first time under the scrutiny of these markets. Indeed, a number of building societies sought formal credit ratings in order to facilitate their wholesale funding operations. (These issues are discussed in greater detail in Drake, 1989.)

Finally, it is important to note that the debate over relative agency costs in mutual and plc financial institutions tends to focus on what may be termed the standard agency problem: i.e. problems associated with the separation of decision-making and risk-bearing functions, and manifested in problems such as management slacking and perquisite taking. A further agency problem, however, relates to the potential conflict between the holders of debt contracts and the holders of equity. Specifically, the nature of the debt contract dictates that if a risky (*ex ante*) investment produces high (*ex post*) returns well above the face value of the debt, equity holders will capture the gains, while debt holders receive only their fixed contractual payments. If, however, the investment fails, then, because of their limited liability, equity holders will face only limited downside risk, while debtholders will face the same downside risk without any compensating upside potential.

It follows, therefore, that equity holders may have an incentive to see the firm investing in highly risky projects even though they may be value-decreasing for the firm, and this tendency may be exacerbated if equity investors have highly diversified portfolio holdings. This effect, generally referred to as the 'asset substitution effect', is an agency cost of debt-financing in plcs and is frequently neglected in the plc versus mutual debate.

It is clear that the asset substitution agency problem is potentially much more serious in plc financial institutions (than non-financial plcs), given that the conflict between equity holders and debt holders will also extend to depositors. The same form of agency problem cannot exist in mutual financial institutions, however, as the depositors are also the owners, which precludes any conflict of interest. Furthermore, as mutual owners have no direct claim on profits, they therefore have no incentive to prefer risky activities. On the contrary, given limited deposit insurance, the owner/depositor in a financial mutual has a positive disincentive with respect to high-risk, value-decreasing projects.

Empirical evidence on agency problems in mutual and plc organisations

The early analysis of mutuality tended to adopt the approach of the managerial theories of the firm and hence to assume that the managers of mutuals would face only weak constraints on the pursuit of preferred goals: i.e. they would exhibit agency costs such as expense-preference behaviour (Nicols, 1967 and O'Hara, 1981). The initial formal analysis of expense preference behaviour and agency costs in financial mutuals, however, tended to produce very mixed results. In studies of mutual and stock savings and loan companies (S & Ls—the US equivalent of UK building societies), for example, Verbrugge and Goldstein (1981) and Verbrugge and Jahera (1981) found that US mutual S & Ls tended to exhibit expense preference behaviour in respect of the labour input.

Blair and Placone (1988), however, pointed out that these studies tended to draw on the literature on the managerial theories of the firm, and hence concentrated on the relatively narrow issue of expense preference behaviour without taking explicit account of more general agency costs. In contrast, Blair and Placone drew on the later property rights and agency costs literature and recognised that, while agency costs may be affected by corporate structure, they may also increase as an organisation becomes more complex but be reduced by the extent of competition in the managerial labour market. We have also argued in this chapter that they are also likely to be reduced as competition in product (output) markets increases. Hence, Blair and Placone formally test for expense preference behaviour in US mutual and stock S & Ls in an empirical model which includes agency costs and the effect of firm organisation. Within this type of empirical approach, Blair and Placone (1988) found no evidence to support the existence of expense-preference behaviour in US mutual S & Ls and no evidence of superior performance by stock S & Ls relative to mutuals. In fact, Blair and Placone found evidence to suggest that small stock S & Ls were more likely to exhibit expense preference behaviour than either large stock S & Ls or mutuals.

An important contribution to the investigation of agency costs in US mutual and stock S & Ls was made by Mester (1989) who pointed out that the earlier tests for expense preference behaviour were based on a methodology developed by Edwards (1977) and assumed the same Cobb–Douglas production technology and cost structure for both mutual and stock organisations. Not surprisingly, Mester established that there were important differences in the cost structures of mutual and stock S & Ls, and Mester (1991) found that, when allowing for this, mutuals had an inefficient output mix which was attributed to the more severe agency problems in mutuals. It is important to note, however, that Mester (1993) actually found the reverse result: i.e. that mutual S & Ls did not exhibit agency problems and were in fact more efficient than stock S & Ls.

According to Mester (1993), one important reason for the difference in the two sets of results is that the 1989 study used pre-deregulation data, while the 1993 study used post-deregulation data. The point was made earlier, in the context of deregulation in the UK mortgage market, that competition is likely to be a significant influence on the behaviour and objectives of financial institutions, and this result strongly suggests that the level of competition in the markets in which firms operate may indeed be an important determinant of the severity of agency problems.

Hence, while Drake (1994) did find evidence of expense preference behaviour in UK building societies (using Mester's methodology), the logic of Mester's analysis suggests that increasing competition will tend to make this type of behaviour increasingly unsustainable. It should also be noted, however, that no comparable studies of UK banks have been conducted and it is therefore not possible to contrast directly expense preference behaviour in UK plc banks and mutual building societies. A recent study by Valnek (1999), however, established that, over the period 1983 to 1993, UK building societies outperformed their plc retail bank counterparts. Of great significance, given the differences in asset structures and risk profiles, is the finding that building societies generated higher risk-adjusted returns on assets than plc banks. Furthermore, Valnek argues that:

> Our results indicate that mutual building societies appear to have outperformed stock retail banks, suggesting that the benefits of mutual organisations may outweigh those of stock organisations. These benefits stem from the merger of the owner and the depositor functions, and from their homogenous clientele: costs related to conflicts between different classes of claimholders ... are thus avoided.

It is clear, therefore, that Valnek's results endorse the inherent efficiency advantage of mutual building societies and are, in part, attributable to the ability of mutuals to avoid agency costs, and particularly those associated with the conflict between debt holders (depositors) and equity holders: i.e. the asset substitution problem in plcs.

A further important contribution to the analysis of agency costs in mutual and stock S & Ls comes from the work of Hermalin and Wallace (1994). Their analysis is one of the few pieces of empirical work in this area to recognise explicitly the two dimensions of the agency problem outlined earlier: specifically, the standard agency problem of lack of effective owner monitoring (typically asserted to be more severe in mutuals), and the problem of asset substitution, which would be expected to be prevalent in stock financial institutions rather than mutuals. Hermalin and Wallace therefore analyse both the efficiency and solvency of stocks and mutuals but recognise that the potential problem of asset substitution suggests the need to control for the different lines of business typically pursued by the two sets of institutions.

Significantly, they find that, in the absence of such controls, stock thrifts are less efficient than mutuals on average, and that this result is mirrored by stock thrifts being twice as likely to fail as mutuals. They argue that:

> A potential explanation is the asset substitution conflict between shareholders and debtholders (depositors). Stock firms are highly leveraged which makes them behave like risk lovers. Risk loving in turn leads stock thrifts to expect lower expected returns in exchange

for greater risk. Given our method of estimating efficiency, lower expected returns translate into appearing less efficient and greater risk means an increased probability of default. Consistent with this explanation, we find that stock thrifts are both more efficient and more likely to remain solvent than are mutuals when we control for the lines of business emphasised. Moreover, the lines of business that stock firms tended to pursue were negatively correlated with efficiency and solvency.

The conclusion arrived at by Hermalin and Wallace, therefore, is that stock thrifts are inherently more efficient than mutuals with respect to the standard agency problems, but that the asset substitution problem results in an additional agency problem which leads stocks to pursue lines of business inconsistent with efficient operations and future solvency. Furthermore, the fact that stock S & Ls were found to be less efficient in the absence of controls for the lines of business, suggests that the impact of asset substitution is potentially more serious and outweighs the impact of the standard agency problem.

Again, this type of analysis has potential implications for the UK. It is well established, for example, that banking tends to be characterised by a so-called 'herd instinct', in which banks enter new and often relatively high risk markets *en masse*. Obvious examples include the acquisition of securities firms after the Big Bang, and the massive exposure in lending to LDCs in the 1970s and early 1980s. This behaviour is easy to rationalise in terms of the asset substitution agency problem, and can explain the relatively poor performance of UK banks in terms of profitability measures such as Return on Equity and Return on Assets (even on a risk-adjusted basis) during the 1980s and early 1990s.

In terms of the conversion process, this analysis also suggests that there are clear systemic benefits to the existence of a continuing and thriving mutual building society sector, in the sense that these institutions tend to adopt a lower risk profile, are not subject to the asset substitution agency problem, and are therefore not subject to the 'herd instinct' to the same degree. This suggests that a financial system characterised by a mixed array of corporate structures such as plcs and mutuals will be inherently more stable than one populated by only the former. This is likely to be particularly significant in economic downturns when, for reasons estab-lished previously, plc financial institutions are likely to be particularly prone to risk-taking behaviour.

In summary, it is clear that, despite the presumption in the literature relating to managerial theories of the firm, agency problems are likely to be more severe in mutual financial institutions, there is no clear evidence to support this. Indeed, certain studies such as Mester (1993) and Hermalin and Wallace (1992) suggest that agency problems (or aspects of agency problems) are less severe in mutuals than in stock institutions. While Drake

(1994) does find evidence of expense preference behaviour in UK building societies, there are to date no comparable studies of UK plc banks. Furthermore, it should be noted that this study utilised data from 1988, only five years after the ending of the BSA interest-rate-setting cartel, and one year after the deregulation associated with the 1986 Act. The evidence from the USA is that increased competition following deregulation tends to reduce or even eliminate potential agency problems. It may be, therefore, that more recent evidence would reject the presence of agency costs, such as expense preference behaviour, in UK building societies. Indeed, as outlined above, Valnek (1999) does find evidence of the superior performance of mutual building societies relative to plc retail banks.

As was established previously, the property rights literature would lead us to expect potential agency problems in any large and relatively complex organisation. The key issues are the measures in place to deal with these potential agency problems and the economic significance of any remaining agency costs. The lack of any strong evidence to confirm the hypothesis that the characteristics of financial mutuals should make them more prone to agency problems and costs seems to be in line with the suggestion in the property rights literature that alternative control mechanisms (such as deposit withdrawals) are in place in financial mutuals to mitigate agency problems. The lack of significant agency costs in practice, combined with the inherent cost efficiency advantage of financial mutuals discussed previously, explains why financial mutuals have competed very successfully with stock or plc institutions in many countries and for many years. We also note that mutual building societies and plc banks are in direct competition with each other in a number of markets. Hence, what would be predicted for a cartelised, semi-monopoly mutual sector would be quite different from the situation where mutuals and plcs are in direct competition with each other.

Size, risk and diversification in mutual building societies

Finally, it is also interesting to note that mutual financial institutions tend on the whole to be highly specialised and relatively low-risk institutions, with the mortgage and life assurance markets providing prime examples. It is also apparent that the waves of demutualisation that have occurred in the 'Anglo-Saxon' economies have generally tended to follow periods of specific deregulation, where mutuals have been permitted to diversify their range of activities, including the possibility of engaging in higher-risk activities. Indeed, the conversion option has often been introduced at the time of deregulation, as in the case of the 1986 Building Societies Act.

While it is clear that mutual financial institutions, such as UK building societies, have traditionally been narrowly focused and relatively low-risk institutions as a direct product of restrictive regulation, it can also be argued that financial mutuals would tend to adopt this profile even in the absence of such regulation. With respect to risk, this reflects the fundamental characteristic of mutuals; specifically their lack of access to significant external sources of capital via specialist risk-takers. The knowledge that capital cannot easily be replaced following the generation of significant losses would be likely to induce the managers of mutual financial institutions to adopt a relatively low-risk profile. Finally, as outlined in the previous section, the fact that mutual building societies are owned by their depositors (debt holders) makes them less prone to the asset substitution agency problem and hence less inclined to risk-taking.

The idea that mutual financial institutions are, on the whole, more likely to be characterised by relatively simple, low-risk business structures is also supported by the relevant property rights literature. Fama and Jensen (1983), for example, argue that:

> Unrestricted common stock is attractive in complicated risky activities where substantial wealth provided by residual claimants is needed to bond the large aggregate payoffs promised to many other agents. Unrestricted common stock, with its capacity for generating large amounts of wealth from residual claimants on a permanent basis is also attractive in activities more efficiently carried out with large amounts of risky assets owned within the organisation rather than rented. Moreover, since decision skills are not a necessary consequence of wealth or willingness to bear risk, the specialisation of decision management and residual risk bearing allowed by unrestricted common stock enhances the adaptability of a complex organisation to changes in the economic environment (p312).

Hence, the property rights literature allows us to explain why large, complex and relatively high-risk institutions such as banks tend to be dominated overwhelmingly by stock or plc institutions, and why (relatively) smaller, more specialised and lower-risk institutions such as savings banks, building societies and life assurance companies are often traditionally characterised by a preponderance of mutual institutions. Equally, while there is no inevitability that mutuals (such as UK building societies) that choose to diversify away from their core activities will convert to plc status, it could be argued that, the more ambitious are their long-term expansion plans (in terms of size, diversity and risk), the more likely they will be to convert at some stage. It is significant in this respect, therefore, that the only building society conversions (planned or realised, stock market flotation or conversion and take-over) to date have involved the relatively larger societies. The logic of this argument also suggests, however, that there is no compelling reason why remaining relatively large mutual building societies (such as the Nationwide), with relatively modest expansion and diversification plans, should not continue to operate effectively with a mutual corporate structure.

It is important to emphasise, however, that there is no ultimate *inevitability* about the relationship between business structure (e.g. diversified versus specialist firms) and organisational form (e.g. mutual versus plc form). The argument is that, in practice, the wider the range of business conducted, and the greater the probability of a firm encountering high risk, the more probable it will be that the plc form will be judged to be the more appropriate organisational form. This is because the members (customers) of a mutual would be less inclined to a (possibly long-term) contractual relationship with a firm likely to be subject to substantial risk. This is especially true if the contractual relationship (e.g. a savings deposit) is such that the customer is subject to a downside risk but does not benefit from the upside potential of sharing in the profits of high-risk ventures. In such a case, it is more likely that specialist risk-takers will provide the risk capital of the firm. However, this does not mean that specialist firms will inevitably be mutual, or that diversified firms will always be plcs.

Summary and conclusions

This chapter has attempted to draw on the literature relating to property rights and agency problems, and on the empirical evidence relating to the comparative performance of financial mutuals and stock (plc) institutions, in order to provide a rigorous framework within which to address the current debate over demutualisation within the UK building society sector. It is hoped that this framework has provided a fresh perspective on the range of views and opinions which surround this highly topical and contentious issue.

The main conclusions of the chapter may be summarised as follows:

1   There are sound economic reasons why mutual financial institutions emerged in certain areas of the financial services market place. These are associated with the intrinsic efficiency advantage of mutuals (by virtue of not having to service an additional stakeholder (shareholder)), and the greater ability of financial, as opposed to non-financial, mutuals to mitigate the agency problems which potentially occur in any large organisation characterised by the separation of risk-bearing and decision-making functions. These characteristics will ensure that financial mutuals can continue to thrive alongside their plc competitors *provided* that is the wish of the relevant agents in the institution, i.e. the customers/owners and the managers.

2   It is likely that agency problems have existed in the past for both UK banks and building societies. There is no strong evidence, either from the USA or the UK, however, to indicate that these agency costs are likely to be more severe in UK mutual building societies than in plc banks. Furthermore, increasing competition and the potential for plc

conversion are both likely to reduce any residual agency costs/expense preference behaviour within the UK building society sector.

3 A number of pressures have been identified that can explain the recent trend towards plc conversion within the UK building society sector:

   i The conversion option accompanied significant deregulation and increased diversification possibilities, as was the case in other countries. It is well established in the property rights literature, however, that the plc form may be better suited to relatively large, diversified, complex and high-risk institutions than is the mutual form. That is not to say that all large building societies which plan to diversify must convert. Nor is it implying that small building societies could not potentially convert. Both theory and the empirical evidence suggests, however, that within the spectrum of possible types of financial institutions, relatively small and narrowly-focused firms (such as savings banks, mortgage lending institutions, etc.) are more likely to be mutual, while *most* large, complex, relatively risky and highly diversified institutions (such as commercial banks and composite insurers) will tend to be stock or plc institutions.

   ii The customers/owners of UK building societies now perceive more clearly than in the past that they are the notional owners of their societies and may therefore have a financial interest in unlocking the value of reserves on conversion.

   iii Increasing competition in the retail financial services market place will have reduced both the attractiveness of, and the potential to engage in, expense preference behaviour on the part of building society managers/executives. This may in itself provide an incentive towards conversion, allied to the fact that managers are likely to be offered share options that will be relatively more attractive the greater the residual degree of 'managerial slack' within the building society (as the society may be correspondingly undervalued by the market on conversion).

4 There is no reason to presume that the recent pace of conversion announcements within the UK building society industry will continue. It is already clear, however, that there is a tendency for the largest building societies to opt for the conversion route, which is entirely in line with the previous arguments. With respect to large building societies that have so far elected to remain mutual, such as the Nationwide, the logic of the analysis presented in this chapter suggests that there is no reason why they should not continue to operate successfully and effectively as mutual organisations. Equally, however, the logic of the analysis would suggest that, on balance, they are less likely to want to evolve into highly diversified, risky and complex financial institutions or 'mutual banks' than are the building societies

that have so far converted or announced plans to convert. In terms of reconciling the interests of the various agents or stakeholders within the organisation, we can see the recent move towards 'mutual dividends' (either annual or by way of reduced lending margins) as a way of simultaneously reducing the relative attraction of conversion and increasing the advantages of mutuality to customers. Similarly, mechanisms designed to reduce the attraction of the conversion option to building society executives may well include measures to improve efficiency and reduce any expense-preference behaviour, such as enhanced profit-related or performance-related pay. It is relevant to point out, however, that such schemes would be difficult to implement in those building societies seeking to demonstrate the benefits of mutuality by deliberately reducing profitability via reductions in lending margins. This would not be the case, however, for those societies adopting the alternative strategy of paying 'mutual dividends' or bonuses to members.

5   Notwithstanding the points made in item 4 above, the logic of our analysis suggests that, over time, the building society industry will increasingly be populated by relatively smaller and more highly focused institutions than has been the case in recent years.

6   Given the inherent efficiency advantage of mutual financial institutions, and the systemic advantages of a mixed financial structure, there are clear economic and welfare benefits to be derived from the continuation of a viable and successful mutual building society sector, albeit less significant in terms of total assets and average size of institution than in the past.

7   In order to derive the maximum benefit from a continuing mutual sector, it is clearly important that the inherent potential efficiency advantage of mutual building societies can be translated into effective pricing behaviour. It is well known from literature of the theory of the firm, however, that price-setting power in any market tends to emanate from the advantages of relative cost efficiency, relative size, or both. It follows from this that there is probably a 'critical mass' in terms of both the number and the relative size of those building societies remaining mutual in respect of significantly influencing pricing behaviour in the various financial services marketplaces.

References

Alchian, A. and Dempsetz, H. (1972) 'Production, Information Costs and Economic Organisation', *American Economic Review*, 5, December, pp. 775–795.
Baumol, W. (1959) *Business Behaviour, Value and Growth*, New York: Macmillan.
Berle, A. and Means, G. (1932) *The Modern Corporation and Private Property*, New York, Macmillan.

Blair, D. and Placone, D. (1988) 'Expense Preference Behaviour, Agency Costs and Firm Organization', *Journal of Economics and Business*, 40, pp. 1–15.

Boxall, A. and Gallagher, N. (1997) 'Mutuality at the Crossroads', *Financial Stability Review*, October.

Cyert, R. and March, J. (1963) *A Behavioural Theory of the Firm*, Englewood Cliffs, NJ: Prentice-Hall.

Drake, L. (1989) *The Building Society Industry in Transition*, London: Macmillan.

—— (1994) 'Testing for Expense Preference Behaviour in UK Building Societies', *Service Industries Journal*, 15(1), pp. 50–65.

Drake, L. and Llewellyn, D. T. (1988) 'A Convergence of Regulation', *CBSI Journal*, September.

DTTI (1995) *Building Societies—A Future or a Past?*, DTTI, July.

Edwards, F. R. (1977) 'Managerial Objectives in Regulated Industries: Expense Preference Behaviour in Banking', *Journal of Political Economy*, 85, pp. 147–162.

Fama, E. (1980) 'Agency Problems and the Theory of the Firm', *Journal of Political Economy*, 28(21), pp. 288–307.

Fama, E. and Jensen, M. (1983a) 'Separation of Ownership and Control', *Journal of Law and Economics*, 26, pp. 301–326.

—— (1983b) 'Agency Problems and Residual Claims', *Journal of Law and Economics*, 26(2), pp. 327–352.

Hart, O. (1995) 'Corporate Governance: Some Theory and Implications', *Economic Journal*, 105, pp. 673–689.

Hermalin, B. E. and Wallace, N. E. (1994) 'The Determinants of Efficiency and Solvency in Savings and Loans', *RAND Journal of Economics*, 25(3), Autumn, pp. 361–381.

Hirschman, A. O. (1970) *Exit, Voice and Loyalty: Responses to Decline in Firms, Organizations and States*, Cambridge, Mass.: Harvard University Press.

Ingham, H. and Thompson, S. (1995) 'Mutuality, Performance and Executive Corporation', *Oxford Bulletin of Economics and Statistics*, 57, pp. 295–308.

Jensen, M. C. and Meckling, W. H. (1976) 'Theory of the Firm: Managerial Behaviour, Agency Costs and Ownership Structure', *Journal of Financial Economics*, 3(4), pp. 305–360.

Kay, J. (1991) 'The Economics of Mutuality', *Annals of Public and Co-operative Economics*, 62(3).

Llewellyn, D. T. (1997) 'The Mutuality *v* Conversion Debate?', LUBC—BSA Project Paper No 2.

Llewellyn, D. T. and Holmes, M. (1991) 'In Defence of Mutuality: A Redress to an Emerging Conventional Wisdom', *Annals of Public and Co-operative Economics*, 62(3).

Mester, L. J. (1989) 'Testing for Expense Preference Behaviour: Mutual Versus Stock Savings and Loans', *The Rand Journal of Economics*, 20, pp. 483–498.

—— (1991) 'Agency Costs Among Savings and Loans', *Journal of Financial Intermediation*, 3, pp. 257–278.

—— (1993) 'Efficiency in the Savings and Loan Industry', *Journal of Banking and Finance*, 17, pp. 267–286.

Miles, D. K. (1991) 'Economic Issues in the Reform of Building Societies Legislation', Mimeo, Birkbeck College, London.

—— (1994) 'Economic Issues in the Regulation of Financial Firms: The Case of UK Building Societies', *The Manchester School*, 62(3), pp. 227–250.

Nicols, A. (1967) 'Property Rights and Behaviour: Stock Versus Mutual Savings and Loan Associations: Some Evidence of Differences in Behaviour', *American Economic Review*, 57(3), pp. 337–346.

O'Hara, M. (1981) 'Property Rights and the Financial Firm', *Journal of Law and Economics*, 24(2), pp. 313–333.

Smith, A. (1904) *The Wealth of Nations* [1776], Reprint, edited by Edwin Cannan, New York: Modern Library, 1937.

Valnek, T. (1999) 'The Comparative Performance of Mutual Building Societies and Stock Retail Banks', *Journal of Banking and Finance*, 23, pp. 925–938.

Verbrugge, J. and Goldstein, S. (1981) 'Risk Return and Managerial Objectives: Some Evidence from the Savings and Loan Industry', *Journal of Financial Research*, 4, pp. 44–48.

Verbrugge, J. and Jahera, J. (1981) 'Expense-Preference Behaviour in the Savings and Loan Industry', *Journal of Money, Credit and Banking*, 13, pp. 465–476.

Williamson, O. (1964) *The Economics of Discretionary Behaviour: Managerial Objectives in a Theory of the Firm*, Englewood Cliffs, NJ: Prentice-Hall.

2 Mutuality through credit unions

A cross-national approach

Olive McCarthy, Robert Briscoe and Michael Ward

In the year 2000, credit unions, as we know them, are celebrating their hundredth anniversary. From humble origins in Quebec, they have developed in different ways and to different degrees in many countries throughout the world. Shaped and influenced by a diverse array of cultures, they face differing socio-economic conditions and levels of support. It is no easy task to write about the worldwide credit union movement; one expert in the field (Professor Ian McPherson of the University of Victoria, British Columbia) has described it as *'a demanding master'*. This chapter confines itself to an examination of the credit union movement in a limited selection of countries: Ireland (the Republic and Northern Ireland), Britain, the USA, Canada, and developing countries. It addresses the issues of size and scale of operation, membership characteristics, mutual status, method and stage of development, legislation, regulation and taxation, and level of services offered. Issues such as age, gender, social class and regeneration will also be examined in the specific credit union movement context. The chapter concludes by discussing the challenges and opportunities facing the worldwide credit union movement, and by exploring the lessons that each of the more local movements might learn from one other.

The prime focus of credit unions is on meeting the financial needs of their members by providing savings and lending facilities at equitable rates of interest. They function according to a set of operating guidelines that reflect co-operative principles and have as their basis the values of equality, equity and mutuality. Credit unions have both social and economic objectives, and work towards the well-being of all members and their community. As financial co-operatives, credit unions are open to the membership of all individuals who can make use of their services. All members must have a common bond, be that of residence, employment or occupation. The owners of a credit union are its customer-members, who each have one vote regardless of their shareholding. Credit unions are democratically controlled, all members having a right to participate in the decisions affecting the credit union. Members can also participate on a voluntary basis by serving at board and committee level or in ongoing office activities. Credit unions are 'not for profit' organisations. Any surplus arising from operations, after reserves have been allocated, must be returned to the members according to their use of the credit union's services.

At a local level, credit unions remain autonomous, but are usually organised on a national basis under a central umbrella body. These central bodies provide various support services and central financial facilities. Being part of a wider movement is important for credit unions, particularly in fostering co-operation and co-ordination at a local and national level, and between national movements at a worldwide level. The World Council of Credit Unions (WOCCU) is the apex representative organisation, representing the movements of eighty-seven countries, which in turn represent over 100 million members in over 37,000 credit unions. In 1998, the total savings held within credit unions worldwide amounted to US$393 billion while total loans amounted to US$292 billion (WOCCU, 1998). The scale and size of operation in the movement in different parts of the world varies enormously. Most unions are concentrated in developed countries (Magill, 1994). North America accounts for 90 per cent of all savings and lending, more than 70 per cent of all members, but only 30 per cent of all credit unions. In contrast, the whole of the African continent has just over 2 per cent of all members, 11 per cent of all unions, but only 0.15 per cent of total savings and lending. Despite the many contrasts, the rapid spread and adoption of the credit union idea throughout the world suggests the ongoing and universal need for mutual and co-operative alternatives to conventional banking systems.

The origins of the modern credit union movement can be traced back to Quebec at the turn of the twentieth century. It was here that Alphonse Desjardins, appalled by rampant usury and the absence of adequate banking facilities for ordinary workers, set up the first *Caisse Populaire*, on which today's credit unions are modelled. Similar credit co-operatives had already proved successful in Germany from the mid-1800s. The *Caisses Populaire* were largely based in small francophone communities in Canada, and stressed the importance of savings and the wise use of money. When the idea spread to the United States in 1909, credit unions, as they became known, were primarily based on associations of employment and occupation, and emphasised the provision of services to members. The movement continued to spread from North America to the rest of the world, mostly from the 1960s onwards and, according to McPherson (1999), developed most easily in countries that had a similar background to the USA and Canada, such as Australia, Ireland and New Zealand. In countries such as Mexico, Kenya, Korea and Sri Lanka, McPherson (1999, p99) asserts that 'credit unions became manifestations of local needs, community structures, family associations, and economic trends', showing the adaptability of their structure to a variety of local circumstances.

The movement continues to spread today through the efforts of national movements and WOCCU. For example, the International Credit Union

Foundation of the Irish League of Credit Unions aids development in selected countries throughout the world, including Albania and the Gambia. WOCCU is implementing long and short-term development projects in countries such as Bolivia, Ghana and Sri Lanka (WOCCU, 1998). The Credit Union Foundation of Australia assists unions in the Pacific islands.

Stages of development

The stages of development of the credit union movement vary considerably between countries. Ferguson and McKillop (1997) attempt a broad typology that is summarised in Table 2.1. In spite of the heterogeneity, they contend that there are three distinct stages of credit union development based on differential asset size. These are the *nascent, transitional* and *mature* stages of development, nascent having the smallest asset size and mature having the largest. Credit union movements in countries such as the USA, Canada, Australia and Korea are cited as examples of *mature* movements. These are typically characterised by deregulation, well-developed financial services, use of technology in service delivery and, of course, large asset size. Movements categorised as being at the *transition stage* of development, such as those of Ireland and the UK, are characterised by a changing regulatory environment, greater product diversification, development of central services and a weakening of reliance on voluntary input. *Nascent* credit union movements have small asset size, voluntarism, some regulation, a small range of services, and rely on outside support; examples include the movements in countries within Central and Eastern Europe. A further contention of the model is that a 'demonstration effect' exists,

Table 2.1 Some features of the typology of credit union development (1)

Nascent	Transitional	Mature
Small asset size	Large asset size	Large asset size
Regulated	Shifts in regulation	Deregulation
Tight common bond	Adjusting common bond	Loose common bond
Emphasis on voluntarism	Greater product diversification	Competitive environment
Serve poor sections of society	Weakening voluntarism	Electronic technology
Singles savings and loans product	Development of central service	Organised trade association
Require wider sponsorship		Professionalisation
High commitment to ideals		Central services
		Product and service diversification

Source: Ferguson and McKillop (1997).

whereby movements at the nascent stage will eventually move to the transition stage, and finally to the mature stage. If this contention is true, credit union movements at different stages have much to learn from one another's successes and difficulties.

A more recent approach by McPherson (1999) proposes three main stages: *the formative stage, the national stage* and *the international stage.* These are summarised in Table 2.2. Credit unions in a movement at its formative stage must typically rely on the support of external agencies for operating and financial resources. Links to local and national networks are also important at this stage, to give legitimacy to the movement. Credit unions primarily need education and training, insurance services and appropriate legislation. At the national stage of development, movements develop national or provincial organisations that engage in joint activities enabling the expansion of credit union activities, such as the introduction of new financial products and the application of new technologies. McPherson asserts that the national stage is one of intense creativity for credit unions, when they begin to have a significant impact on the economy. However, it is also a time of rigorous debate between unions and their activists on issues such as funding, control, managerial competence, and the roles of members and volunteers. The third, international, stage reflects the impact of globalisation; it has not yet been widely experienced by the credit union movement of any country. McPherson asserts that this is because of the community orientations of credit unions.

The remainder of this chapter explores a number of country-specific credit union movements at different stages of development.

The Irish credit union movement

Almost every local community in Ireland is served by a credit union. There are over 550 credit unions throughout Ireland, well spread between urban and rural areas, with a total membership of over two million people and representing a penetration of about 50 per cent of the population (including Northern Ireland). Total assets of the movement are in the

Table 2.2 Some features of the typology of credit union development (2)

Formative	National	International
Outside support	Changing technology	Global operations
Education and training required	New financial products	
Public education and	Enhanced marketing	
promotion necessary	Intense debate and creativity	
Need appropriate legislation	Possible fragmentation	

Source: McPherson (1999).

region of US$4.4 billion, savings are at US$3.8 billion, while total lending is US$2.7 billion.[1] The average union has 4000 members, US$8 million in assets, US$7 million in savings, and US$5 million lent to its members. Each member has an average of US$1750 saved and US$1250 borrowed from their credit union. Clearly, credit unions in Ireland are used by their members for small-time savings and borrowing, although the vast majority of unions are under-lent.

The Irish movement has essentially been a bottom-up development, with the initiative and the wherewithal for establishing unions originating within local communities. First founded in 1959, credit unions in Ireland were a response to the lack of access to adequate saving and borrowing facilities for members of local communities. The profound influence of the Church in the first ten years of development is well recognised, but it is the commitment and mutual needs of the members that have given strength to the movement. Credit unions have mostly been based on the common bond of residence, with only about 10 per cent formed on the basis of occupation or employment. Interestingly, there are more female than male members. The Lansdowne Report (1995) shows that 56 per cent in the Republic of Ireland and 63 per cent in the North of Ireland are female, possibly reflecting the traditional role of Irish women as household managers. Members are well spread across age groups, though there are fewer members at the extremes of the age spectrum. While originally established to meet the needs of the working class, the movement now mainly serves the lower middle and working classes. Farmers and the upper middle class are not well represented among the membership.

As Irish society has become more consumer-driven, credit union members are demanding a wider range of financial services to meet their needs. The current lack of technological innovation in the movement has inhibited its ability to offer as wide an array of services as the conventional banks. Only a very small number of unions offer ATM services. None offer credit cards or cheque book services. However, great strides have been made since the late 1990s towards developing a central computer system that would enable electronic funds transfers. Such a system will be vital in continuing to meet the needs of the members and in staving off any possible shifts in member loyalty, particularly by younger members, towards the conventional banks (McCarthy, Briscoe and Ward, 2000). Co-operation between credit unions in service development and provision is essential.

The Irish credit union movement remains fully mutual, despite the demutualisation of nearly all the Irish building societies and some insurance mutuals. There is some cause for concern, however, about the status of this mutuality. Credit unions in Ireland are not doing enough to show that they are unique within the financial services sector as mutual organisations. Recent attacks by the Irish banking sector over what is perceived as a favourable tax regime for credit unions are worrying. Unions are not liable for taxation on their activities, but members are expected to declare their dividends. Two detailed complaints on the grounds of unfair competition have been made to the European Union by the banking sector on this taxation issue. Credit unions need to make greater efforts to differentiate themselves by creating a stronger sense among members of their unique value as community-based organisations led by volunteers (McCarthy, Briscoe and Ward, 2000). Strategies for doing this would include the encouragement of more active participation by the members, especially youth, in the running of their union, and the strengthening of the existing involvement of credit unions in local initiatives such as housing projects and job-creation schemes.

Since 1966, the movement has had its own tailored legislation. Following wide consultation between the government and the movement, the 1997 Credit Union Act was enacted to consolidate existing legislation and to update the 1966 Act. The new Act has given credit unions greater powers in the provision of additional services while at the same time tightening their regulation. They are regulated by a Registrar of Friendly Societies, with separate Registrars for the Republic and Northern Ireland. Within the Republic, proposals for a new Single Regulatory Authority (SRA) have been made, which will merge all financial services regulation under one central body. This would reflect the experiences of the UK, where all credit unions are now included with conventional financial institutions within a Financial Services Authority (FSA). Interestingly, credit unions in the North of Ireland are not included either within the remit of the FSA or of the SRA. The Irish movement has argued with the Irish government that it should not be included in the remit of the SRA, first, because of the distinctive nature of credit unions; second, because of their existing regulation under the Registrar; and finally, because of their strict self-regulation. In a gesture towards the position of credit unions, a role has been created within the SRA for a Registrar of Credit Unions, which may go some way towards allaying the movement's fears of inclusion in such a regulatory regime.

It could be argued that the Irish credit union movement is engaged in McPherson's (1999) *national stage* of development, by virtue of its changing technological requirements and expanding economic activities. According to Ferguson and McKillop (1997), the Irish movement can be considered to be at the *transition stage* as it moves towards the development of central services and greater product diversification, and as it faces changes in the regulatory framework. Furthermore, a weakening of reliance on voluntarism is already in evidence in many credit unions, as would be anticipated under this model. If a demonstration effect exists, as asserted by the model, the Irish credit union movement needs to act to ensure that the erosion of volunteer involvement that has occurred in mature credit union movements does not also occur in the Irish movement.

The credit union movement in Britain

Despite geographical proximity, the credit union experience in Britain (England, Scotland and Wales) contrasts markedly with that of Ireland. While the number of credit unions is similar, their impact in Britain is considerably less than in Ireland. However, the credit union movement is now the fastest-growing, fully mutual co-operative sector in Britain (Jones, 1999). Their mutual status is in sharp contrast to that of the building societies, which have been demutualising since the end of the 1980s.

In Britain, credit unions have primarily been an urban initiative (Berthoud and Hinton, 1989). The first one was founded in 1964 in London. Growth in the movement was slow until the 1970s, when the retail banks began to pull out of local communities and when the credit union idea began to take root as more and more immigrants from Ireland and the Caribbean took up residence in Britain (Donnelly and Hagget, 1997). Since the early 1990s in particular there have been unprecedented levels of growth although, as previously mentioned, their overall impact is low (Jones, 1999). There are now 430 credit unions with a total membership of 208,000. This represents an average membership per union of about 500. While there has been an almost ten-fold growth in the number of unions since the early 1990s, the average membership per union has remained stable. The movement has a total of US$200 million in assets, US$177 million in savings and US$175 million in member loans. The average credit union in the UK has approximately US$0.5 million in assets, US$0.4 million in savings, and US$0.4 million lent to its members. This represents an average saving and borrowing per member of only an approximate US$800. The overall penetration of the movement is minuscule compared to that of other movements, at only 0.72 per cent of the population. This may, in part, be because of the strength of the Co-operatve Bank, which provides a co-operative alternative in the UK financial services sector. Although the majority of credit unions in the UK are community-based, employee-based ones have more members and more savings per union (Donnelly and Haggett, 1997).

There appear to be no statistics readily available on the characteristics of the members of credit unions in Britain as a whole. A study carried out in Scotland, however, suggests that 69 per cent of members there are female. Over 60 per cent of members are classified as working class. Findings also suggest that more than half of the members are aged over 45 and only a very small minority (5 per cent) are less than 24. If these findings are applicable to the British movement as a whole, then credit unions have much work to do in balancing the profile of members across age, gender and social class.

Since the mid-1980s, development has been assisted by credit union development agencies (funded by local authorities) which employ development workers to 'hand-hold' local communities in establishing a union.

Much of the recent expansion in union numbers and membership in Britain has been attributed to these development workers. Local authorities often provide funding to help credit unions to become established. This method of development has attracted much criticism in that it adopts a top-down approach and results in a less than self-sufficient movement. Regulation is by the Financial Services Authority (FSA, the single regulator for all financial service providers in the UK); a dramatic shift away from the traditional regulatory role of the Registrar of Friendly Societies, (whose role is subsumed under the FSA). Although the Registry's credit union group has been preserved as a separate branch (Swoboda, 1999). Similar regulatory trends are in evidence in Ireland, Canada and Australia.

The level of services provided to members of British credit unions has been severely hampered by inappropriate legislation. The Credit Union Act 1979 was the first piece of legislation enacted; it restricted member shareholding to £5000 per member. Unsecured loans had to be repaid within two years; and secured loans within five years. Membership was limited to 5000 people. These provisions clearly restricted credit union development in Britain. Under the Deregulation Order 1996, these restrictions were relaxed somewhat, increasing the limits on the amounts that can be saved or borrowed and thereby allowing for greater credit union expansion. The Association of British Credit Unions Ltd (ABCUL), the largest (but not the only credit union representative body) is recognised for pushing for legislative change to facilitate the expansion of services (Ferguson and McKillop, 1997). As a result, in 1998, the British government proposed a package of measures lifting some of the restrictions of the 1979 Act and aimed at encouraging credit unions to grow. One of the proposals is to permit unions to provide additional basic services, and to charge fees for doing so, as well as to extend the repayment periods for loans. At present, they are not required to pay any form of corporation tax on profits, as happens in Ireland, but credit union members are required to pay income tax on dividends earned.

The use of technology in service delivery is minimal. Some credit unions have computerised their systems but few would be in a position to offer services such as ATMs and credit cards even if the appropriate legislation did exist. However, the 1999 Treasury Task Force recommends the establishment of a Central Service Organisation (CSO) for the UK credit union movement to 'provide the technical expertise and back office support enabling credit unions to provide a broader range of services' (ABCUL, 2000, p3). It recommends that the CSO be owned and controlled by the movement, in line with similar types of organisations in other countries, such as the US and Canada, where strong central service networks exist.

The UK credit union movement has not been without its problems. Differences of opinion on the philosophical approach to credit union development resulted in divisions within the movement and in the formation of a number of credit union associations. ABCUL, the National

Federation of Credit Unions (NFCU), the Scottish League of Credit Unions, and the Association of Independent Credit Unions are four of the main associations that have been in existence over the past number of years. The 1999 liquidation of the NFCU may help to generate greater cohesiveness within the movement. Other problems that have confounded the movement include the continued lack of market penetration, its stigma as being a 'poor peoples' bank', its over-reliance on local authority funding, and its inability to recruit suitable volunteers (Donnelly and Haggett, 1997). Despite the many difficulties experienced, the future looks bright. Bussy (1999, p214) describes the 'immense political goodwill towards credit unions from both the government and from other public and private bodies'. It is at a *transitional* stage of development according to the typology set out by Ferguson and McKillop (1997), although not as advanced as the Irish movement. According to McPherson's (1999) model, the British movement is probably in an early period of the *national stage* of development, as the national credit union bodies become more active and the provision of central services is being discussed. The movement is in a fortunate position in that it can learn much from the experiences of the Irish, US and Canadian movements.

The credit union movement in the USA

The size of the credit union movement in the USA is very impressive. There are over 10,000 unions, with a total of 70 million members, representing a penetration of the economically active population of just over 50 per cent. Average membership per union stands at 7000, almost fourteen times that of Britain and almost double that of Ireland. Total assets of the US movement in 1998 were almost US$370 billion, total savings were US$323 billion, and total lending to members was US$234 billion. On average, individual credit unions have US$37 million in assets, US$32 million in member savings and US$23 million on loan to members. This represents average savings of US$4600 per member and average loans of US$3300 per member.

Credit union development in the US came largely from the bottom up, although considerable patronage was enjoyed from clergymen, urban reformers and social activists (McPherson, 1999). A proliferation of employee-based and community-based credit unions emerged, although the employee-based ones are dominant today. Community development credit unions, mostly based in local communities, are also in evidence and provide services and support almost exclusively to those on low incomes. The US system is made up of a number of national, state and local-level organisations. Organisations at the state and national levels include credit union regulators, corporate credit unions to provide banking services to unions, and service organisations which aggregate buying power and pool expertise (CUNA, 1999). The provision of central services by CUNA (Credit Union National Association), the main umbrella group for credit unions in the USA, has been a key development within the movement. For example, the Corporate Credit Union Network (CCUN) acts as a credit union for credit unions, providing banking services and central investment channels. CUNA eCommerce offers internet banking facilities, bill payment services, and website design. Such systems are clearly absent from the Irish and British credit union movements where, for the most part, surplus funds are invested with conventional banks, and in secured stocks and bonds. Interestingly, credit unions in the USA are rated highest for customer satisfaction of any type of financial institution (ABCUL, 1999).

At a local level, US credit unions are generally either state-chartered (approximately 40 per cent) or federally-chartered (approximately 60 per cent), and legislative, regulatory and taxation provisions apply according to the charter under which they operate. The enactment of tailored legislation early on in the life of the US movement is one of its distinguishing features (McPherson, 1999) and clearly a lesson that was well learned by the Irish movement. However, legislation in the USA was tight, and deregulation in 1977 was broadly welcomed within the movement. A broader definition of membership was adopted and credit unions were allowed to increase their range of services, so that by the end of the 1970s they could offer mortgages, variable savings accounts, cheque book accounts and credit card facilities. However, with deregulation came mergers, and while the number of members continued to grow, the number of unions declined. The National Credit Union Administration (NCUA) is the federal credit union regulator. State credit union regulation is conducted under the laws of various states. In the early 1990s, interest was shown in consolidating regulation of US financial institutions at a federal level, but was not undertaken. However, a number of individual states are undergoing consolidation of banking, credit union and insurance regulation (WOCCU, 1999) which means that some state-chartered credit unions may come under the authority of a single regulator in the near future.

Membership is split almost equally between males and females. There is a good spread of members across all age groups, although the weakest penetration levels are, as in the Irish context, at the youngest and oldest extremes. The 1998 National Member Survey shows that today's membership consists primarily of middle-age, middle-income individuals. This is not surprising considering that nearly 80 per cent of credit unions are based on occupational type common bonds and that 64 per cent of members are in full-time employment. At the same time, it has been reported that cheque-cashing businesses and pawnshops now outnumber credit unions and continue to grow, their services mostly used by low-income individuals (WOCCU, 1999). This should be of great concern to the credit union movement, which must be careful not to lose sight of the need to serve individuals of modest means. Recent legislation has expanded the criteria for membership once again, allowing credit unions to reach more people. The effects on the membership demographics portfolio will be interesting.

However, the banking sector has been keeping a very close watch on the movement and continues to challenge credit union fields of membership.

The movement has been affected by demutualisation, but not on a large scale so far. The complexity of legislation affecting credit unions has been the cause of some of these conversions (WOCCU, 2000). Between 1995 and 1999, eleven unions converted to thrift associations, while two converted to mutual savings banks. There have also been examples of credit unions adopting stock ownership options. Ferguson and McKillop (1997, p67) come to the following conclusions about the status of mutuality in the US movement:

> From our analysis it is still the case that the benefits of mutuality are well-recognised in the US industry ... Despite the shift to a more business-oriented and professional approach by credit unions, the central value system of co-operative-member-owned institutions is still alive and well. The core value set of credit unions, of course, has to be reinterpreted in the light of constantly changing conditions and adapted to suit evolving conditions, and the evidence is that this entails a constant process of realigning credit union principles and practice.

Interestingly, CUNA has recently established a Project Differentiation Committee to re-emphasise credit union philosophy and commitment to members (NCBA, 2000). Credit unions are being encouraged to draw up a statement of commitment that will communicate their basic principles to members, legislators and consumers. Movements in other countries would do well to learn from this initiative. A brand campaign has also been initiated to help differentiate credit union services from those of other financial institutions.

The movement is clearly at a very advanced stage of development. According to Ferguson and McKillop (1997), it has reached the *mature stage* of development, having among other features, large asset size, loose common bond arrangements, well-developed central services and deregulation. In McPherson's (1999) typology, it is at a very advanced point in the *national stage*. It is interesting that the US movement is currently finding new ways to differentiate itself by highlighting its philosophical principles. Recent legislative changes to the common bond requirements will mean that US credit unions can reach out to more and more individuals. In doing so, they will have to ensure that the needs of people with lower incomes will continue to be met.

The Canadian credit union movement

There are two credit union movements in Canada. One serves the English speaking areas, the credit unions of which are affiliated to the Credit Union Central of Canada (CUCC). The other is the Mouvement Desjardins, which serves francophone communities. The CUCC consists of almost 800 unions and has 4.2 million members. At an average of 5000 members per credit union, these are about 25 per cent bigger than Irish and about 40 per cent smaller than US credit unions. Total assets of the movement are US$32.8 billion, total savings are US$29.6 billion, and total loans to members US$26 billion. The average CUCC credit union has US$41 million in assets, US$37 million in savings and US$32.5 million lent to its members. The average credit union member in Canada has US$8200 in savings and US$6500 borrowed from their credit union. There are 1351 Desjardins credit unions, or *caisses*, with assets in the region of US$70 billion and a membership of 5 million. Both movements have developed somewhat separately but are now finding ways to co-operate in financial product delivery.

Most Canadian credit unions are based on a community common bond and were set up with assistance from churches, universities and other types of co-operatives (McPherson, 1999). Strong links with the wider co-operative movement continue today. Canadian credit union members clearly have far more savings and borrowings than their counterparts in the USA, UK or Ireland. This may be accounted for by the innovativeness of Canadian credit unions in service provision; that is to say, Canadian unions have offered a more comprehensive level of service for longer than any other movement. This complements and enhances their savings and loans levels. They are a 'one-stop shop' for their members in terms of financial services. According to Ferguson and McKillop (1997, p20), Canadian credit unions were the first financial institutions to offer 'extended hours of operation, daily interest accounts, flexible mortgage payments, debit cards, internationally connected ATMs, and other consumer features that have become the norm in financial services'. For example, by 1987 they were offering Electronic Funds Transfers, a service still not offered by the Irish and British movements. By 1994 they were part of a shared network of 15,000 ATMs throughout Canada. The movement is dedicated to a philosophy of total personalised access, the provision of customised financial services by electronic means and by in-branch personal service (CUCC, 1994–5). Home banking is one of the more recent innovations whereby members can complete a range of transactions by connecting online to their union.

Credit unions, particularly those within the Desjardins movement, also support local businesses and community groups. Recently, the Desjardins Movement has been assisting in the creation of co-operatives offering home care services. These are springing up because of government cut-backs in health services and because the population is getting older; home services co-ops provide the support the elderly need to stay in their own homes. This rapidly growing sector recently set up a co-ordinating structure (la Fédération des Coopératives de Services et de Soins de Santé du Québec (FCSSSQ) – the Federation of Quebec Service and

Health Care Co-operatives). The Desjardins Movement has entered into a partnership with this federation, enabling the FCSSSQ to benefit from a range of services and assistance, including provision of premises, publicity and financial and technical support. It has provided an annual grant of $30,500 for three years, has lent a staff member and meets 75 per cent of that staff member's salary.

Canadian credit unions are currently organised in a three-tier structure of local, provincial and national organisations. All local credit unions operate autonomously but are affiliated to a provincial 'central', which provides corporate services and support. The centrals are, in turn, members of the CUCC, which functions as the system's national trade association and financial services provider. Centrals maintain system liquidity at the provincial level, and provide deposit insurance protection, access to payment clearing, and transfers between credit unions. Centrals also provide support to credit unions in marketing, communications, member education, electronic data processing, legal services and public relations. The CUCC maintains system liquidity at a national level and has a broad mandate in the area of credit union development. It also fosters a close working relationship with the Mouvement Desjardins (CUCC, 1990). Proposals were made in 1999 by the National Initiative System Task Force (NISTF), set up by the CUCC, to consolidate the national and provincial centrals into a National Service Entity (NSE). This would give the credit union movement a stronger competitive position in Canada, while retaining the commitment of the movement to its co-operative values and principles. Credit unions and provincial centrals will decide whether or not to approve the consolidation (WOCCU, 1999).

Legislation is on a provincial basis. Centrals are subject to provincial legislation and also to federal legislation under the Canadian Co-operative Associations Act. Regulation of Canadian unions has taken place since 1987 under the Office of the Superintendent of Financial Institutions (OSFI), a single regulatory authority for banks, insurance, trust and loan companies, and credit co-operatives such as credit unions. The OSFI regulates provincial centrals and the CUCC. Provincial regulators continue to regulate individual credit unions, and separate provincial regulation presents some difficulties to the movement when attempting to introduce new products nationally; the NSE, should it be agreed on, would be regulated federally, while credit unions would continue to be regulated at provincial level. The Canadian movement has done much to educate its regulators on the co-operative difference of credit unions (WOCCU, 1999). Educating the regulator and the legislator will continue to be important for all movements regardless of the type of legislation and regulation under which they currently operate. Credit unions in Canada are subject to a variety of taxes, including income tax, property tax, provincial sales tax, goods and services tax, business tax, capital tax, provincial payroll tax, and Canada pension plan and Unemployment Insurance premiums. However, they are still considered by government and the banking sector to operate under low rates of tax compared to other financial institutions in Canada.

While many Canadian credit unions have considered 'going public', most have rejected the idea because it separates membership and ownership (WOCCU, 2000). However, in 1992, it was a Canadian credit union which first issued non-voting shares on the stock exchange. By 1999, proposals were made to the members of the same credit union to dissolve in a share sale to a bank. While these proposals were overwhelmingly rejected by the members, it highlights a worrying possibility for the credit union movements in all countries, not just in Canada.

The Canadian credit union movement appears to have developed at a similar rate to the US movement, although some of their experiences have been somewhat different. Ferguson and McKillop (1997) maintain that the Canadian movement has reached a *mature stage* of development, because of its large asset size, well-developed central services, competitive environment, advanced technology in service provision, and diverse range of products and services. To McPherson (1999), the Canadian credit union movement has advanced through the national stage but is not quite at the international stage.

The credit union movement in developing countries

In aggregate, there are more than 22,000 credit unions serving about 18 million members in both urban and rural financial markets in developing countries (WOCCU, 1998). This averages just over 800 members per credit union. However, the scale and size of the movement varies considerably across countries. Taking the Gambia as an example, there are only ninety members on average in credit unions, with average savings per member of US$42 and average loans of US$26. In Honduras, there are over 3000 members per union, with average savings per member of US$460 and average borrowings of US$430. These differences make it difficult to generalise; however, it is true to say that there are more small credit unions than large ones.

Development is typically aided by outside agencies. WOCCU and the ILCU have both devised strong credit union aid programmes for developing countries. Ferguson and McKillop (1997, p39) assert that 'the start-up of credit unions in developing countries critically requires sponsorship from the wider movement'. However, it is important that unions do not become reliant on such sponsorship, and that development strategies focus primarily on the mobilisation of local savings (WOCCU, 1998). This will be important to secure local commitment and to ensure the financial viability of individual credit unions. Magill (1994) points out that assistance by external agencies is important in enabling credit unions to provide meaningful levels of service to their members when the organisation is still small. He highlights the situation in Latin America in particular, whereby growth in credit unions financed by low-cost funding resulted in their neglecting to adjust their savings and lending policies, and as a result being unable to attract savings.

Much as in the earlier days of the movements in Ireland and the USA, credit unions in developing countries tend to serve people who would otherwise have little or no access to such services. Most provide saving and lending facilities to their members, but few, if any, ancillary services are provided. The use of modern technology in service delivery is virtually non-existent. A key characteristic is that they operate on self-generated capital and tend not to rely on external donations or loans; total savings exceed total loans in the vast majority of developing countries (Magill, 1994). The term 'micro-finance' is often used to refer to the types of services provided. 'Micro-loans' are typically less than US$300 and are provided for micro-enterprises, agricultural use and improving living conditions (WOCCU, 2000).

Occasional, isolated pieces of research hint at the potential for creative involvement by credit unions in community development. A major achievement of the movement in the Solomon Islands has been the development of successful micro-enterprises owned by credit unions. Here, thirty unions have developed their own small-scale co-operative businesses which are proving to be remarkably successful and well-adapted to the local culture. These credit unions own and operate their own small enterprises, financed only by members' funds, union profits or income-generating activities organised by the members. They have found that these businesses seem to work better in this cultural environment than individually-owned firms, and they have started to discourage members from borrowing to set up individually-owned businesses, which might be run more effectively on a communal basis.

In legislative terms, most movements in developing countries operate under outdated laws not specifically designed for credit unions. For example, in many parts of Africa, including the Gambia, they operate under co-operative legislation from the 1960s. Ferguson and McKillop (1997, p39) recognise that an immediate concern in developing countries is 'to seek the legal recognition of credit unions and establish an appropriate regulatory framework'. This is a lesson taught by more established movements. According to the typology set out by Ferguson and McKillop (1997), the credit union movements of developing countries are, generally speaking, at a *nascent stage* of development because of their small asset size, single savings and loans products, and the level of sponsorship required from the wider credit union movement to become established. They continue to lobby governments for appropriate legislation, and they need to promote the credit union ideals to the public. As would be expected according to McPherson's (1999) *formative stage*, they are still reliant on outside support. Despite the challenges faced by movements in developing countries, they share one key advantage in that they can benefit from the lessons learnt from the existing credit union movements (ABCUL, 1999).

Conclusion

Many challenges and opportunities face credit union movements world-wide. The sheer size and scale demonstrates the extent to which it is already an international movement. Baker (1999, p2) suggests that there is an increased need for collaboration between credit unions and their movements. He states that 'there will have to be greater discipline, more co-operation, more planning and more integration. Without these [credit union] strengths would fade away in a new environment that is far more competitive than ever before'. In order to compete, they will need to continue to differentiate themselves from mainstream financial service providers. They will also need to improve service quality while continuing to meet the needs of all members. Finding new ways to harness volunteer input will also have to be a priority. A number of clear lessons for credit union movements emerge from the foregoing analysis.

Lesson 1: National credit union movements need internal cohesiveness

Blame for the slow development of the British movement has been attributed partially to internal differences that caused the formation of a number of different umbrella bodies. On the other hand, the success of movements such as that of Ireland has been attributed partly to its cohesiveness and the ability of credit unions to co-operate with each other in areas such as service provision. The competition faced by many movements in the current financial services environment requires the use of collective muscle. The movement has a far better chance of survival if united, than if divided.

Lesson 2: Appropriate, tailored legislation is essential

Movements that secure appropriate legislation early in their development are, in general, in a stronger position than movements that do not. Provided they can also secure relevant amendments or deregulations, they are free to offer more services and are more easily able to expand their membership bases. The British movement has been dogged by outdated legislation that has severely hampered its growth. The US movement, on the other hand, secured appropriate legislation early in its development as well as deregulations when they were needed.

Lesson 3: A good relationship with government must be fostered

If governments understand the credit union difference they will be more sympathetic to the position of credit unions within the economy. Generating a healthy relationship with the government can help to secure equitable taxation policies and ensure that appropriate legislation and regulation exists. The movement in Ireland demonstrated its strong working relationship with the Irish government in implementing the 1966 Credit Union Act, only seven years after the foundation of the movement, and again in 1997 when the movement was widely consulted on updating and consolidating the legislation.

Lesson 4: Credit unions should, as much as possible, be developed from the bottom up

While assistance may be necessary for emerging credit union movements in terms of finance and other support, it is important that they do not become overly reliant on external assistance. Experience has shown that commitment and dedication to the credit union idea must come from those who need and use its services.

Lesson 5: The distribution of membership should be examined

The movements in the USA, Britain and Ireland show weaknesses in their membership in terms of age distribution. Maintaining a balanced age profile among members will be important in ensuring that the needs of all age groups in society can be met and securing the stability and future of the movement. The British movement appears to serve mostly those on lower incomes, while the US and Irish movements seem to serve mainly those in middle-income brackets. Credit union movements would do well to examine their membership base to ensure that all those who hold the common bond, both male and female, have the opportunity to become members.

Lesson 6: Safeguards against demutualisation of credit unions should be put in place

The ease with which credit unions have been able to change their structures in both Canada and the USA should sound warning bells for movements in other countries. Legislation protecting against such changes needs to be enacted to prevent similar attempts within other movements. The value of mutualist principles should also be promoted more fully to members, given recent trends in the mutual banking sector towards demutualisation.

Lesson 7: Credit unions need to be differentiated from conventional financial institutions

Credit unions in many countries are viewed as being similar to conventional institutions. In a number of countries they are now regulated in a similar fashion to conventional financial institutions, disregarding the strict internal controls in credit unions and their unique co-operative structure. They need to do more to differentiate themselves and to project themselves as a movement. Involvement in community initiatives such as local and national job creation and housing projects may assist this process.

Lesson 8: Volunteerism in credit unions should continue to be encouraged

The level of volunteerism in credit unions declines over time according to the typology set out by Ferguson and McKillop (1997) and as is evidenced in a number of movements. Credit union movements in early stages of development can act to prevent this decline while more developed movements need to find ways to reverse it. They must support the continued training of their activists and members to equip them to participate more fully. On-going research should also be conducted both by those involved in the movement and by academics and findings disseminated widely on a national and international scale.

Note

1   We use the 1998 figures produced by WOCCU, for the most part, throughout this chapter for the sake of consistency across movements.

References

ABCUL (1999) *Credit Union News*, October, London.
—— (2000) *Credit Union News*, January, London.
Baker, C. (1999) 'An Ever-Changing Kaleidoscope', in *Credit Union World*, 1(3), October, Wisconsin, WOCCU, pp. 2–3.
Berthoud, R. and Hinton, T. (1989) *Credit Unions in the United Kingdom*. London, Policy Studies Institute.
Bussy, P. (1999) '*Credit Unions in Great Britain 1997–98*', The World of Co-operative Enterprise 1999, Oxford, Plunkett Foundation, pp. 211–215.
CUCC (1995) *Credit Union Environmental Scan 1994–1995*, Toronto, Credit Union Central of Canada.
—— (1990) *The Credit Union System*, Toronto, Credit Union Central of Canada.
Credit Union National Association (1999), *National Member Survey*, Wisconsin.
CUNA (1999) http://www.cuna.org
Donnelly, R. and Haggett, A. (1997) *Credit Unions in Britain – A Decade of Growth*, Oxford, Plunkett Foundation.
Ferguson, C. and McKillop, D. (1997) *The Strategic Development of Credit Unions*, Chichester, John Wiley.
HM Treasury. (1999) *Credit Unions of the Future*, Treasury Task Force Report, London, November.
Jones, P. A. (1999) *Towards Sustainable Credit Union Development*, London, ABCUL.

Lansdowne Market Research (1995) *Credit Union National Market Research Report*, Dublin.

Magill, J. H. (1994) 'Credit Unions: A Formal-Sector Alternative for Financing Microenterprise Development', in Otero, M. and Rhyne, E., *The New World of Microenterprise Finance*, London, IT Publications.

McCarthy, O., Briscoe, R. and Ward, M. (2000) 'Redesigning the Credit Union for the New Millennium: A Case Study of Ireland', *The World of Co-operative Enterprise 2000*, Oxford, Plunkett Foundation, pp. 119–130.

McPherson, I. (1999) *Hands Around the Globe: A History of the International Credit Union Movement and the Role and Development of the World Council of Credit Unions, Inc.*, British Columbia, Horsdal & Schubart, Wisconsin, World Council of Credit Unions.

—— (1999) 'The Dynamics of Credit Unions: Explaining Diversity in the International Credit Union Movement', *Review of International Co-operation*, 92(1), Geneva, International Co-operative Alliance, pp. 95–107.

NCBA (2000) *Co-operative Business Journal*, 14(3), April.

Swoboda, R. (1999) 'Single Financial Regulatory Authority', unpublished paper, Diploma in Credit Union Studies' Summer School, University College Cork.

WOCCU (1999) 'Is it alphabet soup or regulatory consolidation?' *Credit Union World*, (2) Wisconsin, WOCCU, July, pp. 18–19.

—— (1999) *Statistical Report 1998*, Wisconsin, WOCCU.

—— (2000), What is demutualization? *Credit Union World*, 2(1) Wisconsin, WOCCU, March, pp. 10–11.

3 Housing co-operatives and social exclusion

David Rodgers

Housing investment is capital intense. If you are fortunate, you will have land and property assets bequeathed to you by an earlier generation. If you are doubly fortunate, that earlier generation will also have wielded sufficient political power to protect their (and their inheritor's) assets from the ravages of death and taxes. If you are not in the fortunate position of enjoying the fruits of your forebear's property assets you must provide for your own housing needs in the marketplace for land and property. Land that is suitable and available for housing is a scarce commodity. As has poignantly been observed, the problem with land is that nobody is making it any more. Meeting the housing needs of yourself and your family will be the greatest demand on your disposable income. If you cannot meet this need, which for many will inevitably be the case given that a house and the land on which it stands last longer than any generation of occupiers, your housing needs will only be met if housing is provided or subsidised by the state. If the state does not accept this responsibility, you will be inadequately housed or homeless, a dehumanising fate suffered by many in our society and, by most in the impoverished developing world where governments cannot afford to house the poor. In 2000, in England alone, 66,000 households were living in temporary bed and breakfast accommodation, the highest number since the passage of the Homeless Persons Act in 1977.

The challenge for any modern civilised society is this: how can we meet the housing needs of those in our society who cannot compete in the free market to provide decent affordable housing for themselves and their dependants? What is the best way of doing this? Because of growing demands on land use and the capital intense nature of housing investment, answering this question is a challenge for any society, even for a rich developed nation such as Britain. Seeking to respond positively to this housing challenge is not solely a philanthropic task. It is one that is of mutual interest to all who are concerned about the quality of life and the sustainability of the democratic society in which we live. A classic illustration of this is the role of the new homelessness 'tsar' appointed by the New Labour government in Britain. This person is charged with the task of getting the homeless off the streets. It is a responsibility that has as much to do with the offence that begging and the sight of sleeping bags in shop doorways causes to the voting majority as it has to do with concerns about the plight of those who lack a permanent roof over their heads.

The present generation is not the first to pursue social policies for less than wholly philanthropic reasons. The superb engineering investment our Victorian predecessors made in sewage disposal and water supply was for the public health benefits it gave to the wealthy as much as for the prevention of disease among the poor. The key political issues of today in developed countries are concerns for increased investment in health, education and crime reduction. However, there is a growing realisation that investing in the supply and quality of housing for those who cannot meet their own needs in the free market is of benefit to the whole of society, and should therefore be a higher political priority. This realisation comes from recognition of the link between poor housing and poor health, low educational achievement, and higher crime rates. Add together, poor health, poor housing, low educational achievement, high crime, high unemployment, low workforce skills, high family breakdown rates and lack of access to financial services, and you have a picture of the experience of the poorest communities in British society. This is an experience we describe as 'social exclusion'; the inability to participate in mainstream society. This is a description of disadvantage that the UK New Labour government has embraced and stated its determination to eradicate.

Social exclusion is a diverse phenomenon. In a recent paper it has been defined in this way:

> The term 'social exclusion' concentrates attention on the ways in which significant minorities are excluded from participating in the mainstream life of society; from jobs, education, homes, leisure, civic organisation, and even voting, and on how this disconnection tends to coincide with vulnerability to poverty, crime and family breakdown. It is a useful term in societies in which there is a growing geographical polarisation of access and opportunity so that often quite small areas – a housing estate, an inner or outer urban area – are effectively cut off from life around them. (Perri 6, 1997)

Recently, in the UK, a debate has begun about how the development of mutual policies and strategies can combat social exclusion. It was initiated by Peter Kellner, a well-known political columnist and broadcaster. He used the phrase 'new mutualism' to describe a renewed search for policies that would form the basis for action, in both the public and private sectors, to combat adverse social and economic trends. He first argued the case for this 'new mutualism' at a seminar on the 'Third Way' organised by the UK prime minister, Tony Blair, in May 1998. The British Co-operative Party asked him to develop his ideas to stimulate debate on the role of co-operative and mutual organisations in the New Labour government's search for effective social and economic policies, especially those designed to tackle social exclusion. He did this in the first in a series of New Mutualism pamphlets published by the Co-operative Party (Kellner, 1998). The debate initiated by Kellner is part of the search for new solutions to the social and economic problems created by the self-seeking individualism that dominated the political landscape in the UK during the 1980s and 1990s. It was encouraged by the then Conservative governments led by Margaret Thatcher and her successor John Major, who applauded self-reliance and meritocractic wealth creation through private enterprise. Tax reductions and the privatisation of public service assets encouraged this self-seeking individualism. The free market was given free rein as the boundaries of government were rolled back. These policies aided globalisation and the movement of capital in search of unearned profit, but led to a marked growth of inequality between the richest and poorest in society. They were policies that nurtured the seeds of social exclusion. They were the antithesis of mutuality and solidarity, famously illustrated by Margaret Thatcher's memorable proclamation that 'There is no such thing as society, there are individual men and women and families.'

That human beings have the capacity to act in an altruistic, selfless manner is beyond dispute. In the City of London, near the Barbican, there is a garden of remembrance in the centre of which is a wall, protected from the weather by an open-sided pitched roof, adorned with plaques commemorating those who lost their lives saving or attempting to save others. What is it in our species that gives many people the capacity to risk all, even life itself, for the sake of others? Kellner postulated the view that mutuality and solidarity are part of our genetic make-up, a human quality that has benefited the survival of our species. His view merited further analysis. The first part of *The Third Estate*, the second pamphlet in the New Mutualism series (written by this author, Rodgers, 1999) analyses the validity of this view. It concludes that mutuality or solidarity – acting altruistically for the common good rather than solely for self-interest – is part of our natural human heritage, but like all innate qualities of the human spirit it must be learned through education and the example of others. It argues the case for the application of the principles of co-operation and mutuality to the provision of housing for those unable to meet their own housing needs in the free market.

Housing in the UK is characterised by the divide between ownership and rental. Of the 24 million homes in the UK, approximately 70 per cent, (16.2 million), are owned outright by their occupants or are being bought on a mortgage. The remainder are rented. Of these, approximately 4 million are owned by local authorities, and 1.5 million by non-profit social landlords registered with and regulated by the Housing Corporation (or its Scottish, Welsh and Northern Irish equivalents). The remaining 2.3 million homes are rented from private landlords. Some of the worst housing conditions in the UK are in this private rented sector, where there is no mutuality between the needs of the tenant and the desire of the landlord for a return on the capital value of the property.

In rented housing there is an imbalance of power inherent in the landlord/ tenant relationship. All tenants are dependent for the quality of their housing and the housing services they receive on the benevolence or otherwise of their landlord. Only their basic rights are protected by law. Tenants generally have no control over their housing or their wider housing environment. The exception to this general position is in the small co-operative housing sector. Approximately 10,000 households in the registered social landlord sector are owned by housing co-operatives whose members are the tenants living in the housing their co-operative owns. In housing provided by local authorities, 170,000 households now manage their homes as members of tenant management organisations, the majority of which are co-operatives. In *The Third Estate*, I made the political case for the creation of a new form of tenure in UK property law, one in which rights of occupation of rental housing arise through membership of a democratically controlled housing co-operative.

The publication of the Government's Housing Green Paper 'Quality and Choice' has given added impetus to the housing debate, particularly the rights of tenants to participate in the control of their housing if they so wish (DETR, 2000). It openly acknowledges the need to invest £19 billion to deal with the backlog of disrepair in public, council-owned housing. It also asks open questions about the future of 'social housing', the term used for subsidised accommodation provided by local authorities or non-profit registered social landlords (RSLs). It sets consumer choice and tenant empowerment firmly at the heart of the New Labour government's housing strategies. This is in stark contrast to the last government's policies that were provider-driven, under which tenant majorities on RSL boards were banned, and where tenant control was seen, at best, as just one of the tools for undoing council housing. For the first time in a generation the door is now open for tenants to choose to form a housing co-operative or community-based housing association to take over ownership of their homes. The Green Paper positively encourages transfer of social housing 'to a greater number of smaller bodies that are based in or closer to the communities' they serve (DETR, 2000, p60, para. 7.14). The government's positive attitude to tenant control and ownership in the Green Paper echoes other government statements. The prime minister in his introduction to the Social Exclusion Unit's report *Bringing Britain Together: a national strategy for neighbourhood renewal* stated that: 'Too much has been imposed from above, when experience shows that success depends on communities themselves having the power and taking the responsibility to make things better.' Nick Raynsford MP, in his first speech as Housing Minister to the National Housing Federation's 1999 annual conference, referred to two examples of successful communities as models of what he wanted government policies to achieve. Both were housing co-operatives.

For the past twenty-five years, housing co-operatives have proved themselves to be remarkably resilient and able to create sustainable inclusive communities. The government's support for mutuality in the provision of housing for those who cannot meet their own housing needs in the free market has a pragmatic foundation. It is political support for what has been shown to work and bring positive benefits. Three independent research studies have demonstrated the benefits that mutual co-operative and community housing organisations create (Price Waterhouse, 1995; Clapham and Kintrea, 1998; Gillanders and Blackaby, 1999), benefits that extend beyond the improved management and maintenance of housing. The benefits are best illustrated by example and there are few better places to look than at West Whitlawburn Housing Co-operative in Cambuslang on the south-east fringes of Glasgow, formerly one of Glasgow City Council's sprawling peripheral estates. West Whitlawburn is a demonstration of the capacity of tenants to grasp the opportunity offered by the availability of capital investment to transform some of the worst social housing in Britain into a vibrant thriving community, a place where people want to live rather than to escape from. The benefits of co-operative ownership and control of the regeneration of public housing at West Whitlawburn are self-evident. They extend far beyond the physical improvement of the 543 homes in the former drab, grey, multi-storey blocks where drug dealing was rife and communal areas vandalised and uncared for. Concièrges employed by the co-operative give security to the now-welcoming entrance lobbies and staircases. The Bonus Ball Centre, a community facility built with grant funding from the National Lottery Charities Board and South Lanarkshire Council, has a fitness suite that would be the envy of any city health club, a valuable contribution to individual and community health improvement. A computer training suite, run jointly with Anniesland Further Education College provides IT skills and employment training. Mothers and toddlers meet daily for parenting classes supported by the local health authority and a crèche facility helps parents return to work. The Rollover Café provides cheap, healthy lunches for schoolchildren and runs a healthy eating programme for families. The co-operative has created employment opportunities for eighteen residents, 40 per cent of its forty-six staff.

West Whitlawburn is not unique; the benefits it has created are to be found in differing ways in other housing co-operatives and resident-led housing organisations throughout England and Scotland (Wales and Northern Ireland have not yet developed this type of housing provision). Despite the evident benefits created by housing co-operatives they remain a tiny part of social housing provision. Co-operatives provide and manage less than 1 per cent of the UK's housing stock of 24 million dwellings.

For housing co-operatives to become mainstream providers of housing for those who cannot meet their own housing needs in the free market there must be radical change to the system of social housing administration and finance. The practicalities of the changes needed are set out in the UK Co-operative Council's publication *Co-operative Housing: realising the potential* (1998) and in *Tenants in Control* published by the Confederation of Co-operative Housing (1999). If radical change to social housing provision is to occur, it is necessary for those who understand the benefits of co-operative housing to persuade those who control housing policy and administer it that the development of housing co-operatives benefits society as a whole. This is as great a challenge as that faced by our progressive Victorian ancestors who needed to persuade their contemporaries – who understood little of the science of bacteriology – of the benefits of investing for the common good in water supply and sewage disposal.

The challenge of persuading our contemporaries that housing co-operatives bring positive benefits to society as a whole, rather than just benefits solely to the communities who live in them (benefits which comfort the liberal minority rather than the tax-paying majority), is not an easy political task. While not easy, it is one that the advocates of applying co-operative and mutual principles to housing can approach with confidence. Persuasion centres on two key arguments; first, that applying the principles of mutuality in housing through the positive promotion of housing co-operatives and other community-led housing providers unlocks the potential of socially excluded communities in a way that is of benefit to the whole of society. The second key argument is more esoteric but none the less valid. It is that, if we are to protect democracy and the rational rule of law from extremism and authoritarianism, democracy must be deeply rooted in our society, and housing co-operatives are a vital way of nurturing democracy's roots. Let us look at each of these arguments.

Housing co-operatives unlock the potential of socially excluded communities in a way that is of benefit to the whole of society. As stated previously, three independent research studies have demonstrated the benefits that mutual co-operative and community housing organisations create; benefits that extend beyond the improved management and maintenance of housing. The most in-depth study was carried out by management consultants Price Waterhouse and published in 1995. It looked at co-op performance over a number of years and compared it with the best of traditional social landlords. Price Waterhouse concluded:

> The findings of this research demonstrate that there are significant and worthwhile benefits associated with Tenant Management Organisations (TMOs) especially those which give tenants effective control, tenant management co-operatives or autonomy, par-value housing co-operatives. These take the forms of not only more cost-effective services, especially the speed and quality of repairs, but also in terms of wider social and community benefits, as through the acquisition of new skills and experience which can be important to many residents in social rented housing. Some of these benefits are quantifiable in

financial terms; some cannot be appropriately expressed in money terms and others are unquantifiable, but nevertheless real. The case study TMOs have, in general, delivered higher levels of resident satisfaction across a wide range of housing services. While resources are required in the short-term for setting up TMOs, the benefits arising from this initial investment can be expected to produce longer-term saving and benefits which more than outweigh the set-up costs. (1995, p122)

What are the benefits that extend beyond the improved management and maintenance of housing, an improvement that in itself is beneficial to society as it helps to maintain the quality of housing for subsequent generations? The personal benefits are the learning of new skills and the development of latent talents. The social benefits created by housing co-operatives arise from the informal social support networks that develop in communities where people know each other and share their needs and aspirations. These informal social support networks are vitally important to ensuring the least possible demand on the state, because where they do not exist it is the state that, of necessity, steps in to provide the support that is not found within communities themselves. Informal support networks exist within all communities but research on, and practical experience of, co-operatives shows that they exist to a greater degree within housing co-operatives and other mutually-administered communities. This is because the day-to-day task of exercising mutual responsibility for the management of housing provides a foundation for their development. It enables neighbours to get to know each other and to find out who can be trusted to act for mutual benefit rather than just for selfish gain.

The development of these mutual support networks is of growing importance for a society, such as that in Britain, where there is a growing number of elderly people who, without such networks, will need state support. In the Netherlands, co-housing schemes for the elderly, where there is an element of communal living and where elderly people choose to live together for mutual support, are common, well-established and highly successful.[1] Similar projects have yet to develop in the UK. There are many bureaucratic impediments to their development, as the gloriously named 'Growing Old Disgracefully' group of older women in London who want to establish a co-housing scheme are finding. The experience in the Netherlands shows that by living together and providing mutual support, elderly people make fewer demands on health and social services, and enjoy a better quality of life. That such mutual housing provision for the elderly would benefit older people and taxpayers alike is illustrated by the decision of Lambeth Council to charge elderly and disabled people for previously free support services such as 'meals on wheels' and assistance with shopping. The introduction of charges is reported to be necessary, in part, to generate additional income to meet the higher than budgeted cost of an external contractor administering housing benefit, a task at which it is appallingly inefficient (reported in *Streatham, Clapham and Dulwich Guardian*, 7 September, 2000, p3). This is a classic illustration of why radical change in the way the UK administers housing and related services for the poor and disadvantaged is needed, radical change in which the principles of mutuality have a vital role to play.

Housing co-operatives benefit their members and society as a whole in many ways too. Recently a delegation of housing managers and journalists from Austria visited housing co-operatives in London. Austria has a well-established co-operative housing sector. The oldest housing co-operative in Austria still active today was founded in 1895. When visiting Hazel Housing Co-operative in South East London, the visitors discussed with co-op committee members the relatively low incidence of property and car crime in the co-operative in comparison to the surrounding council and housing association estates. The chair of Hazel Co-operative, Della Read, explained that it was because the community knew each other and were prepared to challenge strangers. The polite English challenge described by Ms Read as 'Excuse me, can I help you?' caused amusement to the Austrians, who explained that in their culture the challenge made by co-op members would be more robust but none the less effective. Della Read explained the reason why co-op members were willing to challenge strangers who might be intent on crime. As well as the desire to protect themselves and their neighbours' property, they also knew that a break-in would cause damage to the property the co-op owned, damage that would take time, effort and co-op money to repair.

Through exercising mutual responsibility for their housing, co-op members also grow in stature personally and socially. Those who become active members develop new skills and abilities in ways that benefit other aspects of their lives. This is what Perri 6 refers to as the development of human and social capital that would otherwise remain dormant. He describes human capital as:

> arguably the most valuable form of capital today ... not just formal qualifications and skills, but more subtle ones: knowing how to behave at work, knowing how to please a customer, knowing how to work in a team and most importantly, being able to spot an unexploited opportunity and find a way to make use of it. (Perri 6, 1997, p5)

These are work-related examples of what constitutes human capital. Those of us developing housing co-operatives would add other soft skills such as knowing how to listen; learning to resolve differences of opinion by discussion rather than by conflict; learning to accept the will of the majority while respecting the opinion of the minority; and learning to lead without usurping the rights of the led. If these skills have not been learned previously, housing co-operatives provide another opportunity for them to be acquired because they are essential for the effective working of the co-operative. Perri 6 argues that policy to regenerate poor areas today would more sensibly start with learning rather than the state of the physical environment. This is precisely what happens in the development of a housing co-operative where the education and training of new members is an essential prerequisite for the establishment of the co-operative.

Perri 6 goes even further in arguing that human capital needs to be matched by social capital. By this he means 'the quality of contacts people have and the networks they plug into, and the norms of trust, reciprocity and goodwill, sense of shared life across the classes and capacities that these ties afford'. Again, sharing responsibility for housing through membership of a co-operative creates the opportunity for the development of this social capital. Trust is the foundation on which mutuality and reciprocity within communities is built (an issue I analysed in depth in Rodgers, 1999, section 1).

A study by Nottingham University for the National Institute for Adult Continuing Education (NIACE) gives an insight into why participation in a housing co-operative or other voluntary organisation creates opportunities for the development of human and social capital (Elsdon *et al.*, 1995). The researchers looked at what people gained from participation in a wide range of voluntary organisations as diverse as pigeon-fancying clubs, tenants' associations and church choirs. They concluded that participation led to increased knowledge, skills and confidence, and enhanced the ability of participants to control their own lives. The study identified two distinct types of learning, both of which were beneficial to individual development, and to the development of human and social capital. The first was 'premeditated learning': learning that related directly to the organisation's purpose and function. In a housing co-operative, an example of this would be learning skills related to budgeting and financial control of the co-operative, skills that are clearly transferable to home and work. The second type of learning was described as 'unpremeditated learning': the learning of new skills that related only indirectly to the primary purpose of the organisation. These are 'soft' skills that are largely personal and social ones such as working in a group, learning to organise and run meetings, learning to listen and so forth. These skills, although unpremeditated because they are not what the person joined the group to learn, are equally valuable and transferable to other life situations. Such unpremeditated learning is definitely the result of participation in a housing co-operative. Not everybody succeeds in learning these skills, and failure to do so causes loss in interest in participation, but in a successful co-operative the learning by members of new hard and soft skills is a distinctly beneficial outcome of the co-operative's activities.

The study also found that the later a person left formal education the more likely it was that they would participate in a voluntary organisation and gain these skills. This is an important finding for housing policy. Those who live in the publicly-subsidised rental housing sector tend towards the lower quartile of the population in both income and educational attainment. They tend to have on average a lower 'terminal educational age'. They are therefore less likely to be involved in voluntary organisations of any type and therefore less likely to have the opportunity of acquiring skills through the premeditated and unpremeditated learning the report describes. Involvement in managing housing through a housing co-operative creates the opportunity for skills development which such communities would not otherwise have, with all the personal and social benefits this brings.

If these arguments are not sufficient in themselves to persuade policy-makers and the public that investment in housing co-operatives brings benefits to the whole of society (and better value for tax-payers' money than investing in traditional landlords) then there is another equally compelling 'benefit for the whole of society' argument. It is that housing co-operatives underpin and protect democracy. They do so in a sector of society where other grass-roots democratic organisations increasingly do not reach. The case to be made is that co-operatives are therefore vital to the health and continuation of the democratic government that British society values and holds dear. With the collapse of the Soviet bloc, the dangers to democracy are as much from inside British society as external. It is threatened from within by a growing disillusionment with and lack of participation in formal democratic political processes. The ease with which our society can be held to ransom by dissidents was shown by the effects of last year's blockade of fuel depots by disgruntled farmers and hauliers. As TUC secretary, John Monks, reminded us, it was a lorry owners' strike which helped to bring down the democratically elected Allende government in Chile and brought the right-wing human rights abuser General Pinochet to power in the 1970s (report in *Guardian*, 15 September, 2000). The lack of participation in formal democratic politics by the socially excluded in our poorest neighbourhoods is one reason why such neighbourhoods provide some of the most fertile recruitment territory for the undemocratic, racist far-right.

Part of the problem with democratic politics is that decisions affecting the lives of British citizens are taken by politicians and government institutions remote from those they affect and not accountable to them. Everyday lives are affected by a plethora of government quangos and executive agencies, from the Advertising Standards Agency to the Welsh Administration Ombudsman. These are run by officials and appointed boards that are only remotely accountable to the electorate via their responsible minister and his or her accountability to Parliament. This accountability is also at risk of being weakened, ministers having recently been criticised by MPs for making policy statements outside the House of Commons. Even the democratic role of local councillors is in danger of being minimised in the cause of modernisation, although the need to seek efficiency in the running of local government is irrefutable. The centralisation of political power in such organisations may be convenient for government, but it is unhealthy for democracy. We need a strategy to move from a form of democracy that is primarily representative to one that is fundamentally participative. An attribute of political power is that, rather like energy, it can neither be made nor destroyed. It exists in one form or other within a society. If political power is centralised it cannot be exercised locally. If it is devolved the centre must let go of it, as the devolution and elections for the Welsh and Scottish Assemblies and the election of London's mayor have graphically shown.

The same principles apply to housing. In housing provided by a traditional council or housing association, power and authority rest with the landlord. In these organisations tenants are disempowered and can only seek to influence their landlord individually or by collective action through tenants' associations. Progressive landlords permit tenant representatives to sit on their boards and committees, but this does not alter fundamentally where political power rests. It simply moves representatives into existing decision-making structures. The management of such housing does little to encourage political participation or to improve the health of our democracy. The most progressive of social landlords will share power over the management of their housing. This they do through joint management boards or local area committees on to which tenants elect their representatives. This power-sharing brings political power closer to the people who are affected by a landlord's decisions, but it does not place it directly and democratically in the hands of consumers of housing services.

The word 'empowerment' is used frequently in the debate about shifting the balance of power between landlord and tenant. It is a dangerous word that is used too often without proper understanding. Empowerment, like inoculation, implies a passive process; something that is done to someone or a community rather than something a person or community achieves for themselves. Power is not given to tenants or communities. The balance of power transfers when communities of tenants understand enough about the issues that affect the control of their homes and trust each other enough to exercise power responsibly and take control of their housing environment. It is an active process of taking hold of the levers of power, not a passive one of accepting what is offered.

The tenants of housing co-operatives and other types of community landlords have the right to vote on major policy matters that affect their housing and to elect accountable representatives to take day-to-day management decisions for them. Political power over housing and its environment is devolved, as far as it can be, to the residents themselves. By participation in a housing co-operative or other mutual landlord, the poorest in our society learn how to use democratic processes to improve the quality of their lives and their neighbourhood. The participation in formal constitutional decision-making processes in a well-governed housing co-operative teaches respect for the effectiveness of democracy as a means of social governance. It helps to root democracy deeply within the fabric of British society, not least because distributed political power is harder to usurp. There is no better case than this for encouraging mutuality in housing and promoting the establishment of housing co-operatives.

Notes

1   A co-housing scheme is the Americanised term used to describe a type of housing co-operative in which members can have a varying equity interest and in which there is an element of communal living and shared living space. They are common in Denmark and the Netherlands and are beginning to develop in the United States. See *We're in Charge: Co-housing communities of older people in the Netherlands, lessons for Britain*, by Maria Brenton, Policy Press/The Housing Corporation, 1998, ISBN 1-86134-133-4; and *Co-housing* (second edition) Kathryn McCamant Charles Durrett, 10 speed Press, ISBN 0-89815-539-8.

References

Clapham, D. and Kintrea, K. (1998) 'Sustainability and maturity of community-based housing organizations', *Journal of Co-operative Studies*, 31(1), pp. 30–38.
Confederation of Co-operative housing (1999) *Tenants in Control*, London.
DETR (Dept of the Environment, Transport and the Regions) (2000) *Quality and Choice: A Decent Home for All*, Housing Green Paper, London, DETR.
Elsdon, K. T. with Reynolds, J. and Stewart, S. (1995) *Voluntary Organisations: Citizenship, Learning and Change*, NIACE.
Gillanders, G. and Blackby, R. (1999) *Models of Resident-controlled Housing*, London, Office for Public Management.
Kellner, P. (1998) *The Third Way*, Pamphlet No. 1, London, Co-operative Party.
Perri 6, P (1997) *Social exclusion: time to be optimistic*, London, DEMOS Collection No. 12.
Price Waterhouse (1995) *Tenants in Control: An Evaluation of Tenant-led Housing Management Organisations*, London, HMSO.
Rodgers, D. (1999) *The Third Estate*, Pamphlet No. 3, London, Co-operative Party.
UK Co-operative Council (1998) *Co-operative Housing: realizing the potential*, Manchester, UKCC.

4   Consumer co-operatives in retrospect and prospect

Johnston Birchall

Strictly speaking, a consumer co-operative is non-mutual. It is owned entirely by individual members, customers who choose to pay a small fee for a membership share. It is controlled by a board elected by those members, and practices open membership so that anyone who wishes can join. Yet in most countries customers do not have to be members in order to shop at the 'co-op'. When co-operative principles were codified in the form of the 'Rochdale Principles' in 1844, the Rochdale 'pioneers', as they were known, did not bother to specify that customers should be members; it was taken for granted that they would be. At that time, there were three main incentives for shopping co-operatively: the quality of the goods, price, and the dividend. By far the most persuasive of these was the last – the quarterly payout of significant amounts of money (that could be taken in cash or left to earn interest in a share account), calculated as a percentage of a member's purchases in that quarter. Not to be a member would have been irrational. This condition continued in the UK and in several other countries until the 1970s, when increased competition and a lack of business integration between societies led to their abandoning the dividend in favour of a new strategy of low prices or discounts paid out to all customers. Managers began to copy the retail strategies of their multiple-chain competitors, and membership ceased to have much meaning. The one notable exception is Japan, where in the early postwar period the co-op's competitors forced it to be fully mutual, insisting that all customers have to be members. It is significant that the Japanese co-operative movement is, on several criteria, the most successful in the world.

As we shall see further in this chapter, in some other countries the situation is now changing; membership is becoming more central to strategies for emphasising the difference between co-ops and their competitors, and for stressing the 'co-operative advantage'. For this reason, and also because they are such large and comparatively successful forms of member-owned business, it is worth seeing consumer co-ops as being significant for 'mutuality'. In this chapter we shall be outlining the origins of the idea, and tracing its development from the founding fathers of Rochdale in 1844 to the present day, both in the UK and in other countries that have developed their own co-operative movements. Then we shall be asking whether this now very old form of mutual business still has a continuing purpose on behalf of consumers. Evidence will be reviewed for the effectiveness of co-ops in meeting their purposes, and the radical question will be asked as to whether the still considerable assets of the sector are being used to their best advantage. Then we summarise one recent chain of events – the attempted demutualisation of Europe's largest consumer co-op, the Co-operative Wholesale Society (CWS). The attempt failed, and we shall be drawing lessons from this for the future of consumer co-operatives.

The origins of consumer co-operation

In 1760, the shipwrights who worked in the British Navy's dockyards at Chatham and Woolwich did something very unusual. They bought and began to run their own flour mills. From there the idea spread along the coast to other ports such as Hull (1795), Whitby (1812), and Devonport (1816). From milling, they went into baking, and in 1816 the skilled artisans of Sheerness opened their own general store, and the classic association of consumer co-operation with shopkeeping had begun (Cole, 1944). We do not have to look far for their motives; this was a simple case of market failure. They were suffering from local monopolies of millers and bakers which resulted in high prices and adulteration of the flour. In his classic study of food during the British industrial revolution, Burnett says that in general monopoly was not important, but that it *was* prevalent in flour milling (1989, p95). Production was based on water or wind power that was limited to certain locations, and so entry into the market was difficult, and existing producers could easily fix prices. Consumers were tied to their localities by the poor communications of the time, and had to use local suppliers. The result was, as one report published in 1767 put it: 'Millers have indeed within a few years raised immense fortunes, and with incredible expedition; and bakers in general thrive and get rich in a proportion far beyond what is seen in other trades' (quoted in Potter, 1899, p42). Had this issue been experienced more recently, we might have expected the shipwrights to campaign for new laws banning food adulteration, to appeal to a government anti-monopolies commission, complain to their local authority consumer protection department, to boycott the producers, or to have their case taken up by a consumers' association. None of these options was available, so they simply went into production for themselves.

This simple idea that consumers can, if they so wish, go into business for themselves, mutually providing for their own needs, can be traced from these flour mill societies right through to modern consumer co-operatives around the world. The historical development of consumer co-operation in the developed world follows closely that of industrialisation in each country (Birchall, 1997a). It is not surprising that the first co-operative movement grew up in the first country to industrialise, Great Britain.

Consumer co-operatives are predicated on a division between consumer and producer that is a characteristic of industrialisation (Polanyi, 1957). They take their place among several working class self-help movements which began in the mid- to late eighteenth century and matured in the late Victorian period (late nineteenth century) as a set of highly respected and well regulated mutual institutions: they included also the friendly societies, trade unions and building societies (Hopkins, 1995).

There were more attempts at co-operation, but the first successful one began in 1844 when the 'Rochdale Pioneers' opened a store in Toad Lane, Rochdale, which became a source of inspiration and guidance for the consumer co-operative movement all over the world. It was very successful in two senses. First, it showed that consumer-controlled businesses could compete effectively against private traders. At a time when wholesale and retail markets were undeveloped and inefficient (Jeffreys, 1954), the Pioneers virtually invented retail management via branch stores, and through co-operative wholesaling were able to organise distribution much more effectively than their competitors (Birchall, 1994). Second, the Rochdale society laid down some basic principles that would ensure both business success and democratic control by consumers. There was the 'dividend principle' by which surpluses were distributed regularly to members in proportion to their purchases. There was a principle of giving no more than a fixed and limited return on shares, which were not revalued in line with the value of the business but remained at their original value. Together these principles meant that there was a sound economic reason for being a member and shopping as much as possible at the 'co-op', and that the organisation could not deform into an investor-owned business. The low cost of entry, combined with an open membership principle, meant that all but the poorest could afford to join (and even the poor could pay their share in instalments). There was an incentive to encourage others to join, because, other things being equal, the larger the membership, the lower would be the expenses and the higher the dividend. There was the principle of one member having one vote regardless of the size of shareholding, an education principle that encouraged societies to spend part of their surpluses on educating their members, and a principle of political and religious neutrality. All of these contributed towards a high quality of member participation in decision-making. There was a prudent principle of cash trading which, though it had the effect of excluding the very poor who relied on weekly credit from small shopkeepers, ensured that the business would survive in bad times. Finally, there was a principle of supplying only pure and unadulterated products, which meant that at a time of almost universal adulteration and short measures the co-operatives could be trusted to work wholeheartedly in the interests of consumers (Holyoake, 1907).

By the end of the nineteenth century there were 1439 co-operative societies in Britain, with over 1.7 million members and a turnover of more than £50m a year. The Co-operative Wholesale Society (CWS), as well as being one of the largest wholesalers in the world, was also a major grower, manufacturer and importer, bringing to the British consumer the benefits of cheap food from abroad and cutting out the 'middle man' throughout the supply chain. By 1914 the movement was a well-established institution, celebrating an unbroken history of growth in every direction that had already lasted seventy years.

At around the same time as the Rochdale Pioneers were opening their store, similar experiments were being carried out in other countries, but it was only when promoters in each country discovered the Rochdale 'system' with its dividend on purchases that their own movements began to take off. In Switzerland during the 1860s, existing societies such as the Zurich Consumverein converted to the Rochdale system, and by 1904 there were 204 societies, with their own wholesale society and national union. In France, by 1907, there were 2166 societies, with over 600,000 members. The Belgian movement was inhibited by religious and political divisions, but even so by 1905 there were 168 societies with a national federation. In Italy, by 1904, there were 1448 registered societies, with around a third as many again unregistered. In Germany, early development was mainly of rural and urban credit banks, but by 1905 a central union of consumer co-operatives had 787 societies in membership, along with 260 attached to the credit banks. Their wholesale society was explicitly modelled on the highly influential English CWS.

In Russia, by the time of the 1905 Revolution there were nearly a thousand societies, with 300,000 members. After this, a more liberal political climate led to rapid growth, so that by the time of the Bolshevik Revolution they had become a vital part of the supply chain. Other central and eastern European countries also established small, but nationally federated, co-operative sectors, and some can boast co-operative-type stores as old as that of the Rochdale Pioneers. In Japan, by 1907, there was a society 'in every town of any importance' (Vacek, 1989, p1033). However, their expansion was checked by a government suspicious of independent associations. At the start of the First World War all the countries of Western Europe and Scandinavia, Russia and several countries in central and eastern Europe had well-developed consumer co-operative sectors. The largest was still the British movement, with three million members, but the Germans, with 1.7 million members, were not far behind.

Developments during the interwar period

It has been a curious but understandable feature of consumer co-operative history that, except in countries where they have been suppressed, they have tended to prosper during wartime. Governments come to rely on their distribution systems to meet basic needs, and the populace comes to a new understanding of the fairness and integrity of retailers who believe in putting the consumer first. By the end of the First World War, in which 'the Co-op' in Britain distinguished itself by introducing voluntary rationing before the state intervened, and by refusing to profiteer, there were over three million members. In 1917 it took the unprecedented step of setting up its own political party, and in 1918 had its first Member of Parliament elected. The Co-operative Party then entered an alliance with the Labour Party, and ever since has had several 'Labour and Co-operative' MPs and Lords in Parliament, as well as many local 'Labour and Co-op' councillors. The movement grew steadily during the interwar period. By the start of the Second World War, 'the Co-op' consisted of 1100 societies, controlling 24,000 stores, and having 40 per cent of the market in butter, 26 per cent of milk, 23 per cent of grocery and provisions, 20 per cent of tea, sugar and cheese, and so on. When rationing was introduced, 28 per cent of the population – 13.5 million people – registered with the Co-op (Birchall, 1994, ch8). It employed a quarter of a million people in retailing and another hundred thousand in manufacturing and distribution. With 155 factories, the CWS was one of the biggest businesses in the world.

In all countries with established co-operative movements, this was also a time of steady expansion. Because they were dealing in basic commodities, co-operatives tended to stand up to the shocks of economic depression and mass unemployment. In times of trouble, member loyalty tended to increase, even if for a while their total spending went down. In most countries the rise of big city societies and powerful national wholesale societies led by 'monarchical' managers enabled the building up of very large, modern businesses. But there were structural weaknesses: the Co-op tended to deal in a narrow range of staple food products, there were too many small societies, and these were concentrated mainly in industrial working-class areas. The movement was tending to grow organically, along lines of least resistance rather than by planned development (Birchall, 1997a). However, these weaknesses did not become noticeable until after the Second World War.

During the interwar period, the idea of consumer co-operation became more firmly established in North America. In Canada, it took root most firmly among the mining communities of the Atlantic Provinces. Here, for similar reasons as in mining villages in Western Europe, people co-operated to overcome the 'truck system' by which mine-owners supplied goods needed by their workforces in company stores. In Eastern Nova Scotia, they were aided by the adult education system developed by the Antigonish movement, which stressed the importance of co-operatives to the local economy (Fay, 1938). Growth was checked, though, in countries taken over by Fascist or Communist governments; autonomous consumer-owned businesses and totalitarianism did not mix. In Italy, Germany, Austria, Japan and Spain the movement was destroyed as an independent force. The threat from Communism was more subtle. In Russia, by 1918, there were 26,000 societies with 9 million members. The Bolsheviks extended co-operatives so they became an almost universal provider, though in the process they killed off the voluntary nature of membership. Lenin realised he had made a mistake, and in 1924 tried to restore their autonomy. However, once lost, it proved impossible to restore, and in 1935 Stalin completed the process by abolishing all the urban consumer co-operatives and confiscating their assets, without compensation to the then 10 million members. Despite these setbacks, by 1937 the International Co-operative Alliance had in membership 50,000 consumer co-ops with nearly 60 million members.

After the Second World War

After the war, the movement in the UK continued to expand. It was at the forefront of innovations such as self-service and supermarketing, but these hid underlying structural problems. With over 1000 societies, a range of different-sized shops, many of which were too small, and with a lack of integration between societies and their wholesalers, the movement began to lose ground to the multiple chains. By the late 1950s, the Co-op had 11 per cent of the retail trade, and the multiples 22 per cent, but the Co-op stopped growing and then began a long decline. What had been its strengths – local loyalties, the cherished independence of each society, a prejudice in favour of letting managers emerge 'from the ranks' and against those who were university educated – all these began to work against the Co-op. There was no lack of detailed analysis of what was wrong (see Co-operative Independent Commission, 1958), but there was weak central direction and a determination among societies to continue trading until they had to merge in order to survive. Mergers have reduced the original 1000 societies to forty-six (as at the year 2000), but faced with some of the most effective and efficient multiple retailers in the world the movement has declined steadily until it now has a market share of just under 4 per cent. It has been overtaken by three multiple chains in its strongest area, food retailing, where it has around 7 per cent of the market.

The German movement was reconstituted after the war, and by 1953 had nearly two million members. However, as in the UK, it faced stiff competition. Though the German co-op continued to grow it lost market share; by 1965 it had 8.6 per cent of the market, multiple stores 19.3 per cent and the wholesalers' purchasing groups 31 per cent (Brazda, 1989). The response was also similar. Instead of paying dividend to members, co-ops began to offer rebates to all customers, thus weakening the vital connection between membership and economic returns. Similar too were the reports on the structural weaknesses of the sector, attempts to organise mergers being hampered by weak central direction, and the resistance of small societies determined to keep their autonomy even at the risk of extinction. As in Britain, a plan for regionalisation took shape slowly and mergers took place out of weakness rather than in a planned way. In the early 1970s, in response to mounting debts, societies began to convert to a conventional limited company form, and amalgamated in one central organisation, Co-op Zentrale AG, which by 1980 was back in profit. However, weak accountability structures and fraudulent management led to further drastic reorganisation until by 1989 the movement had only thirty-seven societies, with 650,000 members. Some of the healthiest societies, such as Co-op Dortmund, resisted the conversion to a joint stock company. This society, by continuing to pay attention to member relations and pay a traditional dividend, remained highly successful (Brazda, 1989). By 1988, it had nearly half a million members and over 14 per cent of local retail trade. However, stagnating retail trade and intensified competition led to a withdrawal of shares by members, the sale of stores, and the society's eventual dissolution (Kurimoto, 1999).

A similar story can be told in other Western European countries. In Austria, a too-rapid expansion in the 1970s led societies into a serious debt burden, and eventual amalgamation into one Konsum Austria. It is interesting to note that in the UK some co-operative revivalists have promoted the idea of one national society; in the case of Austria stagnation and the concealing of the crisis from consumer-members led, in 1995, to the national society's (and therefore the whole movement's) bankruptcy (Schediwy, 1996). In the Netherlands, in 1973, the movement had to be sold off to the private sector. In France, in 1985, around 40 per cent of the movement was sold off (Schediwy, 1989).

Consumer co-operators in the Scandinavian countries also faced strong competition and the need to rationalise the number of societies. They made a better job of it than their southern counterparts. In Finland, in 1983, thirty-nine regional societies belonging to the 'E-Movement' formed Co-op Finland, the third biggest company group in the country, which did manage to achieve commercial viability, though with this taking precedence over 'social conscience' (Schediwy, 1989). A second grouping, SOK, maintained their conscientious stance, keeping open small shops in rural areas and living off massive reserves built up in better times. Eventually drastic restructuring was needed, but this succeeded and the movement gained 23 per cent of the market (together, the two movements now have a creditable 35 per cent of the market). In Sweden, by 1970, market share was 18 per cent and membership over 1.6 million (Schediwy, 1989). Yet by the mid-1980s the movement was in trouble. Instead of amalgamating into one national organisation, the Swedish co-ops decided to form a retail group, maintaining their democratic structure but accepting the discipline of a single business organisation. There are now 102 societies, with 2.2 million members and a rising market share (Ag, 1995). In Norway, 400 societies have joined a buying group, with a corporate identity imposed by their national body, NKL. Again, market share has risen slightly, proving that amalgamation is not always the only alternative to local autonomy (Sivertsen, 1993).

Two success stories are the movements in Switzerland and Italy. At first, the postwar history of the movement in Switzerland follows the usual one of decline, with the closure of small shops, resistance to mergers, even the giving up of dividend in favour of rebate stamps which so devalued the idea of membership. Yet a strong central union imposed structural reforms, so that by 1983 market share had increased to 12 per cent of retail trade. One unique factor which partly accounts for the turnaround was that Co-op Suisse faced competition from another consumer co-op, Migros, founded as a conventional, and highly successful retailer, and then in 1940 given to the customers by its owner (Hasler, 1985). By 1970, its twelve regional societies had 872,000 members and a 9.4 per cent share of the market (Setzer, 1989). In Italy, we might have expected the gradual decline seen in other countries, but because of the relative backwardness of the retail trade the co-ops have experienced 'expansion and growing social recognition' (Setzer, 1989, p853), though with only a small share of a fragmented retail trade.

The best example of a successful consumer co-operative sector in the postwar period is undoubtedly Japan. Here the movement was recon-stituted after the war under one federation. It grew quickly so that by 1947 there were 6500 societies acting as bulk-buying organisations feeding entire populations. Despite political opposition from private traders, which led to laws prohibiting sales to non-members and consumer co-operative banking, and preventing expansion beyond prefectural boundaries, the movement continued to grow. By the mid-1960s it might have suffered from the same kinds of processes of stagnation and decline as occurred in most Western European movements, but three new elements ensured continued success. One was the invention of the '*han*' or joint buying group. This rebuilt member participation from below, giving a key role to women members (most of the *han* were organised by women as housewives), and enabling societies to consult members regularly, involving them in product testing and consumer campaigns. The second element was the development of co-op branded goods by the national federation, goods that gained a reputation for quality, freedom from adulteration, and environmental friendliness. Third, co-operative leadership and management were revitalised by an influx of educated people who had experienced the very successful university co-operative movement, and they brought to the movement new direction and expertise. They managed to do what other movements had thought was impossible: to make large-scale organisation compatible with member democracy and organisational efficiency. Though there are now nearly 600 co-ops, the top thirty account for 60 per cent of turnover. And though 20 per cent of households are members, the average spend is low and in the bulk-buy groups is restricted to a basic range of goods, so market share is only 2.6 per cent (Nomura, 1993). It is, however, the largest retail chain in a very fragmented market, and it leads the field in the efficiency of its distribution system, the advanced use of new technology, and the development of larger stores.

However, it also faces problems. Recently, the pre-eminent reputation of the Japanese movement was dented when Co-op Sapporo and two other co-ops on the same island got into economic difficulties; the Japanese Consumer Co-operative Union had to step in with a rescue operation (Kurimoto, 1999).

A brief evaluation of the consumer co-operative form

The above outline history of the development of the consumer co-operative in the developed world has shown just how large it has become and how economically successful, at least until its decline in some countries since the early 1980s. It does not show to what extent the needs, views and interests of consumers have been advanced by this form of consumer self-supply, and how it compares to other ways of representing consumer interests, such as campaign groups or local government consumer protection services. A thorough evaluation of their contribution would take a major research effort, which has yet to be carried out (a cross-national study led by Brazda and Schediwy, published as a two-volume series in 1989, deals more with the economic issue of strategies for survival in the face of competition). Here we shall confine ourselves to some broad generalisations about five key indicators of success, from the consumer point of view:

- democratic control by consumers;
- ability to reward members with lower costs and/or better quality than their competitors;
- ability to protect consumers against market failures;
- influence on government consumer policy; and
- ability to meet new demands from 'ethical consumers' and environmental groups.

We shall confine ourselves also to a comparison between two widely differing co-operative sectors, in the UK and Japan.

Democratic control by consumers

There is no doubt that the societies set up as part of the Rochdale movement were highly democratic. There was one person, one vote regardless of shareholding; directors were held to account through quarterly members' meetings; and higher-level organisations were organised on the principle of federation, with the national level Co-operative Union organising annual congresses, referred to quite unselfconsciously as the 'parliament' of the movement. Commentators of the time confirm that day-to-day decision-making was characterised by tolerance, attention to detail, and open debate, backed up in many societies by a commitment to member education (Holyoake, 1907). Most societies were small, and the interest of managers was kept in check by rules restricting the proportion of employees who could be elected to the board. At first, women were excluded from office, not by rule but by social convention, but the Women's Co-operative Guild, founded in 1883, was able to train and encourage women to become co-operative board members, local government councillors and magistrates (Gaffin and Thoms, 1983). By the interwar period, there were some very large societies, but reports expressed satisfaction with the democratic side of the movement (Webb, S. and Webb, B., 1921; Carr-Saunders *et al.* 1938). Postwar, oligarchies emerged, led by powerful individuals, and low levels of participation were reported, with only a tiny percentage of members, and with fewer contested elections (Ostergaard and Halsey, 1965). It was in the smaller societies that apathy had begun; in the large city societies elections were contested by political party groups, which kept the democratic process alive. The excessive power of top managers was illustrated by the slow pace of mergers, and there were some spectacular failures of governance by boards that allowed managers to negotiate merger terms to their own advantage. Recently, there have been genuine reforms: new directors are now offered training through an Institute of Co-operative Directors, member relations departments have secured the resources to mount effective member recruitment campaigns, and a recent report on corporate governance has prompted rule changes enforcing control by elected boards. The largest societies have evolved complex voting patterns based on regional committees, and elections are becoming more contested.

The experience in the other European countries where the movement has survived has followed a roughly similar pattern. It might have done the same in Japan, but for some unique factors that have encouraged the Japanese movement to maintain a high level of democratic control throughout the postwar period. In the 1960s they invented the *han*, bulk-buying groups of five to ten households, mainly led by women, which became the basic building block of the movement. The *han*, along with groups based on co-op stores, elected representatives to local committees, who then elected higher committees, which enabled even the largest societies such as Co-op Kobe to remain truly democratic. They began to reinforce this process by consulting members regularly through the *han*, engaging them directly in product testing, social activities, volunteering and consumer campaigning. In this way, it seems the Japanese societies have solved the problem faced throughout the postwar period by European co-ops – how to restructure into larger organisations without losing touch with the members (International Joint Project, 1995).

Ability to reward members

In Britain, one of the main incentives to membership was always the dividend. It has been estimated that £50 million were returned to members in Britain before the First World War (Birchall, 1994). The effect was enhanced by being spread among so many working-class people, and because the dividend was often a means of small savings that allowed people to survive during recessions (Holyoake, 1907). Later, societies were criticised for giving too much dividend – sometimes up to 12 per cent of purchases – which excluded the poor because prices were kept high. Other incentives were the good quality of products, the reliability and honesty of the employees, and an antipathy towards advertising, which they felt was unnecessary. However, by the 1970s, dividend had been replaced in most societies by discount stamps given to all customers, and membership lost its meaning. The continued need to compete with well-capitalised multiple chains led to the ending of all incentives, and the 'Co-op' was felt to be no different from any other retailer. Recently some regional co-ops and the largest society, CWS, have reintroduced dividend using electronic swipe cards linked to computer systems, which automatically record a member's entitlement (Birchall, 1998b). Although this is not strictly dividend (which has to be declared after surpluses are made), it is an incentive to customer loyalty, and a basis on which the sense of membership could be renewed.

In other European countries, again the picture is similar. Co-ops in Norway have also reinstated the dividend using electronic cards. However, Migros in Switzerland shows that there are alternative 'social dividends'; it channels its surpluses into community education activities for members. In Japan there has always been less emphasis on the dividend – rarely does it exceed 1 per cent of sales. Because customers have to become members in order to trade with the co-op, other incentives can be given, such as the provision of high-quality, pure products, and social dividends such as community facilities. Co-op Kobe, for instance, has built and maintains large, purpose-built community centres in each locality within its region. Because the Japanese movement is a most efficient and modern retailer, it has avoided the vicious circle of low profitability and inability to afford member benefits. Regional co-ops provide generous community facilities that in other countries would be supplied by local authorities.

Ability to protect consumers against market failures

As soon as the co-operative sector became large enough, it tended to work against cartels and price-rings. For instance, when in the 1880s shipping companies imposed a price rise, the CWS simply set up its own shipping line. In the interwar period it successfully broke price-rings in the soap trade, tea imports, flour-milling, and baking (Redfern, 1938). Where prices were fixed by government marketing boards, co-ops reduced the price by giving dividend. The use of dividend was opposed by manufacturers, who organised a boycott of the Co-op; again, the movement went into its own production of goods such as lightbulbs, radios, and gramophones. Since the Second World War, the movement in the UK has not been strong enough to affect markets on behalf of consumers, though its insistence on keeping open small, loss-making shops should perhaps be seen as an attempt to mitigate the effects of market changes on those less mobile customers who bear the social costs (Birchall, 1987).

In Japan, in the interwar period, the co-op promoter, Kagawa, organised a consumer boycott of producers who would not sell to the co-ops, but again they were not strong enough to radically affect the markets. Postwar, they began to affect the retail trade through strong advocacy of consumers. For instance, they ran a campaign exposing the poor quality of milk and its adulteration by producers, and directly linking up with agricultural co-ops to ensure a pure supply for co-op members. The movement's share of the milk trade grew rapidly from 1 to 4 per cent. Since then, they have continued to link up with agricultural co-ops to guarantee purity and quality, and developed new lines such as an environmentally friendly washing powder. In the mid-1980s private traders campaigned against the movement, but a government commission found it acted as a 'countervailing power on consumers behalf' and should be supported (Takamura, 1992, p51).

Influence on government consumer policies

Considering its size, the consumer co-operative movement in Britain had very little influence on consumer policy until after the First World War. The exception was the campaigning Women's Co-operative Guild, among whose successes was the inclusion of maternity benefits in the 1911 Insurance Act, and the payment of the benefit direct to women (Gaffin and Thoms, 1983). The setting up of a Co-operative Party should have meant a powerful consumer advocate in Parliament, but the record is a disappointing one, of a party tied to the Labour Party and, until recently, lacking in ideas (Carbery, 1969). The Parliamentary Committee of the Co-operative Union, acting as a trade association, had some success, but by the 1960s it had been overtaken in this role by the Consumers' Association, an organisation dedicated to campaign and research on behalf of consumers. Recently, it could be argued that all-party groups in Parliament have been more effective, for instance in protecting building societies from predatory take-overs, and promoting co-operative housing (Graham, 1998; Love, 1998). In Japan, the movement has suffered from a quite hostile political climate, because of the political power of the private traders linked to the ruling liberal democratic party. Its impact on government consumer policy has also been limited.

Ability to meet the demands of ethical consumers

The movement in the UK has been quite responsive to ethical demands. During the 1960s, the main issue was a boycott of South African goods, which showed how effective consumers could be when they could vote as to whether a retailer stocks certain goods. More generally, the CWS has been committed to rigorous testing of products for purity in order to produce the Co-op brand, though the impact of this was lessened by a lack of publicity. In the 1970s, the UK Co-operative Bank began an ethical stance, being the first to introduce free banking and publish its charges. It now has a full set of ethical and environmental policies which are endorsed by its customers through market research (Birchall, 1998c). Its parent company, CWS, has launched an 'honesty in labelling' policy and has become the foremost retailer of 'fair trade' products. On the other hand, its competitors are also joining in with ethical stances of their own, realising that the 'ethical consumer' is a significant part of their market. A new consumer co-operative has been launched called 'Out of this world', which provides information on products through a computer and assures its members that all their ethical concerns will be considered. Clearly, there is potential for consumer-owned businesses to map out new areas of ethical concern and in so doing to attract new members. In Japan, the ethical stance of the movement regarding pure food and the environment is already well established. The latest ethical concern is with a growing elderly population. The *han* groups are expanding into welfare work; and becoming less of a women's movement, and more a community movement involving working men and women of all age groups (Takamura, 1992).

The attempted demutualisation of CWS

Before we make a final evaluation and look at the prospects for consumer co-operatives in the future, it is important to learn the lessons from the one attempt at demutualisation that has occurred so far. As we have noted, co-operative sectors have sometimes demutualised in order to restructure and to bring in new institutional investors such as trade unions and co-operative banks, but they have never been attacked from outside.

The Co-operative Group (CWS) Ltd is the biggest consumer co-operative in Europe (measured by turnover). Founded in 1863 as the wholesaler and manufacturing arm of the British retail co-operative movement, it is now in reality a group of businesses engaged in food and non-food retailing, funerals, milk production, travel agency, optical services, car sales and garage services, agriculture, engineering and property investment. Among its subsidiaries it has two that are themselves big businesses: the Co-operative Bank and the Co-operative Insurance Society (CIS). Although it sold its food-manufacturing arm in 1994, and is no longer a traditional wholesaler, it co-ordinates a buying group, the Co-operative Retail Trading Group (CRTG), and is responsible for negotiating with manufacturers to produce 'Co-op brand' products. Because it has absorbed, rationalised and invested in over fifty societies, many of which were making a loss, its ownership structure is a complicated hybrid of corporate and individual members. Its corporate shareholders include fifty retail co-operative societies and 120 other co-operatives, and half a million individual members who join through the Society's stores. Its position in the co-operative sector is crucial. In the words of its current chief executive, Graham Melmoth, 'A strong, broadly-based CWS is the rock on which the consumer co-operative proposition stands' (quoted in Birchall, 1998b, p16).

However, when the media began to be interested in the CWS early in 1997, as a result of the rumours of an imminent take-over bid, financial journalists were quick to point to the group's under-performance compared to conventional investor-owned companies. Media criticism also focused on the failure of attempts to merge CWS and the second largest co-operative retailer, CRS (a merger that has since taken place, but only after CRS experienced losses it could not sustain). Under a previous chief executive, CWS had been concentrating on becoming an effective retailer, but had not been emphasising its co-operative nature. With Graham Melmoth's appointment late in 1996, CWS began a strategic review of its business. The Co-operative Bank was growing rapidly, partly because of the development of bold ethical and environmental policies that caught the imagination of existing customers and encouraged many new ones. It was embarking on yet another venture called 'Inclusive Partnership', which emphasised its honesty and sense of responsibility towards all those affected by its business. The Bank had proved that the co-operative form, if defined concretely in terms of an ethical business and backed by a vigorous advertising campaign, could prove a positive advantage in the competition with conventional investor-owned banks. Other parts of the CWS Group lacked such a positive image, though the retail arm had been presented as 'the 'responsible retailer', launching campaigns, for example, on the honest labelling of foods, the customer's 'Right to Know', and healthy eating. On Melmoth's appointment, the 'co-operative differ- ence' began to be stressed. A dividend card was developed that records customer discounts every time they buy from a CWS outlet. Clearly, before the take-over bid, CWS was already trying to establish a new corporate image based on its co-operative nature, but this was interrupted by the need to fight an unexpected battle for its very survival.

Co-operative market share of retailing has been falling steadily since the mid-1950s, from a high point of 12 per cent to below 4 per cent. One consequence has been that the CWS's food factories have been under-used, and the Board decided they would like to sell them. In 1994 they accepted an offer from Andrew Regan, an entrepreneur who bought the food manufacturing arm for £111 million and then, after closing some factories and boosting profits in others sold them on, making a net profit thought to be around £3 million. Regan then planned to buy and asset-strip CWS itself; he had backing from the City of around £1.2 million, the value of CWS's holdings being thought to be between £1.8 and £2 billion. Regan's strategy was reported as being to make an offer for the CWS to its Board, which could only be accepted if the organisation were converted to a company. The Board would then call a general meeting of members to vote on the proposal, and if they backed it, a formal bid would be made. Press speculation had it that Regan planned to keep the food business and to sell the Co-operative Bank (reputedly to the Allied Irish Bank), and the CIS.

However, the complex CWS representative process stood in his way. Because of its unique history, CWS has corporate members and individual members. In accordance with co-operative principles, voting among corporate members is weighted according to the value of purchases made and *not* by one organization, one vote, or by the value of shareholdings. Corporate members are themselves co-operatives, with their own individual members, who therefore exercise very indirect control over CWS through their representatives. Individual members of CWS Retail are organised into branches, which elect representatives to regions and then to a block of seats on the Board. Unlike building societies and other large consumer co-ops, individual members do not vote directly in CWS annual general meetings, only in their branch and regional meetings. In these respects, CWS democracy is much less direct than that of other co-operative and mutuals, being designed to balance the interests and powers of two very different types of member. There is another important difference between CWS and mutuals in the financial service sector: CWS, like other consumer co-operatives, has an active and committed base of members who are already involved in its democratic process. Members of the Board are much more answerable to their own members, whether these are individual members of CWS or of the societies in membership of CWS.

The bid from Regan's investment company, Lanica, never materialised. CWS found out that one of their senior managers was leaking large amounts of information to the demutualisers, and a High Court injunction was granted, preventing use of the information so provided. CWS also began to investigate further the extension to the Hobson supply contract, finding that a mysterious payment of £2.4 million had been paid to a Cayman Islands account. Because of the taint of illegality, and because of the strenuous defence put up by CWS, the financial backers of the bid pulled out. CWS directors were able to send the bid back to the senders 'unopened and unread'.

Evaluation of the 'Lanica Affair'

How should we evaluate this, the first ever hostile attempt to take over a consumer co-operative society? There is not much theoretical generalisation to draw on when it comes to comparing the inherent efficiencies of one form of private sector business with another. Compared with the intense interest of public choice theory in the relative merits of public and private service delivery organisations (see Pollitt and Birchall, 1998), this is an underdeveloped area; as Bager points out, theorists are more concerned with what organisations do than with what they are (Bager, 1994). Buckland and Thion suggest 'Organisational form is a consequence of the nature of the agency problem presented, and the mode of its resolution' (1991, p357), and that non-plc forms have been set up to solve problems of market failure in the 'normal' market. Consumer co-ops are an example of collective consumers solving their own agency problems. This was certainly true in the early days, with food adulteration, inefficient, credit-based private retailing, and underdeveloped wholesale distribution (Birchall, 1994). However, it is difficult to apply this insight to the current co-operative sector, whose existence is based more on institutional inertia, the interests of managers in keeping it trading, and the cushioning effect of large asset bases tied up mainly in property, than on any perceived need to solve agency problems in today's market. In a simple sense, CWS exists because it has continued to exist. As we have noted, it is under-performing compared to its competitors. This could point to inherent weaknesses of organisational form, but equally could be a legacy of its role as an 'ambulance' for financially weak retail societies, and of the commitment of its directors to keep open less profitable community-based shops. It has certainly not been trading on a level playing field with its competitors. There is some strength, also, in the argument that co-operatives' 'bottom-line' is different, and that they should not be compared directly with investor-owned businesses. However, while going some way to defend a low profit to capital ratio, this argument does not explain why co-operative societies have been under-performing on several other key indicators such as retail sales per square metre of store space. Regardless of their ultimate goals, they are simply not as good at retailing as their multiple chain competitors.

This point is softened somewhat by examples of regional co-operative societies in some parts of Britain that are performing well, both in turnover and profitability, in comparison with similar retailers. The key to success seems to have been good management, a strong local identity, development of profitable non-food business such as funerals, travel agency and car sales, and a business strategy of upgrading existing town centre and community-based stores rather than attempting to enter the superstore market where their competitors are strongest. In some instances, notably in travel and funerals, they have broken price rings operated by their competitors and met Buckland and Thion's expectation that non-plc forms will flourish where markets are failing.

In order to prove the hypothesis that co-ops are inherently less efficient than plcs in the retail sector, one would have to take all of these points into consideration, and then focus on some other key variables that have been identified as affecting performance: for example, ability to raise capital, differences in managerial incentives, and governance and accountability structures, between the co-operative and plc forms. Co-operatives are unable to raise money through share issues, and tend to borrow more from banks. However, they have had some advantages over their competitors: they have inherited a strong asset base in commercial and industrial property and can raise funds from their members through non-voting preference shares. In 1958, the seminal 'Gaitskell Report' on the consumer co-operative sector in the UK estimated that there was more than enough capital to support an enormously ambitious modernisation programme (Birchall, 1994). However, since then, the asset base has mostly been squandered in stemming trading losses, and the potential for raising money from members has not been fully exploited (see Kurimoto, 1999).

There are certainly differences in management incentives: co-operative managers cannot receive share options, though their salaries and bonuses do keep up with those of their competitors. There was, until the 1980s, a tendency to recruit from within, thus ensuring the loyalty of co-operative staff but not always guaranteeing competence. However, there has been a great deal of movement of top managers between the sectors, and co-operative boards seldom complain of an inability to recruit people of talent. More serious is the charge that the governance of co-operatives allows managers to under-perform because directors put more value on social aims and preservation of existing jobs than on profitability. During the postwar period, there has been a gradual separation of two aspects of the organisation that had previously been held together: the business enterprise, and the membership association (Stryjan, 1994). There had always been tensions between these two aspects of a co-operative, but they had been held together by one fundamental mechanism: the regular payment of dividend on purchases. Neglect of the membership base and abandonment of dividend have meant that there has been literally no one to complain when co-operatives return low profits.

In many societies, managers and directors have been insulated from almost all pressure from members. They have been able to hide poor trading results, and remain unaccountable until they have had to ask members to endorse a merger with a larger co-operative because the society was effectively bankrupt. The restoration of dividend through the electronic card might induce members to put pressure on their managers for higher returns. A more likely alternative will be the forming of a membership group interested altruistically in providing a 'social dividend'. One regional society, the Oxford, Swindon and Gloucester, has begun to allocate a small percentage of surpluses to a development fund for new co-operatives, to be matched by local authority funding, and this has revived interest in the performance of the society by local activists. However, many societies still have an accountability deficit.

Can the CWS prevent further attempts to take it over? There is no doubt of the determination of co-operative managers and directors to defend the Society. The review that had been begun before the take-over bid produced a fundamental restructuring of the business, a new retail trading strategy concentrating on the Society's strength in convenience stores and small supermarkets, and a new focus on the CWS as a family of businesses, emphasising the potential synergies between them. There was also an ongoing commitment towards changing the organisational culture, with a training course in 'Co-operative Values, Principles and Future' being extended to all 35,000 staff, and with a stated determination to change from a 'command and control' style to one of empowerment. In October 1997, the CWS Board introduced some rule changes that would make it more difficult for a hostile take-over to succeed, such as requiring card votes for changes of rules, and higher thresholds for the numbers required to call special general meetings. They could have played down membership altogether, but to their credit the Board declared a commitment to expanding and encouraging a more active membership base, accepting that in the long run this is the best defence against take-over.

Other societies have also made rule changes and restricted membership to people who lived in their trading area, making them sign a declaration of support for co-operative principles or prove their loyalty to a particular store before allowing them to join. However, legal barriers to conversion will always be limited by the need to safeguard the rights of individual members. In the future, the continued existence of co-operatives will depend on their ability to compete effectively in the markets in which they operate, and to provide benefits to members that they cannot get from conventional companies. These will include both material rewards and the satisfaction that comes from ethical trading. Co-operatives have to call out to, and to have faith in, the loyalty and commitment of their members.

Can consumer co-operatives justify their continued existence?

Why should co-operatives survive? This question has been raised most urgently by the attempted demutualisation, some of whose supporters argued not just that there was an economic incentive for conversion, but also a kind of moral imperative to make good use of assets that were currently being under-used. There are three kinds of argument in favour of the continued use of these assets by co-operatives: arguments derived from a critique of capitalism; arguments derived from co-operative principles; and arguments about market failure. They each have two aspects to them, which tend to merge but need to be kept separate: an ideal argument about how the co-operative form ought to be superior or will be in the future; and an argument derived from real instances of successful co-operative action.

It is possible to create systematic models of political theory that value different types of organisation for reasons to do with ultimate values such as liberty, equality and fraternity, and second-order values such as democracy and self-help (Birchall, 1988, 1997b). Here we shall note how various authors have defended co-operative forms from an idealistic perspective. Ephraim Gil provides a high-level argument for a 'practical strategy of long-range evolution' towards a co-operative economy (1998, p5). It contains a critique of the existing, mainly capitalist, system: that it puts profits before people, displaces workers, relocates where labour is cheaper and so on. A counter-strategy of local economic development in which capital is under local control would put great stress on co-operatives and mutuals. Stanley Maron contrasts competitive capitalism and what he calls 'consensual economics', pointing out that unrestrained capitalism has caused economic chaos and acute problems of redistribution (Maron, 1998). He believes that a new class of consumers is being formed in the global market that is the potential foundation for a new communitarian economics. Obviously, despite the high level of abstraction in such arguments, the role of CWS and similar organisations is seen to have great potential. A less abstract argument is provided by Gray and Mooney, who see co-operatives as being rooted in class practice, and conversions as having the effect of a permanent loss of 'class instruments' that removes them from possible availability during periods of class mobilisation (1998, p42). Their argument applies specifically to agricultural co-ops and their conversion to plcs, but it might well apply to consumer co-ops if they are seen, as they traditionally have been, as part of a wider set of working-class institutions. However, it is difficult to envisage a scenario in which organisations such as CWS would become a focus of class action; the traditional links with the labour and trade union movement have almost completely withered (and in any case it could be argued that the class basis of the co-ops' customers has always included artisans and lower middle classes). More generally, arguments for a 'social economy' or third sector distinct from, and challenging, public and private for-profit sectors, have some salience, and a defence of CWS and similar organisations could be mounted on the basis that their conversion would be a loss to this sector. The smaller the sector, the less influential, and the less able to demonstrate a different set of corporate values.

The second kind of argument derives from co-operative principles. Co-operatives are constituted as democratic organisations on the basis of one person, one vote; they return surpluses to members in proportion to trade and not to capital; and so are designed to have a different relationship between people, capital and economic results. It can be argued that these in-built principles are an indirect critique of the plc form, and represent an alternative model of exchange, with people taking precedence over capital. Though they are not anti-capitalist, they have the potential to embody alternative values and so should be preserved (Michelsen, 1994). Gray and Mooney identify a rhetoric of member-ownership and control among co-operative advocates that allows us to see 'co-operatives as different types of organisation by design and purpose, by aspirations and relationships between stakeholders' (1998, p45). This kind of argument does not depend on co-operatives always living up to a particular set of values, merely on their existing as an alternative form. Their existence is in itself a challenge to orthodoxy. However, one can see how limited the argument is when faced with evidence that this form is less efficient and effective than the plc. One cannot escape the need to evaluate the actual practice of co-operatives.

The third kind of argument is one we have already met, the argument from market failure. Anheier and Ben-Ner argue that, in a perfect world of pure private goods and perfect information, we would not care what type of organisation provided goods and services (1997). In reality there are externalities and a lack of information, and if this causes a structural deficit between producers and consumers, consumer co-ops are one option. However, there are other options such as state regulation, consumer associations, or self-regulation by the producers, and a good case could be made out for a historical shift, in Western Europe at least, from the consumer co-operative model to these other alternatives. Economic theory is good at specifying the conditions under which co-operatives might arise, but less good at explaining their continued existence. For instance, Femida Handy (1997) offers two major explanations for the existence of non-profits: contract failure (the inability of plcs to generate trust among consumers), and government failure (the inability of governments to meet the needs of public-service users). The co-existence of non-profits and for-profits is explained by the fact that they cater for heterogeneous demands. However, Handy's most convincing example derives from the elderly care sector, where there are acute problems of information and trust, and it cannot account for the co-existence of consumer co-ops that (until the recent attempts to emphasis the 'co-operative difference') have seemed intent mainly on copying their competitors. Again, we come back to the uncomfortable conclusion that consumer co-ops exist because they have existed, and no one has yet attempted to take them over or convert them from within into a for-profit form.

Conclusion

The success of CWS in defending itself against a hostile take-over bid does not show that consumer co-operatives in general are safe. We have noted that, because of its complex ownership structure and the illegal way in which its opponents operated, CWS has enjoyed certain advantages that other co-ops would not have under similar circumstances. In particular, the loyalty of its members was never put to the test. However, in the UK, the shock caused to other consumer co-operatives has led them to strengthen their constitutional defences, and to take steps to develop an active and loyal membership. Their best defence may be in not being a very attractive prospect for take-over in the first place. Their continued poor performance relative to their competitors in the food sector makes them (with a few notable exceptions) less obviously worth asset-stripping than was the CWS with its large banking, insurance, funerals, travel and other businesses. On the other hand, with the competition in the UK food sector becoming more intense, and the development of new retail sites giving way to growth by acquisition, some of the town centre assets of regional co-operative societies may come under intense scrutiny, and the loyalty of their members may yet be put to the test.

What does the case of the CWS show about whether consumer co-ops are inherently less efficient and effective than their competitors? There are three reasons why the City might back a take-over bid: because there are substantial reserves that can be released by demutualisation, because the targeted business is under-performing but has substantial assets, or because it is performing well and can add value to a competitor's business. The first reason applies to financial services, but not to co-operative retailing; co-operative reserves tend to be fully utilised. However, CWS shows that the second and third reasons can both be present at the same time: under-performing in food retailing, CWS also has substantial businesses – banking, insurance, travel, funerals – that are outperforming the competition. This indicates that the question as to whether consumer co-ops are inherently less efficient than their competitors can only be answered in relation to each retailing sector. The nature of the competition, the relative advantages of having an established market presence, the ability to differentiate by marketing the 'co-operative difference', vary by sector.

For academic observers, the attempted take-over gives a new salience to the 'reproduction perspective', which sees the continued existence of co-operatives as an ongoing achievement, 'a project that has to be reinvented anew every day' (Stryjan, 1994, p75). It also questions the traditional dichotomy between the business and the association; instead of seeing these as irreconcilable, we begin to see them as complementary; under threat of take-over, members become both investors in the business and protectors of the association. Case studies of failed co-operatives show that development of the business away from a sound membership base tends to be unsuccessful; ultimately, democratic deficit leads to unsound business structure (Kurimoto, 1999). The CWS take-over bid also shows that it might lead to loss of the business, when members are asked to vote to dissolve the association. In consequence, CWS and other regional societies have begun to take some tentative steps towards the reintegration of the business and the association. They realise that members give them a potential business advantage over their competitors as well as forcing managers and directors continually to justify the continued existence of the co-operative. If they are unsuccessful, co-operative advocates will have to begin to address seriously the question of whether their assets can be better used in other ways. If they are successful, they will demonstrate that there is still a limited but useful place in the market for the consumer co-operative form.

References

Ag, L. (1995) 'Swedish retail co-operation in transition' in *The World Co-operative Enterprise*, Oxford, Plunkett Foundation.

Anheier, H. and Ben-Ner, A. (1997) 'Long-term changes in the size of the for-profit, nonprofit, co-operative and government sectors', *Annals of Public and Co-operative Economics*, 68, pp. 335–353.

Bager, T. (1994) 'Isomorphic processes and the transformation of co-operatives', *Annals of Public and Co-operative Economics*, 64, pp. 35–57.

Birchall, R. J. (1987) *Save Our Shop: the Fall and Rise of the Small Co-operative Store*, Manchester, Holyoake Books.

—— (1988) *Building Communities: The Co-operative Way*, London, Routledge.

—— (1994) *Co-op: The People's Business*, Manchester University Press.

—— (1997a) *The International Co-operative Movement*, Manchester University Press.

—— (1997b) 'Co-operative values and principles: a commentary, *Journal of Co-operative Studies*, 30(2), pp. 42–69.

—— (1998a) 'The Lanica Affair: an attempted takeover of a consumer co-operative', *Journal of Co-operative Studies*, 31(2).

—— (1998b) *To Change the Face of Banking: a Short History of the UK Co-operative Bank*, Meiji University Guest Lecture Series No. 3. Tokyo, Meiji University.

Brazda, J. (1989) 'The consumer co-operatives in Germany', in Brazda, J. and Schediwy, R. (eds), *Consumer Co-operatives in a Changing World*, Geneva, International Co-operative Alliance.

Buckland, R. and Thion, B. (1991) 'Organisational structures, objectives and agency relationships in banking services', *Annals of Public and Co-operative Economics*, 62, pp. 355–389.

Burnett, J. (1989) *Plenty and Want: A Social History of Food in England*, London, Routledge.

Carbery, T. F. (1969) *Consumers in Politics: a History and General Review of the Co-operative Party*, Manchester, Manchester University Press.

Carr-Saunders, A. M., Sargant Florence, P. and Peers, R. (1938) *Consumers' Co-operation in Great Britain*, London, George Allen & Unwin.

Cole, G. D. H. (1944) *A Century of Co-operation,* London, George Allen & Unwin.

Co-operative Independent Commission (1958) *Report*, Manchester, Co-operative Union.

Fay, C. R. (1938) *Co-operation at Home and Abroad*, London, P. S. King.

Gaffin, J. and Thoms, D. (1983) *Caring and Sharing: The Centenary History of the Co-operative Women's Guild*, Manchester, Holyoake Books.

Gil, E. (1998) 'Advancing co-operation in an unco-operative world – issues of transformation and survival', *Journal of Rural Co-operation*, 26(1–2), pp. 5–20.

Graham of Edmonton, Lord (1998) 'The survival of the co-operative and mutual sectors', *Journal of Co-operative Studies*, 30(3), pp. 11–16.

Gray, T. and Mooney, P. H. (1998) 'Rhetorical constructions and co-operative conversions: a comment', *Journal of Rural Co-operation*, 26(1–2), pp. 37–48.

Handy, F. (1997) 'Coexistence of nonprofit, for-profit and public sector institutions', *Annals of Public and Co-operative Economics*, 68(2).

Hasler, A. A. (1985) *L'Aventure Migros*, Berne, Federation des Cooperatives Migros.

Holyoake, G. J. (1907) *Self-help by the People: The History of the Rochdale Pioneers*, London, Swan Sonnenschein.

Hopkins, E. (1995) *Working-class Self-help in Nineteenth Century England*, London, UCL Press.

International Joint Project on Co-operative Democracy (1995) *Making Membership Meaningful*, Saskatchewan, Centre for Study of Co-operatives.

Jeffreys, J. B. (1954) *Retail Trading in Britain 1850–1950*, Cambridge University Press.

Kurimoto, A. (1999) 'Renewing the membership basis for raising investment and patronage', *Journal of Co-operative Studies*, 32(1), pp. 50–60.

Love, A. (1998) 'Building societies in the UK: a politician's perspective', *Journal of Co-operative Studies*, 31(1), pp. 3–11.

Maron, S. (1998) 'Competitive or consensual economics?' *Journal of Rural Co-operation*, 26, pp. 65–78.

Michelsen, J. (1994) 'The rationales of co-operative organisations: some suggestions from Scandinavia', *Annals of Public and Co-operative Economics*, 65(1), pp. 13–34.

Nomura, H. (ed.) (1993) *Seikyo: A Comprehensive Analysis of Consumer Co-operatives in Japan*, Tokyo, Otsuki Shoten.

Ostergaard, G. and Halsey, A. H. (1965) *Power in Co-operatives*, Oxford: Basil Blackwell.

Polanyi, K. (1957) *The Great Transformation: the Political and Economic Origins of Our Time*, Boston, Mass. Beacon Press.

Pollitt, C. and Birchall, J. (1998) *Decentralising Public Service Management*, London, Macmillan.

Potter, B. (1899) *The Co-operative Movement*, London, Swan Sonnenschein (NB: Beatrice Potter later became Beatrice Webb).

Redfern, P. (1938) *The New History of the CWS*, London, J. M. Dent.

Schediwy, R. (1989) 'The consumer co-operatives in Sweden', 'The consumer co-operatives in Finland', and 'The consumer co-operatives in France', in Brazda, J. and Schediwy. R. (eds), *Consumer Co-operatives in a Changing World,* Geneva, International Co-operative Alliance

—— (1996) 'The decline and fall of Konsum Austria', *Review of International Co-operation*, 89(2), pp. 62–68.

Setzer, J. (1989) 'The consumer co-operatives in Italy' in Brazda, J. and Schediwy, R. (eds), *Consumer Co-operatives in a Changing World*, Geneva, International Co-operative Alliance.

Sivertsen, S. (1993) 'The strategy of Co-op Norway', *Review of International Co-operation*, 86(4), pp. 99–101.

Stryjan, Y. (1994) 'Understanding co-operatives: the reproduction perspective', *Annals of Public and Co-operative Economics*, 65(1), pp. 60–77.

Takamura, I. (1992) 'The co-operative movement in Japan', *Review of International Co-operation*, 85(1), pp. 49–60

Vacek, G. (1989) 'The consumer co-operatives in Japan' in Brazda, J. and Schediwy, R. (eds) *Consumer Co-operatives in a Changing World*, Geneva, International Co-operative Alliance.

Webb, S. and Webb, B. (1921) *The Co-operative Movement*, London, Longman.

5 Mutuality and public services

Lessons from the 'new leisure trusts'

Richard Simmons

The postwar period, during which many of the welfare provisions of Western states were either created or consolidated, has often been characterised as one of political and social consensus over the range and level of public services to be provided. In common with the growth of mass-production techniques in the private sector, under the welfare state umbrella many services grew incrementally in a fairly standardised or 'mass-produced' way in what have since become known as Fordist solutions. However, from the end of the 1970s, mass-produced, 'one-size-fits-all' services have become less and less sustainable given a growth in consumerism, whereby consumers have become progressively more vocal in the demands they place upon public services, as well as other patterns of social, political and economic change. As a result, since the early 1980s there has been an ongoing process by which public services have been reorganised and restructured in a movement away from the previous rigidity of provider-dominated bureaucratic administration towards more flexible forms of organisation.

Across Europe, in particular, these developments have led to a range of new opportunities for the growth of co-operative and mutual structures in the provision of public services (see Ullrich, 2000). Some examples include the development of medical and health care services, and day care nurseries in Sweden and Finland (Stryjan, 1994; Pestoff, 1998; Mietinnen and Nordlund, 2000); home care and disabled services in Spain (Caballer *et al.*, 1994; Vidal, 1994); day care, community shelter and home help services in Italy (Ranci, 1994); health care services in Switzerland (Wagner, 1994); and community service centres in Austria (Holzmann, 1994). Co-operative housing has been growing as an alternative to public-sector provision of rented housing. In Britain, there has been a 'voluntary transfer' of some local authority housing stocks to new structures, including tenant management co-operatives and (in Scotland) community ownership co-operatives (Clapham *et al.*, 1998; Scott, 2000). There has been a similar transfer in some locations of former local authority residential care homes and contracting of home care services to care co-operatives (Spear *et al.*, 1994).

Good reviews of these initiatives are available in the literature cited above. This chapter considers the case of one particular development in Britain which has, so far, been less widely investigated; the transfer of responsibility for public leisure services to new leisure trusts (NLTs). The first section considers the wider process of public-sector reform, examining the change context since the 1980s from a number of perspectives. The second section considers the recent development of NLTs, some of which have been created as charitable companies, some as multi-stakeholder co-operatives. Finally, the third section brings the insights of the first two sections together, considering how the case of the new leisure trusts in Britain might contribute to a debate about the more general potential for co-operative and mutual structures in the provision of public services.

The policy context: recent reform of the public sector

This section considers the policy context that has given rise to 'the trend towards greater use of non-profit and co-operative agencies in the delivery of public services' (6, 1994). The recent development of opportunities for co-operative and mutual enterprise in the field of services formerly provided by governmental bureaucracies appears to have its roots in a complex yet inter-related range of factors which have guided public sector change since the 1980s. Particular focus is given here to recent public sector reform (PSR) and its effects. PSR is occurring worldwide for different reasons, at different speeds and through different means (Litvack *et al.*, 1997), yet despite such variety some common themes have emerged. PSR has largely been sustained by continued fiscal pressure originating from the end, in the mid-1970s, of the 'golden age' of uninterrupted postwar economic growth (Pierson, 1998). However, there have also been related pressures for change in the role and structure of government (OECD, 1996; Pollitt *et al.*, 1997). Toonen and Raadschelders sum it up in this way:

> we can just as well think of the 1980s and 1990s as the Adaptive Capacity Reform Age. For some systems this has required that they engage in managerial activities and innovations, in others that they loosen up and flexibilise their intergovernmental systems or stifling state-society embraces (1997, p1).

They distinguish between three types of reform that have guided PSR during the 1980s and 1990s (see Table 5.1). They argue that while it is obvious that increased efficiency, productivity and parsimony have been important and often the stated purpose of PSR since the early/mid-1980s, the quest for efficiency through 'managerial' reform has coincided with (i) an often understated, underlying concern for increased stability, adaptive capacity, and economic robustness through 'structural' reform; and (ii) a concern to consider distributive issues through 'policy' reform.

Table 5.1 Types of public sector reform

Types of reform	PSR objectives[a]	Sets of core values[b]
1 'Managerial' reforms (increasing efficiency within given constraints)	Efficiency and productivity	Parsimony, economy and the mission to 'keep it lean and purposeful'
2 'Structural' reform (increasing the level of system survival, adaptive capacity and stability of a dynamic government system)	Savings (redefinition of the nature of the state)	Reliability, system maintenance and the mission to 'keep it robust and resilient'
3 'Policy' reforms (increasing or decreasing equality by changing policy entitlements and government programmes)	Entitlements and equality	Fairness, equity rectitude and the mission to 'keep it honest and fair'

Source: After Toonen and Raadschelders, 1997.

Notes: [a]After Lane, 1995; [b]After Hood, 1991.

While reform has been implemented to differing degrees in different countries and regimes, some widely noted 'trajectories' have embraced such policies as privatisation, marketisation, decentralisation and devolution (Pollitt *et al.*, 1997, 1998; Pollitt and Summa, 1997), and more recently, partnerships. A common theme here has been the dismantling of former state hierarchies and the 'agencification' of public services. As Clarke and Newman observe, 'the dispersal of power forms a uniting thread that underpins a variety of new systems and mechanisms' (1997, p29). In one form or another, these ideas have had a relatively widespread effect on the landscape of public services.

A significant proportion of the reform of the public sector has focused on local government. In many countries this most basic unit of government is changing in response to pressures both from central and regional governments and from users of public services who are growing more self-confident and assertive of their rights (Kirkpatrick and Martinez Lucio, 1995). In the UK the trend has been towards the 'enabling' local authority that no longer provides all its services but contracts them out to independent profit-making and non-profit agencies (Clarke and Stewart, 1988; Ridley, 1988). The implication is that the purpose of the authority is to govern on behalf of the community, rather than necessarily to provide services directly. Similar changes have occurred elsewhere in Europe and beyond. For example, in Scandinavia, decentralisation has been accompanied by a 'free local government' experiment that has given them great freedom to determine their own priorities, including substituting area organisation for functional committees (Batley and Stoker, 1991). In France and Southern Europe there has also been a trend towards decentralisation and local autonomy. In Germany, the espousal of subsidiarity has been restated at the local level. In fact, in most countries, to a greater or lesser extent, there has been a move towards creating new relationships with private-sector or non-governmental organisations, either following the UK model of contracting out or based on a more collaborative model of partnerships (Worrall *et al.*, 1996; Lorrain and Stoker, 1997). Smith (1998) identifies six dimensions to this change:

1 Competitive tendering

Local government engages less in the direct provision of services to the public and more in the specification of policy objectives, met by a variety of external agencies sponsored by or under contract with the authority. Local government's role is to assess needs, set priorities and then monitor the performance of a range of competing providers. In Britain, 'compulsory competitive tendering' (CCT) was introduced during the 1980s, creating an internal market through a 'client-contractor split', and exposing service departments to external competition. In this way, new impetus was to be given to government ideals of efficiency, cost containment and consumer choice. Moreover, in the process of drawing up and negotiating the service contract, local authorities were to be forced to clarify and formalise the aims and objectives of service delivery. However, while efficiency gains were often reported, gains in quality were less common. Furthermore, with its highly detailed contract specifications and significant monitoring and inspection, local authority contracting under CCT often led to an adversarial client-contractor relationship which created additional, if largely hidden, transaction costs (Boyne, 1998).

2 Consumerism

Recipients of public services are seen as customers. Strategies include user groups, advisory bodies, one-stop-shops, and marketing communications. Customer contracts are established which specify standards of service and means of redress, with statements of customers' rights and information on performance levels.

3 Strategic planning

The capacity of local councillors to plan strategically for the overall welfare of their areas is strengthened. Comprehensive surveys of community needs and of the resources available form the basis of the strategy.

4 Influencing other organisations

Other agencies are persuaded to achieve prescribed ends. Influence, regulation and co-operation with other agencies (public, private and voluntary) are used in order to meet community needs using contracts, partnerships, co-ordination, facilitation, advocacy, consultation, and grants-in-aid.

5 Stimulating 'pluralist collectivism'

The development of local community organisations is encouraged, in order to represent interests and provide local services. The focus is on local government using its powers and influence to encourage the growth of the non-profit sector – for example, through voluntary organisations, trusts and co-operatives. Local government then monitors, supports and regulates this 'third sector' provision.

6 Participation in policy-making

The rights of citizens are highlighted (rather than those of mere consumers) to make choices affecting the development of their communities. Through openness, accountability and participation in decision-making, services are provided 'with and by', rather than just 'for' the public (Stewart and Stoker, 1988).

Local administrations in different countries have drawn differently from the above dimensions according to their individual circumstances. One important result, as Walsh has observed, is that 'the public service is becoming a network of interacting agencies in which organisational boundaries are blurred. The network of agencies replaces the integrated governmental organisation as a unit of analysis', reflecting a move from local government to 'local governance' (1997, p32). However, in 'a major unintended consequence' of PSR, Rhodes (1997a) contends that such networks resist government steering. As a result, concern has emerged over the issue of 'fragmentation' in the system of local services (e.g. Jervis and Richards, 1996). It may be argued that these unintended changes have contributed to the new institutional environment in which opportunities for the development of co-operative structures now arise. Davis (1996, p5) asserts that '[fragmented] governmental systems need a capacity for integration. In a fragmented system different policy agendas have to be brought together and new forms of relationship must be built'. In support, Reid (1995, p134) observes that 'policy implementation at local level is increasingly dependent upon securing the collaboration and co-operation of, and between, groups of diverse service-providing agencies, many of which are independent in the sense that they are outwith direct statutory control'. This need for co-operation has seen a growth in local networking and partnerships (Stewart, 1996; Pierre, 1998; Johansson and Borell, 1999). For Mullins,

> the term 'partnership' disguises the differing approaches taken by organisations to co-operation. Some organisations take an

entrepreneurial and competitive approach, carefully choosing which partners to co-operate with in order to promote their strategic objectives. Others are seen as more collaborative, being prepared to commit resources to longer-term relationships, exercising less choice over partners, and working towards more collectively defined goals. (1998, p136)

In the first instance, the relationship might be based on a 'transactional' approach, one which derives from treating the transactions with which the partnership is concerned as discrete, economic exchanges conducted formally and relatively impersonally. By contrast, in the second scenario, a 'relational' approach might be more likely, entailing 'long term social exchange between parties, mutual trust, interpersonal attachment, commitment to specific partners, altruism and co-operative problem solving' (Duberley, 1997). These latter themes have recently become more commonplace, with key issues surrounding how to design long-term relationships with other agencies so as to produce synergy and collaborative advantage (Huxham, 1996; Huxham and Vangen, 2000). Hence, Rhodes (1997b) notes that the language of networking and partnership has increasingly come to indicate the importance of trust and diplomacy. Kay asserts that 'a primary strength of mutuality is that it facilitates the development of such relational contracts ... It is only necessary to look at the culture of some of the more successful mutual organizations to see the reality of this' (1991, p315). However, while there has recently been increasing recognition of the value of co-operation in the provision of public services, such arrangements have also been recognised as holding potential challenges to both probity and democratic accountability (Davis and Walker, 1997; Rhodes, 1997a).

The case study of the 'new leisure trusts' in Britain draws on key elements of the changes that have occurred in response to these various forces acting on the public sector. It looks for evidence of the effects of managerial, structural and policy reform, and how new leisure trusts are being developed at the local government level. It looks at the ways in which transfer to a new organizational form may have produced value changes and (following Pollitt *et al.*, 1998), changes in organisational performance, accountability and control.

The case of the new leisure trusts

As a study of the use of co-operative structures in the provision of public services, we consider public leisure services in Britain. Here, concepts of 'market failure' and 'merit goods' have provided ongoing rationales for the public provision of leisure services, predominantly in sport, play, libraries and the arts. However, traditionally there has been a reluctance for direct state intervention in leisure, because of its distinction as a 'private sphere' that is thought to be not properly the object of public policy (Whitsun, 1987). It is recognised that 'a commitment to service the public's recreation interests is too open ended to be practical ... recreation interests are too diverse' (Roberts, 1978). As a result, local authority leisure services have occupied an ambiguous position between ideologies of welfare and the market, and public provision has developed alongside that of the private and voluntary sectors in a 'mixed economy' (Coalter, 1990).

This section examines the voluntary transfer of responsibility for leisure services to legally independent, not-for-profit organisations created from existing local authority providers. These new leisure trusts (NLTs) have generally been established in one of two forms: industrial and provident societies (IPS) operating as multi-stakeholder co-operatives for the benefit of the community; or companies limited by guarantee (CLG), operating in the more 'philanthropic' model of charitable trusts. These organisational types share at least the potential for certain features in common, such as an absence of profit motive, a public service ethos, and stakeholder-inclusive board structures. Consultancy reports produced for local authorities considering this form of transfer have generally been inconclusive about which organisational form is the most appropriate. Nevertheless, the externalisation of local authority services has been recognised as a growth opportunity for the use of co-operative structures (e.g. ICOM, 1997; Gosling, 2000), and following the well-known example of Greenwich Leisure in South London there has been widespread interest in adopting this approach. An important question arises as to whether the use of the co-operative organisational form may provide for potential advantages that go beyond those associated with other forms.

The recent development of NLTs by British local authorities plots a middle ground between the public and private sectors. Trusts had already been used for some time in new towns, where special administrative and financial procedures applied in making arrangements for the ownership and management of community facilities (Curson, 1996). Until recently, however, despite proving themselves both 'robust' and 'stable' vehicles, trusts had not been more widely used because of the general desire by local authorities to retain full operational control over facilities (Sports Council, 1994). Nevertheless, the developments during the 1980s and 1990s in the political and managerial environment for leisure services, as detailed in the previous section, has led in many locations to a change of approach. It is worth noting, that the development of NLTs has not been the direct result of central legislation, but rather of the continuous pressures placed by central government on local government finance. In Britain, the 1979–97 Conservative government set about reviewing the role and finances of local government with particular vigour, viewing it as 'wasteful, profligate, irresponsible, unaccountable, luxurious and out of control' (Newton and Karran,

1985, p116). There were two main outcomes:

1   The introduction of an unprecedented series of additional financial cuts and controls on both capital and revenue expenditure (Travers, 1998). However, local authorities deployed a range of strategies in the face of this tighter financial stringency (Wolman and Peterson, 1981; Wolman, 1984; Elcock, 1994), and in some ways NLTs have been created as a result of local authorities' 'creative defence' of local leisure services (Simmons, 2000).

2   A review of the structure and function of local government. The emerging 'enabling' concept proposed a reduction in direct provision through such mechanisms as privatisation, marketisation and decentralisation. As a result, the dogma of direct provision could no longer easily be sustained, and in some locations NLTs have come to be seen as a politically acceptable alternative to direct provision.

The transfer of leisure services to a NLT is just one of the options currently available to local authorities as they respond to this changing environment (Sports Council, 1995). Yet the number of new Trusts is growing steadily, and the new Labour government remains keen to encourage partnership working with suitable external organisations (DETR, 1999). Hence, it seems likely that this form of transfer will remain on the policy agenda. The question remains: How can trusts provide solutions? The answer lies in the assessment of claimed advantages and disadvantages for such a change. The remainder of this section focuses on how local authorities are going about taking the 'Trust option'.

These issues were investigated in a recent research project conducted by this author at Brunel University, which found that there still remain extensive opportunities for the development of co-operative structures in local leisure services. The reported experience of NLTs confirms that in most cases it was the financial attractions (tax advantages and significant savings on national non-domestic rates) which produced the stimulus for partnering. Since local authority budgets remain under severe pressure, there are widespread expectations that even more authorities will follow suit. However, while it is the financial pressures emerging from slashed local authority budgets that have led to the growth of new leisure trusts, this should be seen as only one of the necessary conditions for a successful transfer. In addition, it is necessary to ensure that the quantity and quality of services provided will at least be sustained without threat to the viability of the new organisation. It is also necessary to ensure that all major stakeholders will accept and stay committed to the new structures for the delivery of the service (Employee Ownership Options, 1999). The research looked at key issues that arise for various stakeholders following transfer: issues of performance, accountability and control. Whether they are constituted as co-operative (IPS) or charitable (CLG) structures, the discussion of these issues is central to the consideration of the new leisure trusts in action.

Performance

Performance issues included financial aspects, the quality and quantity of services, the quality of management, and the maintenance of social welfare objectives. It was found that, in relation to the latter three aspects, change was often positive, although relatively marginal. First, the quality and quantity of services as previously defined under CCT remained largely stable or benefited from increased investment. Second, officers often claimed that the quality of management benefited from the 'single-issue focus' that transfer provided. Third, trusts remained committed to the pursuit of social objectives, if only to justify the continued provision of service grants from their 'parent' authorities. The one area where significant change was reported was in financial performance. Large-scale tax savings are an obvious advantage for trusts, yet further savings have often been made via other routes, such as having the flexibility to negotiate with a wider range of suppliers, and gaining efficiencies in staff costs. Innovations in service delivery, pricing and marketing have often also provided the basis for future revenue growth. The net result has been the potential, now being realised in many locations, to reduce the annual service grant provided by the local authority, and in effect to provide the same (or slightly more) for less.

It is too early to tell whether IPS or CLG forms have inherent advantages for performance. The initial 'big bang' financial benefits (savings on tax and business rates) are common to both, and at this early stage in NLTs' development serve to cloud underlying performance trends. In the longer term, the success of these organisations will depend on the strategies employed, and it is here that the opportunity exists for co-operatives to promote themselves as the bearers of a distinctive set of values and principles set down by the International Co-operative Alliance in 1995:

- Voluntary and open membership;
- Democratic member control;
- Member economic participation;
- Education, training and information;
- Autonomy and independence;
- Concern for community; and
- Co-operation among co-operatives (see Birchall, 1997).

While in theory both charitable and co-operative forms could share in their commitment to at least the first six of these principles, in practice this appears to be unusual. Membership in any meaningful sense is not generally available to employees of charitable structures, while it is an important aspect in co-operatives, with, for example, a reported take-up at Greenwich Leisure of 90 per cent of eligible staff (ICOM, 1997). While both forms of organisation have innovated by involving staff in strategic and corporate-level working, it is unusual for workers in charitable structures to have either the democratic worker-member representation found on most co-operative Boards or the economic participation of co-operative members (Greenwich worker-members are asked to make a commitment of £25 for a single non-distributing share). Such employee involvement has been claimed by co-operative NLTs to have been important in moving the culture of these organisations forward. For example, at another co-operative, Wycombe Leisure, all staff have been involved in the formulation and agreement of a new set of company values, and have been involved in business planning and target-setting for the organisation (Wycombe Leisure Ltd, 1997). Autonomy and independence, and concern for community, are principles that are carefully guarded by both charitable and co-operative structures, and are of fundamental importance to the performance of both forms of organisation. However, in the last of the above list of principles, co-operative NLTs can claim a further potential advantage in their ability to co-operate with one another. Fruitful relationships have been developed among IPS leisure providers in such aspects as securing economies of scale through joint procurement, and making savings by sharing payroll costs (Sesnan, 1998).

Despite this analysis, the major changes in performance currently appear to be common to both IPS and CLG forms. This might suggest that it is simply the new-found autonomy of these organisations that has led to the reported positive outcomes, as opposed to the organisational form employed. If so, it might also imply that leisure services might as easily have been privatised. However, the impact of autonomy on performance cannot be considered in isolation where the public has an interest in services. Arguably, 'third sector' organisations such as NLTs provide an appropriate fit with public leisure services' profile between the ideologies of welfare and the market, and provide a solution to trust problems among payers and service users (6, 1998). The issue of trust is important. The creation of NLTs as multi-stakeholder structures, governed by workers, service users, council members, community and business representatives, even academics, provides a counterweight to problems of self-interest attributed both to publicly-owned monopolies and to private-sector enterprise (e.g. LeGrand, 1998). However, trust in these new structures is likely to be effective only when limited and conditional rather than absolute (Gray, 1998), and there is consequently a need to balance the potential benefits of increases in autonomy on performance with countervailing new arrangements for accountability and control.

Accountability and control

The common assertion that accountability is lost as services are devolved from the public sector was not entirely supported in this research, although there are often unanticipated changes in accountability, monitoring, control and feedback structures. In practice, the notion of partnership employed by the new trust and its 'parent' authority is crucial. Hence, for the service-user constituency, elected council members may still perceive themselves to be democratically accountable through the ballot box for policies agreed in the annual service agreement, even though the responsibility for service delivery has transferred to a trust. Trust managers may argue that their new-found autonomy allows them to respond better to the concerns of service users, and that it is this form of accountability that is ultimately important. What emerges is a more equivocal picture. Accountability relationships appear to have been blurred by the involvement of both council and trust in the provision of services, with, in the worst case scenario, two potential effects: buck-passing and scapegoating between the two partners, and confusion for the citizen-consumer. Even where experience reflects a more positive situation, the 'shared' nature of accountability within this form of partnership appears to work on the somewhat flawed assumption of an unproblematic division between policy and implementation. In reality this may lead to at least two relatively complex problems.

First, ongoing, underlying tensions may arise where parent authorities are perceived to be (re)politicising issues that are properly the managerial concerns of the trust, and vice versa. Hence, for both partners, there is a need to underpin the achievement of financial benefits with a positive approach to partnering. This requires proper planning on both sides, not just that of the trust – some parent authorities have initially been guilty of viewing the trust option as simply a financial arrangement, without appreciating or evaluating the full range of implications. There is also widespread recognition of the need for the careful building of relationships between partners, with less conflictual contract arrangements than were found under the previous regime of compulsory competitive tendering (CCT). If sufficient care is taken, trusts, whether IPS or CLG, offer clear potential for the development of complementary cultures and attitudes based on trust, mutual respect for objectives, flexibility and open communication.

Second, further tensions may arise for parent authorities because they are responsible for simultaneously contributing to the partnership whilst exercising control. Leisure facilities are generally leased to the new trusts by the parent authority in whose ownership they remain. In addition, a deficit grant of around 50 per cent of operating costs is often provided by the authority. It is not uncommon, therefore, for the Council to retain a strong interest in how these resources are used, and it may seek to express its influence through a range of mechanisms:

- Places on Board of Trustees (limited to 19.9 per cent in England and Wales);
- Linkage of annual grant to Trust business plan/service level agreement;
- Conditions within leases and licences; and
- Joint consultative bodies.

It has been suggested that these methods may not be as effective as direct control (ADLO, 1997). However, our research found that control over the annually-variable grant and service agreement, allied to the ultimate sanction of terminating leases, appears to have provided parent authorities with two significant 'levers' which it may use to negotiate with the trust, thereby providing robust ongoing influence. This influence is generally acknowledged to be very strong, although parent authorities now have to 'bob and weave' in a constant process of negotiation and renegotiation, both formal and informal, with the trust. If there has been a movement away from the authoritative relationships previously enjoyed by elected members over service delivery, in most cases this has not had any deleterious effects. Important issues emerging from the political process may still be brought forward – for example, through formal representation of the council on the Board. Furthermore it has been widely acknowledged, in some cases even by councillors formerly solely responsible for the governance of provision, that trust board members drawn from a range of backgrounds and perspectives enhance the level and quality of debate over service level issues. In this way, the emerging multi-stakeholder trust structures provide potential new ways of doing business, working in tandem with parent authorities to meet strategic goals in a manner that builds on the strengths of each to the benefit of both.

A fairly positive picture emerges from this analysis of performance, accountability and control in co-operative and other NLT structures. However, the movement away from the aggressive 'transactional' contracting which was a feature of CCT and direct council control to partnerships focused more on 'trust-based' (or 'relational') arrangements raises a further complex problem. Trust-based arrangements may have positive effects that can help to lift quality and control costs, but also negative effects if relationships become too 'comfortable', with trust being shared between self-serving actors from either side of the newly-created partnership (Seal and Vincent-Jones, 1997). The looser definition of responsibilities that is a feature of the new relational contracts generally leads to a greater degree of ongoing communication and negotiation, both formal and informal. Nevertheless, the full details of the relationship and what makes it work successfully may well be 'opaque' to outsiders (Walker and Davis, 1999), and the potential arises for such arrangements to lead to complacency – or at worst corruption. As yet there is little evidence to suggest that there are any such problems in relation to NLTs. However, these are early days for the new trusts, and the interest of key stakeholders remains strong at this stage. As Lindsley *et al.* (1995) have shown, the level and intensity of this interest often wanes as routines become established and organisational stakeholders begin to view the NLT as being successful. In this scenario the degree of ongoing communication and negotiation is reduced and, as people take their 'eye off the ball', complacency (or worse) can set in. Moreover, difficulties may remain in ensuring that the new relationships not only work in the public interest but are also seen to do so. It is surprising to note that few NLTs, whether IPS or CLG, have yet gone far enough to develop the fuller involvement and participation of service users and their local communities (Lowenberg, 1997). This might at least encourage greater transparency and understanding, while potentially also developing capacity and strengthening connections within these constituencies. The opportunity beckons here for the unique advantages provided by multi-stakeholder organisations to develop more widespread involvement. For co-operative structures based around the 1995 principles there may be a number of natural advantages in this respect – in particular, open membership, the formal recognition and protection of member-stakeholder interests and the ballot.

NLTs are not unique in having had to confront these kinds of issues. In the UK and beyond there has traditionally been a reluctance from local government to acknowledge fully or to engage with the third sector as a partner in the provision of public services (Salamon, 1995; Pestoff, 1998; Garside, 2000). It is only more recently that the strategic transfer of services has become less of an anathema, to the point where local government itself has even acted as 'midwife' to the birth of local agencies (Painter *et al.*, 1997). As this trend develops, so the opportunities for co-operative structures in the provision of these services should grow. However, a number of key issues present themselves from the above analysis. In the concluding section we shall examine how consideration of these issues would be valuable at this time for policy-makers in both the public and co-operative sectors.

Insights for public policy

There are a number of issues raised in the above analysis of NLTs that are salient for policy-makers involved in the development of 'alternative' structures to deliver public services. Four that appear to be more widely applicable are: the impacts of reform and changed incentive structures; the implications of multi-stakeholding; relational contracting and inter-organisational 'distance'; and re-emphasising the co-operative difference.

The impacts of reform and changed incentive structures

The case of leisure trusts shows that there has certainly been 'structural reform' to create both a more focused organisation, and one in which significant tax savings become possible. There has also been 'managerial reform', with an increase in autonomy and an adaptation of organisational values that has given the new trusts the ability to balance the commercial and social aspects of leisure service provision more comfortably than the in-house contractors who preceded them. These have been obvious and fundamental changes, and their importance should not be underestimated. However, just as important (although much less obvious) has been a further unintentional change, involving 'policy reform'. It may be argued that the need to ensure the viability of contracts under CCT in a climate of financial cuts had led to a downward spiral in addressing the social objectives of the service (Fisher, 1998) (see Figure 5.1).

The incentive for the contractor (in which local authority 'clients' fearing the political fallout of contract failure were often complicit) was therefore to maximise revenue opportunities by replacing subsidised activities with others chargeable at a market rate. In this way, following this incentive may have led to policy reform 'by default' through changing policy entitlements. In the NLTs, the downward spiral has been stabilised temporarily as the financial pressures illustrated in Figure 5.1 have been eased. It can also be argued that incentives for the new trusts have also changed. The pressure

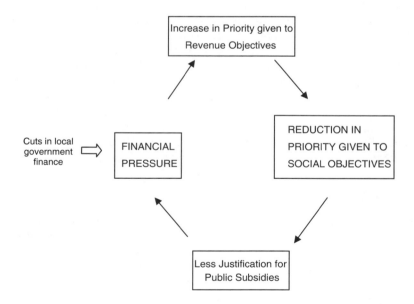

Figure 5.1 A downward service spiral
Source: After Fisher, 1998.

now is to justify subsidies under the parent authority's grant funding regime and so protect the grant that can amount to around half of the trust's total revenue. In doing so, it appears that the renewed pursuit of social objectives has become a key organisational strategy.

For other service areas, there are equally important implications for the establishment of co-operative and other 'third sector' service delivery structures. Even for services where tax savings are less important, such as housing, structural reform extends access to capital finance previously prohibited by public-sector borrowing regulations (Birchall *et al.*, 1995), thereby creating 'synergy' through the leveraging of extra resources (Peters, 1998). Similarly, for most services, the increased autonomy that is typical of managerial reform is often associated with increased activity rates and responsiveness, which at least have the potential to enhance a 'new' co-operative's efficiency and effectiveness (Pollitt *et al.*, 1998). Finally, changed incentive structures may also have an effect on policy reform in other services, particularly where a newly-formed co-operative has a continued relationship with a governmental funding body linked to the way it operates. The nature of these effects will be dependent upon the characteristics of the service and its environment. However, if they were to be anticipated by both co-operative and public-sector policy-makers they could form part of a planned approach to partnership and co-working, rather than the largely unintentional consequence found in many new leisure trusts.

The implications of multi-stakeholding

On a more general level of incentives, it has already been argued that third-sector organisations provide a potential alternative to problems of self-interest in private-sector enterprise ('profit motive') or publicly-owned monopolies ('producer domination'), and with it a solution to trust problems among service users (6, 1998). However, problems of self-interest are not automatically avoided in co-operative and other third-sector organisational forms despite their 'non-profit' status and commonly-held aspirations to inclusiveness. For example, in relation to co-operative structures, Hargreaves has observed that 'too often democratic principles have been negated by rigid managerial hierarchies and poor communication' (1999, p12). Hence, while narrowly-defined profit motives may be absent, problems of producer domination may persist. It may be argued that multi-stakeholding has the potential to minimise these effects. In the NLTs it is widely acknowledged that involving a range of stakeholders has generally enhanced the level and quality of debate over key issues. In this way, synergy has not only been created in these new organisations by leveraging extra financial resources, but also by bringing together of a range of stakeholders in their governing structures (Huxham and Vangen, 1996, 2000). The initial evidence suggests there is a future for multi-stakeholding in these emerging new structures.

Nevertheless, there is some resistance in co-operative circles to multi-stakeholding, based on the perceived need for control to be vested in only one stakeholder group – or at least for one group to have primacy. It is argued that the very democratic nature of co-operative structures may contribute to managerial ineffectiveness (Hargreaves, 1999). The choice that appears to beckon here is between the 'noise' created by disparate interests using their voice in the democratic process, and fractured communication leading to the 'moribund consensus' of single-stakeholder domination. Against this, supporters of multi-stakeholding assert that it is possible, indeed essential, to draw a balance between these positions. They argue that multi-stakeholding promotes a dialogue between stakeholders and reduces the asymmetry of information and power between them. This provides for an alignment of objectives and agreement on action (Huxham and Vangen, 1996) as well as a system of checks and balances to help to avoid the corrupting influence of absolute power (Pestoff, 1995; Turnbull, 1997). Hence, for Pestoff (1998, p106), multi-stakeholding holds out the prospect that 'domination and control will be replaced by co-determination and co-ordination, by participation and involvement'. Moreover, any consequent increase in the transaction costs of decision-making will be offset by the synergic benefits. It has already been stressed that the participation and involvement of service users is particularly important in ensuring that public services both operate in the public interest and are seen to do so.

Is the perceived need for control to be vested in only one stakeholder group really a necessary condition? Or, as Blackley (1996) has advocated, does co-operation work 'precisely because it shares ownership, control and benefits equitably – because it provides a structure within which mutual understanding and trust can be built and tensions amicably (or at least democratically) resolved?' No doubt the current debates will continue, but if there is a particular advantage to be gained here, it appears to remain for the co-operative sector to drive it home.

Relational contracting and inter-organisational 'distance'

Governmental bodies are likely to continue as key stakeholders even where responsibility for the delivery of public services is transferred to third-sector organisations, including co-operatives. It is likely that the use of public money and/or physical resources will still be central, and therefore that this key relationship, as exemplified by that between NLTs and their 'parent' authorities, will remain. Walsh (1997) uses the 'contract metaphor' to describe how 'independent agencies' relate to governmental bodies through contracts and quasi-contracts, and how subsequently exchange relationships replace authoritative orders as the means of co-ordination and control. It is the extent to which govern-mental control is retained in these relationships that is of particular importance here. Following structural changes, there is commonly a dilemma in balancing the potential benefits for performance of increased agency autonomy with political requirements for accountability and control.

Two key issues are involved in achieving this balance. First, the nature of the contract/quasi-contract is important. Relational-type contracts tend to work best for complex services, owing to the difficulty of specifying complex services in sufficient detail (Deakin and Walsh, 1996). As Kay (1991) has asserted, co-operatives may have a 'natural advantage' in the administration of relational contracts, which depend for their ongoing success upon building firm relationships based on trust and diplomacy. It should therefore be of little surprise that the provision of public services by co-operatives tends to focus on the human services (health, social care, housing, leisure), where the greatest complexity is generally found. One important reason for this complexity is that users tend to act as co-producers in the services they consume. For Pestoff (1994) this is an additional reason why co-operatives, which often require both membership and active participation, may again hold a 'natural advantage' in the provision of such services.

Second, the manner in which the independent agency is regulated is also vital. If a lot of control is required by governmental bodies, the model followed by NLTs, with Board representation in conjunction with other mechanisms such as fail-safes and financial penalties, appears to provide a good vehicle for robust ongoing influence. However, the governmental body needs to remain clear that exchange relationships will replace authoritative orders as the means of co-ordination and control. As Stoker (1997) argues, a key feature of the new providers is their independence, and that governmental bodies have to learn to 'let go'. The balance for the governmental body is therefore one of regulatory 'distance'. Too much interference may fracture the relationships on which the quality of the service may depend, while danger to effective working also arises from being seduced into 'too cosy' a relationship (Painter, 1996; Painter and Isaac-Henry, 1997). The concept of inter-organisational 'distance' is also important for the new organisations. Here a balance must be drawn between the need for autonomy of action and the need to maintain credibility and legitimacy in managing and implementing public programmes (Kumar, 1996). Interestingly, in this way, neither party, while technically autonomous as a principal in its own right, may be able to make significant movements independently from the other without introducing counterproductive tensions or strains into the relationship.

The balance between organisational autonomy and governmental control and influence remains at the heart of the developing system of 'local governance'. An insight into this process, alongside an understanding of the design features in a regulatory system, should form a fundamental part of our understanding of the relationships upon which local service delivery is coming to depend.

Re-emphasising the co-operative difference

As the delivery of public services comes increasingly to involve the use of third-sector organisational forms (including co-operatives), issues of performance, accountability and control of the new service providers become increasingly salient for policy-makers. The above analysis attempts to define how improved performance may emerge from processes of structural, managerial and policy reform. It shows how enhanced accountability may be achieved through the embracing of multi-stakeholding and meaningful user involvement, and how the balance of control may be optimised through the appropriate use of contracts and regulation. The evidence from the new leisure trusts and the literature on other public services seems to imply a generally positive impact following the transfer of responsibilities from governmental bodies. Anticipated negative implications are increasingly being recognised as implementation issues that can be minimised or eliminated through a planned approach to transition management. Co-operative structures may provide certain potential benefits that are unique to this form of organisation, in spite of the fact that many of the 'headline' benefits could also be more or less provided by different organisational forms (Pestoff, 1995; 6, 1998). The underlying assertion is that the potential for these additional benefits provides good reason for enthusiasm over the use of co-operatives to deliver public services (see also ICOM, 1997; Hargreaves, 1999; Gosling, 2000).

While it appears that such enthusiasm would not be misplaced, and that the transfer of public services represents a genuine opportunity for the development of co-operative structures, there is also a sense that more needs to be done if their full potential is to be realised. Birchall (2000) has noted the recent tendency towards 'mimetic isomorphism', whereby competing organisations in the public, private and third sectors take on similar characteristics. Co-operatives must ensure that their performance is at least comparable with that of other organisational forms, and so a degree of similarity is to be both expected and welcomed. Beyond this, there seems little to be gained from the simple emulation of other forms. Indeed, for many commentators, achieving a 'co-operative advantage' is contingent on astute management of the 'co-operative difference' (e.g. Davis, 1999). Arguably, what is different about co-operatives is the way in which a distinct set of co-operative values is put into practice, particularly inclusive member-ownership arrangements and the opportunities this provides for active stakeholder participation. As yet, there is not enough evidence that public policy-makers or co-operatives themselves are paying enough attention to developing these inherent advantages. They have to learn to capitalise on the 'co-operative difference'.

References

ADLO (Association of Direct Labour Organisations) (1997) *Leisure Trusts – Key Issues for Local Authorities*, Briefing Paper 48, Manchester, Association of Direct Labour Organisations.

Armstrong, H. (1997) Speech to Local Government Association Conference, London, 3 June.

Batley, R. and Stoker, G. (1991) *Local Government In Europe*, London, Macmillan.

Birchall, J. (1997) 'Co-operative values and principles: a commentary', *Journal of Co-operative Studies*, 30(2), pp. 42–69.

Birchall, J. (2000) 'Some theoretical and practical implications of the attempted takeover of a consumer co-operative society', *Annals of Public and Co-operative Economics*, 71(1), pp. 29–54.

Birchall, J., Pollitt, C. and Putman, K. (1995) *The Difference That Makes For Autonomy: A Comparative Study of Opted-out Schools, Hospitals and Housing Associations*, Paper at Housing Studies Association Conference, Edinburgh, September.

Blackley, S. (1996) *Multi-stakeholder Structures – Will They Fly?*, http://csf.colorado.edu/co-op/coop-bus/96feb/0069.html

Boyne, G. (1998) 'Competitive tendering in local government: a review of theory and evidence', *Public Administration*, 76(3), pp. 695–712.

Caballer, V., Ruano, E. and Vivas, D. (1994) 'Organisations in the social economy in health care and social services: an overview', in 6, P. and Vidal, I., *Delivering Welfare*, Barcelona, CIES.

Clapham, D., Kintrea, K. and Kay, H. (1998) 'Sustainability and maturity of community based housing organizations', *Journal of Co-operative Studies*, 31(1), pp. 30–38.

Clarke, J. and Newman, J. (1997) *The Managerial State*, London, Sage.

Clarke, M. and Stewart, J. (1988) *The Enabling Council*, Luton, Local Government Training Board.

Coalter, F. (1990) 'The "mixed economy" of leisure', in Henry, I. (ed.), *Management and Planning in the Leisure Industries*, London, Macmillan.

Curson, T. (1996) *Can You Place Your Trust In Them? The Role Of Charitable Trusts In Leisure Management*, Brighton, LSA.

Davis, H. and Walker, B. (1997) 'Trust-based relationships in local government contracting', *Public Money and Management*, 17(4).

Davis, H. (1996) 'Quangos and local government: a changing world', *Local Government Studies*, 22(2), pp. 1–7.

Davis, P. (1999) *Managing the Co-operative Difference*, Geneva, International Labour Organization.

Deakin, N. and Walsh, K. (1996) 'The enabling state: the role of markets and contracts', *Public Administration*, 74(1), pp. 33–48.

DETR (Department for the Environment, Transport and the Regions) (1999) *Achieving Best Value Through Partnership*, Paper 7, Warwick Best Value Series, London, DETR.

Duberley, J. (1997) 'Factors impacting upon the nature of the contracting relationship', *ESRC Research Programme: An Organisational Behaviour Approach to Local Authority Contracting*, Working Paper, Sheffield Hallam University.

Elcock, H. (1994) *Local Government*, 3rd edn., London, Routledge.

Employee Ownership Options (1999) *Externalisation of Public Services*, http://www.employee-ownership.org.uk/external.html

Fisher, K. (1998) 'Best value: yes, but what does it mean?', *Recreation*, Jan/Feb.

Garside, P. (2000) *The Conduct of Philanthropy*, London, Athlone Press.

Gosling, P. (2000) *New Mutualism: a new solution for renewed councils?*, London, Co-operative Party.

Gray, P. (1998) *Rebuilding Trust*, Paper at NEXUS Conference, London, 3 July.

Hargreaves, I. (1999) *New Mutualism: in from the cold*, London, Co-operative Party.

Holzmann, A. (1994) 'Between welfare state and civil society: a case study on local community service centres in the Austrian province of Tyrol', in 6, P. and Vidal, I., *Delivering Welfare*, Barcelona, CIES.

Hood, C. (1991) 'A public management for all seasons?', *Public Administration*, 69(1), pp. 3–19.

Huxham, C. (1996) *Creating Collaborative Advantage*, London, Sage.

Huxham, C. and Vangen, S. (1996) 'Managing inter-organizational relationships', in Osborne, S. (ed.), *Managing in the Voluntary Sector*, London, International Thomson Business Press.

Huxham, C. and Vangen, S. (2000) 'Ambiguity, complexity and dynamics in the membership of collaboration', *Human Relations*, 53(6), pp. 771–806.

ICOM (1997) *The Case for Democratic Employee Ownership in Externalisation of Services*, Leeds, ICOM.

Jervis, P. and Richards, S. (1996) *Three Deficits of Public Management*, University of Birmingham.

Johannson, R. and Borell, K. (1999) 'Central steering and local networks: old-age care in Sweden', *Public Administration*, 77(3), pp. 585–598.

Kay, J. (1991) 'The economics of mutuality', *Annals of Public and Co-operative Economics*, 62(3), pp. 309–319.

Kirkpatrick, I. and Martinez-Lucio, M. (1995) *The Politics of Quality in the Public Sector*, London, Routledge.

Kumar, S. (1996) 'Accountability: what is it and why do we need it?', in Osborne, S. (ed.), *Managing in the Voluntary Sector*, London, International Thomson Business Press.

Lane, J. (1995) *The Public Sector: Concepts, Models and Approaches*, 2nd edn, London, Sage.

LeGrand, J. (1998) 'Ownership and social policy', *Political Quarterly*, 69(4), pp. 415–421.

Lindsley, D., Brass, D. and Thomas, J. (1995) 'Efficacy–performance spirals: a multi-level perspective', *Academy of Management Review*, 20(3), pp. 645–678.

Litvack, J., Ahmad, J. and Bird, R. (1997) *Rethinking Decentralization at the World Bank*, http://www-wbweb4.worldbank.org/courses/ebel/revisit6.html

Lorrain, D. and Stoker, G. (1997) *The Privatization of Urban Services in Europe*, London, Pinter.

Lowenberg, P. (1997) *Partnering for Service Delivery: Securing Best Value Through New Forms of Procurement and Service Agreements*, London, LGMB.

Miettinen, A. and Nordlund, A. (2000) 'Institutional limitations for providing co-operative welfare in Sweden and Finland', *Journal of Co-operative Studies*, 33(1), pp. 39–52.

Mullins, D. (1998) 'More choice in social rented housing?', in Marsh, A. and Mullins, D. (eds), *Housing and Public Policy*, Buckingham, Open University Press.

Newton, K. and Karran, T. (1985) *The Politics of Local Expenditure*, London, Macmillan.

OECD (1996) *Executive Summary – Ministerial Symposium on the Future of Public Services*, http://www.oecd.org/puma/gvrnance/minister/summary.html

Painter, C. and Isaac-Henry, K. (1997) 'Relations with non-elected agencies: local authority good practice', *Public Money and Management*, 17(1), pp. 43–48.

Painter, C. (1996) 'Local authorities and non-elected agencies: the dilemmas of multi-dimensional relationships', *Local Government Policy-Making*, 23(2), pp. 18–25.

Painter, C., Isaac-Henry, K. and Rouse, J. (1997) 'Local authorities and non-elected agencies: strategic responses and organizational networks', *Public Administration*, 75(2), pp. 225–245.

Perri 6 (1994) 'Introduction', in 6, P. and Vidal, I., *Delivering Welfare*, Barcelona, CIES.

Perri 6, P. (1998) 'Ownership and the new politics of the public interest services', *Political Quarterly*, 69(4), pp. 404–414.

Pestoff, V. (1994) 'Beyond exit and voice in social services: citizens as co-producers', in 6, P. and Vidal, I., *Delivering Welfare*, Barcelona, CIES.

Pestoff, V. (1995) 'Local economic democracy and multi-stakeholder co-operatives', *Journal of Rural Co-operation*, 23(2), pp. 151–167

Pestoff, V. (1998) *Beyond the Market and State*, Aldershot, Ashgate.

Peters, B. (1998) ' "With a little help from our friends": public–private partnerships as institutions and instruments', in Pierre, J. (ed.), *Partnerships in Urban Governance*, London, Macmillan.

Pierre, J. (1998) 'Public–Private Partnerships and Urban Governance', in Pierre, J. (ed.), *Partnerships in Urban Governance*, London, Macmillan.

Pierson, C. (1998) *Beyond the Welfare State: The New Political Economy of Welfare*, 2nd edn, Cambridge, Polity Press.

Pollitt, C. and Summa, H. (1997) 'Trajectories of reform: public management change in four countries', *Public Money and Management*, 17(1), pp. 7–18.

Pollitt, C., Birchall, J. and Putman, K. (1998) *Decentralising Public Service Management*, London, Macmillan.

Pollitt, C., Packwood, T., Hanney, S., Rothwell, S. and Roberts, S. (1997) *Trajectories and Options: An International Perspective on the Implementation of Finnish Public Management Reforms*, Helsinki, Ministry of Finance.

Ranci, C. (1994) 'The role of the third sector in welfare policies in Italy', in 6, P. and Vidal, I., *Delivering Welfare*, Barcelona, CIES.

Reid, B. (1995) 'Interorganisational networks and the delivery of housing services', *Housing Studies*, 10(2), pp. 133–149.

Rhodes, R. (1997a) *Understanding Governance*, Buckingham, Open University Press.

Rhodes, R. (1997b) 'From marketization to diplomacy: it's the mix that matters', *Public Policy and Administration*, 12(2) pp. 31–50.

Ridley, N. (1988) *The Local Right: Enabling Not Providing*, London, Centre for Policy Studies.

Roberts, K. (1978) *Contemporary Society and the Growth of Leisure*, London, Longman.

Salamon, L. (1995) *Partners in Public Service: Government-nonprofit Relations in the Modern Welfare State*, Baltimore, MD, Johns Hopkins University Press.

Scott, S. (2000) 'The people's republic of Yoker: a case study of tenant management in Scotland', *Journal of Co-operative Studies*, 33(1), pp. 15–38.

Seal, W. and Vincent-Jones, P. (1997) 'Accounting and trust in the enabling of long-term relations', *Accounting, Auditing and Accountability Journal*, 10(3), pp. 406–431

Sesnan, M. (1998) *Sports & Leisure Trusts – The Way Forward?*, Paper at ILAM Greater London Region Seminar, 20 January.

Simmons, R. (2000) 'Partners in trust', *Leisure Manager*, January.

Smith, B. (1998) 'Enabling and the 1993 Local Government Act in New South Wales', *Public Administration*, 76(3), pp. 559–578.

Spear, R., Leonetti, A. and Thomas, A. (1994) *Third Sector Care*, Open University, Milton Keynes, Co-operatives Research Unit.

Sports Council (1994) *Trust Management of Sports and Recreational Facilities*, *Recreation Management Factfile Datasheet*, London, Sports Council.

Sports Council (1995) *Management Options for Local Authority Leisure Service Provision*, Recreation Management Factfile Datasheet, London, Sports Council.

Stewart, J. and Stoker, G. (1988) *From Local Administration to Community Government*, London, Fabian Society.

Stewart, J. (1996) *Moving Partnerships Forward*, Paper at Policy and Performance Review Network Conference, Warwick, 8–10 July.

Stoker, G. (1997) 'Privatization, urban government and the citizen', in Lorrain, D. and Stoker, G. (eds), *The Privatization of Urban Services In Europe*, London, Pinter.

Stryjan, Y. (1994) 'Understanding co-operation: the reproduction perspective', *Annals of Public and Co-operative Economics*, 65(1), pp. 60–77.

Toonen, T. and Raadschelders, J. (1997) *Public Sector Reform in Western Europe*, Paper at Conference on Comparative Civil Service Systems, Indiana University, 5–8 April, http://www.indiana.edu/%7Escrc/toonen11.htm

Travers, T. (1998) Change *for Local Government: A Commentary on the Government's Proposals for Local Authority Finance*, York, JRF.

Turnbull, S. (1997) 'Stakeholder co-operation', *Journal of Co-operative Studies*, 29(3), pp. 18–52.

Ullrich, G. (2000) 'Innovative approaches to co-operation in health care and social services', *Journal of Co-operative Studies*, 33(1), pp. 53–71.

Vidal, I. (1994) 'Non-profit organisations in the administration of social services in Catalunya', in 6, P. and Vidal, I., *Delivering Welfare*, Barcelona, CIES.

Wagner, A. (1994) 'The significance and function of social welfare associations in Switzerland', in 6, P. and Vidal, I., *Delivering Welfare*, Barcelona, CIES.

Walker, B. and Davis, H. (1999) 'Perspectives on contractual relationships and the move to best value in local authorities', *Local Government Studies*, 25(2), pp. 16–37.

Walsh, K. (1997) 'Markets and the public service', in Lorrain, D. and Stoker, G. (eds), *The Privatization of Urban Services in Europe*, London, Pinter.

Whitsun, D. (1987) 'Leisure, the state and collective consumption', in Horne, J., Jary, D. and Tomlinson, A. (eds), *Sport, Leisure and Social Relations*, London, Routledge & Kegan Paul.

Wolman, H. and Peterson, G. (1981) 'State and local government strategies for responding to fiscal pressure', *Tulane Law Review*, 55(3).

Wolman, H. (1984) 'Understanding local government responses to fiscal pressure: a cross-national analysis', *Journal of Public Policy*, 3(3), pp. 245–264.

Worrall, L., Collinge, C. and Bill, T. (1996), *The Strategic Process in Local Government: A Discussion Paper and Extended Bibliography*, Paper at LGMB Conference, London, 12 June.

Wycombe Leisure Limited (1997) *Annual Report*, Wycombe, Wycombe Leisure Limited.

6 Mutuality in insurance and social security

Retrospect and prospect

Deborah Mabbett

For much of the twentieth century, insurance against risks faced by householders was understood as an inherently mutual activity. A group of people pay premiums into a pool from which benefits are paid out to those among them who suffer a loss from the insured contingency. To ensure that the arrangement will be sustainable, the premiums must reflect the loss rate (the probability of the event occurring). This rate can be learned from the experience of the scheme, and it constitutes a shared characteristic of the group. Excessive claiming by some members affects the premiums of all. If the group is sufficiently socially proximate, members will be able to police claims and guard against moral hazard. The group also has an incentive to restrict its membership to those with similar risk characteristics; that is, to guard against adverse selection.

We can contrast this understanding of insurance with that which developed in shipping and other commercial activities. Premiums levied also reflect the loss rate, but the insurer does not rely primarily on pooling similar policies. Instead, the insurer stakes its capital to ensure that losses can be covered. Mutual insurers also need to hold capital reserves against the risk of ruin that can arise from an uneven flow of claims, but mutuals were able to operate with lower reserves than commercial insurers. (Some early mutual constitutions allowed the society to call on members when faced with excess claims; another model was to combine an insurance and savings scheme, with the latter providing the needed reserves.)

By the end of the twentieth century, the commercial understanding of insurance had largely displaced the mutual understanding, at least in Britain. Successful mutuals had grown too large to benefit from the small societies' methods of controlling claims. The desire to avoid adverse selection had to be put to one side if it was not to turn into a recipe for decline, with societies failing to recruit new members. Sophisticated methods for differentiating between individuals when estimating the probability of loss contributed to the 'fine-tuning' of premiums and reduced the perception of group inter-dependency. 'Providers' of insurance assumed a separate identity to 'members', and competition between providers became increasingly robust.

At the same time, the development of the state social security system eclipsed some of the areas of insurance first developed by mutual associations. In the next section, I explain how, after the passing of the 1911 National Insurance Act, friendly societies were subjected to a process of 'creeping nationalisation', becoming in effect agencies of the state in delivering sickness insurance. This agency relationship suffered from a number of problems and the societies did not prosper. During the Second World War, William Beveridge drew up a report setting out a comprehensive welfare state, but was keen to see a role for friendly societies retained in the implementation of his proposals. After the war ended, the Labour government elected in 1945 brought most elements of the Beveridgean welfare state into being, but opted for a centralised, state-run insurance scheme. As a result, the system of income-smoothing and risk-bearing in the British economy has come to be characterised by a clear separation of state social security provision from its private counterparts. This contrasts with the situation on the Continent, particularly in France, where mutual insurance associations have been incorporated into the social insurance system.

The 1980s saw a series of measures adopted by the Conservative governments to promote the coverage of private insurance and thereby facilitate the curtailment of the state system. It soon emerged that the incentive structures of private providers did not necessarily lead to a socially desirable pattern of insurance provision. This was revealed particularly by the pensions mis-selling scandal (when insurers persuaded people to move from occupational to personal pensions, often at a loss to their eventual entitlement), but also by the general problem of excessive fees and charges.

There are three types of solution to these problems. One is to reverse privatisation and revive state provision. Another is to tighten regulation of private providers. Regulation operates partly by restricting the decisions of private managers and partly by influencing their incentives (e.g. by fines). The key difference between a regulatory solution and state provision is that, in the former, competition between providers can be implemented. Competition may help to promote cost-effectiveness; however, it is also possible for competition to have perverse consequences. The third option is to address the governance structure of private providers to make them more responsive to the public interest. The principle of mutuality was revisited in the 1990s by some participants in the pensions policy debate, notably Frank Field (1996), in the course of the search for better governance structures for insurance. However, this approach has not been pursued by the Labour government. The background to this debate is discussed in the third section.

Friendly societies and social security provision between the wars

In Britain, a national health insurance scheme was created in 1911 to provide medical services and cash benefits. The following discussion concentrates on cash benefit (sickness benefit) administration, which was conducted by 'Approved Societies'. Societies had to meet two main conditions to be approved to administer sickness benefits:

(1) that the Society shall not be conducted for profit, and
(2) that its constitution shall provide for its affairs being subject to the absolute control of its members (Royal Commission on National Health Insurance, 1928, p92).

In specifying these conditions, Parliament drew on the model provided by the friendly societies that had been established in the course of the previous century. About 40 per cent of those to whom the 1911 Act applied were already members of friendly societies. However, the Act also allowed commercial companies (i.e. with non-customer shareholders) to participate in administering sickness benefits, but they had to establish a separate branch which complied with conditions (1) and (2) above. The commercial companies that established approved society branches were primarily companies engaged in selling life insurance and insurance to meet funeral costs. In the terminology of the time, they were 'industrial assurance companies' or 'industrial assurance collecting societies'; they are referred to below as industrial offices.

A standard rate of compulsory contribution to health insurance was set in the 1911 Act, along with a basic structure of benefits. If a society had surplus income, it could offer additional benefits. This was subject to the approval of the Ministry of Health, which determined, at five-yearly intervals, how any surplus accrued by a society should be divided between reserves and additional benefits. These were the only possible destinations of the surplus: surplus income could not be extracted from the society by members and/or owners in any other form. The government paid a subsidy to the sickness benefit scheme. The initial amount of the subsidy was two ninths of benefits paid and administrative costs incurred for men insured, and one fourth for women (women had a higher rate of sickness absence than men). Subsequently, this was changed to two ninths for all, and then cut to one seventh for men and one fifth for women in 1926. Apart from the crude differences in the subsidies for men and women, the main adjustment for different risks taken on by the societies was the system for crediting against 'reserve values' related to the age of society members (Royal Commission on National Health Insurance, 1928, ch. VII). The inadequacies of subsidy differentiation meant that the financial position of societies, and therefore their ability to pay additional benefits, differed markedly according to the risk characteristics of their memberships (1928, p115).

Whiteside's (1983) account of the Approved Society system emphasises the advantages to the government of using 'private agencies for public purposes'. In particular, she documents how the rate of government subsidy was cut over the course of time. Civil servants governed the allocation of surpluses between additional benefits and reserves. It was therefore open to the government to pursue a conservative benefits policy, cause the societies to accumulate reserves, and then cut the state subsidy to the scheme. In the first fifteen years of operation of the system, claims ran at lower levels than expected, and many societies accumulated large surpluses. The Royal Commission recommended that the basic rates of benefit and the range of risks covered be improved, but this recommendation was not implemented. In the latter part of the 1920s, claims rose strongly, but the government pressed for tougher administration rather than reverse the cuts in subsidy it had made (Whiteside, 1983, p177). The government's desire to save money (by causing societies to build reserves, and then cutting the subsidy) exceeded the incentive of societies to control claims. 'Even the most profitable societies became subject to official scrutiny' (Whiteside, 1983, p177); this is significant because profitable societies had the prospect of providing additional benefits to encourage them to be 'responsible' in administration.

The government also required the societies to meet part of the cost of maintaining rights to sickness benefits for members who became unemployed and were unable to keep up their contributions (Whiteside, 1983, pp175–176, 183–184). Related measures increased the amount of pooling of contributions between approved societies, culminating in the Treasury's 1931 proposal (which was defeated) that all funds should be pooled. The Treasury favoured pooling in order to minimise the level of government subsidies or loans that would have to be given to loss-making societies, but, as the Government Actuary pointed out, pooling would remove the last traces of financial incentive for 'responsible' administration.

Another feature of the government's evolving relationship with the approved societies was that it gradually increased its powers to intervene in the running of societies. The Ministry of Health persuaded the Royal Commission that its powers to supervise the societies were inadequate and its sanctions insufficiently flexible. The government could withdraw approval from a society, effectively meaning that its business would have to be disbanded and transferred to other societies, but this was seen as 'too drastic' for most problems which arose (Royal Commission on National Health Insurance, 1928, p110). The government's preference was to enhance its 'day-to-day' powers of intervention, thereby gradually transforming its arms-length contract into a closer working relationship.

The government was dealing with two main types of providers: friendly societies and industrial offices (there were also small numbers covered by trade unions and employers' provident funds). The Royal Commission did not make much play of the differences between these institutions. It did not accept industrial offices' suggestions that administrative allowances were too low for societies that did not have voluntary workers, and expressed reservations about the contracting-out of administration from some societies to their commercial parent companies (1928, pp252–255). However, the

Commission's main concern was the inequality of benefits, and the industrial offices were not implicated in the selection of members to improve benefits ('cream-skimming'), as discussed below. The Commission did note that the requirement that a society's affairs were 'subject to the absolute control of its members' was not effective in the case of larger societies: while the rules in theory provided for member control, this was more semblance than substance (p97). In making this point, size rather than constitution was seen as the key issue.

Unlike the Royal Commission, Beveridge made a strong distinction between the friendly societies and the industrial offices when he reviewed the system for his 1942 Report. He recommended that industrial offices should cease to be involved in the administration of social insurance. However, he favoured a continuing role for the friendly societies under his unified national insurance scheme. Beveridge argued, in effect, that the friendly societies and the industrial offices had quite different incentives for participating in the administration of social insurance, and that the incentives of the friendly societies were compatible with the aims of the government, while the incentives of the industrial offices were not.

What were these incentives? Since surpluses could only be used for the benefit of customers, not outside owners, the interwar structure for sickness benefits would appear to be well-suited to the mutual form of organisation. A company with outside shareholders would, by contrast, have no apparent interest in running such an operation. However, the industrial offices were interested in participating in the compulsory scheme. One reason was that they could bundle additional products ('voluntary' insurance) with their administration of the compulsory component. Bundling took several forms: the two types of product could be linked at sale, they could be linked in the administration of contribution accounts (where the grant from the government contributed to economies), and they could be linked in the claims process, if the contingencies insured were the same. Beveridge was highly critical of the life insurance and funeral benefit policies that industrial offices bundled with their administration of the state scheme. Friendly societies also sold their own products, but they were more likely to offer sickness insurance to top up the inadequate benefits provided by the state scheme. Beveridge argued that the voluntary insurance sold by friendly societies was socially useful, whereas that sold by industrial offices was not. This argument is discussed in more detail below.

Beveridge did acknowledge one claim to participation on the part of the industrial offices. By including these operations, the state took advantage of their vigorous recruitment and collection activity. When the 1911 scheme was set up, five million people belonged to friendly societies but seven million needed a home:

> It is arguable that . . . if the industrial life offices had not seen in this the
> opportunity to build up through State insurance connections for their

own lines of business, a substantial proportion of those compelled to pay contributions would have failed to become members of any Approved Society. In that case the State would have had itself to undertake direct administration of sick benefit. (Beveridge, 1948, p76)

In 1911, the government arguably lacked the bureaucratic capacity, and certainly lacked the inclination, to engage in this task.

Why were the industrial offices active in selling to those not in friendly societies? Might the friendly societies have expanded their business more after 1911 if the industrial offices had not competed it away? The answers to these questions revolve around the propensities of the two types of society to be selective in the business they took on: to 'cream-skim'. If an insurer has only a single risk pool (i.e. levies the same contributions and provides the same benefits to all) and takes on high-risk business, the benefits that can be expected by low-risk members of the pool deteriorate. In a mutual society, low-risk members will not want to expand their pool to include high risks, because this will reduce their benefits (for approved societies, the prospect of paying additional benefits would recede). The mutuals therefore guarded against adverse selection via their restrictive recruiting policies.

Cream-skimming is also a feature of competitive insurance markets in which the participants are capitalist firms. In a competitive market, an insurer who is able to exclude high risks will be able to attract low-risk customers from those insurers who have failed to be selective. The unselective insurer will have to raise premiums or reduce benefits, ending up with a business covering only the high risks refused by other insurers. It might therefore be thought that industrial offices would want to sell their voluntary products to the 'cream' and avoid high risk customers, but this was not so. A great deal of their business was in the sale of life policies, tailored to the desire of the lowest income groups to avoid a pauper's funeral. They made good profits on selling policies to people in insecure and unstable employment, because of the stringent rules operating which led to the lapsing of policies when policy-holders did not keep up their contributions.

Aside from the overall growth in their business, the main indication that the industrial offices were less selective than the friendly societies comes from their insurance of women compared with men. They insured 55 per cent of women but only 40 per cent of men in 1938 (Beveridge, 1948, p77). The connection between sex and risk characteristics is apparent in the distribution of additional benefits: 63 per cent of men belonged to societies giving additional benefits, but only 28 per cent of spinsters and widows, and 20 per cent of insured married women belonged to such societies (Beveridge, 1942, p27). As Beveridge concluded in his study of mutual associations: 'The societies which showed themselves most ready to be all-embracing were those whose sponsors had a financial interest outside insurance for sickness, that is to say, the industrial life offices' (1948, p78).

By the time the Beveridge Committee was taking evidence, virtually everyone agreed that the provision of unequal sickness benefits under the approved society system was indefensible (Beveridge, 1942, p28). However, if societies could not offer additional benefits to their members, they would not have the incentive for responsible financial management that came from being able to offer better benefits to members through sound administration. (Of course, the problem of cream-skimming was that societies could offer better benefits by selection of risks, rather than by sound administration.) If additional benefits were to end, so also would the basis for financial independence of societies. However, Beveridge argued that friendly societies should still be able to participate in the social insurance system as 'responsible agents'. In the current terminology of principal–agent theory, we might say that Beveridge thought that the incentives of friendly societies as agents could be aligned with the objectives of the government as principal. How could alignment be achieved without financial independence? The key was the friendly societies' administration of their own (i.e. voluntary) sickness benefit insurance. Beveridge saw the administration of the state scheme as being undertaken in tandem with voluntary insurance, so that the incentives for responsible administration of the latter would 'spill over' to the former.

Beveridge was quite aware of the problems of administering benefits via an independent agency, but held to the view that only industrial offices would present these problems. He argued that

> the Industrial Life Offices, so far from having any motive for careful administration of disability benefit, would have a direct economic motive to be liberal with the money of the Social Insurance Fund, in order to obtain or retain customers for industrial assurance [burial policies etc.] and to increase the profits of their shareholders or the pay of their staff. (1942, p32)

Far from having the potential to be 'responsible agencies', industrial offices had incentives that detracted from the attainment of government policies. Beveridge saw no possible 'synergies' between the industrial offices' administration of their voluntary business and social insurance. This was because of the nature of the business the industrial offices were engaged in. They did not have a local structure for scrutinising claims in an effective way, and so specialised in insurance against death because the facts were easy to ascertain. Because moral hazard problems in this type of insurance were thought to be slight, industrial offices did not even have to ascertain that the policy-holder had an insurable interest (i.e. that s/he would experience a loss on the insured event occurring at least as great as the insurance payable). This had resulted in industrial offices selling policies in breach of Acts of Parliament intended to prevent gambling. By contrast, friendly societies concentrated on offering insurance against contingencies where there really was an insurable loss, and indeed the success of their business required them to verify those losses and guard against moral hazard.

The Coalition's White Paper on Social Insurance (1944, Part I) rejected Beveridge's proposals for the inclusion of friendly societies. It argued that, at most, one-third of the population was covered by friendly societies which fulfilled Beveridge's conditions of having substantial resources of their own involved in voluntary provision and an efficient sick-visiting system. Furthermore, societies did not offer benefits that really 'lined up' with the state benefit: they did not pay long-term benefit and it would be in their interest to treat applications for long-term state benefits leniently. If friendly societies' incentives were not aligned with the objectives of the government, they could not be trusted as 'responsible agents'.

The societies lobbied intensively against the government's rejection of their case, but, finding the Labour Minister of National Insurance (James Griffiths) unbending, and sensing that they had lost the battle, they changed tactic. An alternative model, whereby the societies would act as 'paying agents', was put forward. On recommittal of the 1946 Bill to the House, it was proposed that the Minister should 'utilise the Friendly Societies through the operation of Regulations. Such a course could make the voluntary Friendly Societies a part of the Minister's administrative machinery in the same ways as ... the Post Office and the Unemployment Exchange' (Goodrich, 1946). While this arrangement would have saved the faces of Labour MPs who had given a pledge to support friendly societies prior to the 1945 election, it was also rejected. A state machinery was needed anyway for those (the majority) who were not members of societies. The underlying problem in moving from the responsible agency to the paying agency model is that the prospect of substantial savings in state administrative effort receded greatly: a paying agency must be subject to close supervision and control, which may as well be accomplished by incorporation into a hierarchical bureaucracy.

One important problem with Beveridge's argument for friendly society administration is that it rested on the elision of a particular type of business with a particular type of society (friendly societies with sickness benefits; industrial offices with death benefits). The parallel payment of voluntary sickness benefits was the key to operating as a responsible agency, not a non-profit-making structure or a constitution incorporating governance by members. For Beveridge, the elision of the nature of the business and its institutional form was not just historical chance: it was a reflection of fundamental features of insurance, and in particular, of the need for discretion in administration.

> Insurance of wage-earners against sickness has never in Britain presented itself to business men as in itself good business. The solution of the critical problem of combining sound finance with the

sympathetic administration which is essential in this field has been the achievement of the friendly societies. (Beveridge, 1948, p81)

Similarly, the development of unemployment insurance rested on mutual aid through trade unions. By contrast, burial insurance (and subsequently life insurance) appealed to 'the business motive of gain ... involving payment of a single sum on an event which could be established without difficulty' (ibid.). One surprising consequence of Beveridge's interest in the particular characteristics of decision-making on sickness insurance was that he expressed reservations about the efficacy of state administration, doubting whether the state could 'combin[e] soundness with sympathy' as did the friendly societies (1948, p84).

Embedded in Beveridge's discussion is a distinction between 'mere' mutuality (an institutional structure in which profits are returned to members, and members have voting rights in the appointment and governance of managers) and constitution as a friendly society, where members are bound by 'good fellowship' and relationships go 'beyond the narrowly contractual' (Yarrow, 1993, p27). However, the special ethical basis of friendly societies was already on the wane by the time Beveridge wrote *Voluntary Action*. Beveridge recognised that the relationship with the state in administering sickness benefits had contributed to changing practices: approved societies became 'more official and less personal' (1948, p79). Societies with the structures and resources to participate in administering state benefits did not feature close ties between members. In his final speech in the House on the arrangements with friendly societies, Griffiths stressed that if Beveridge's condition that no society should be admitted unless it paid substantial benefits from its own funds were to be accepted, nearly all the small friendly societies would be excluded, yet these were the very ones with the 'human touch' extolled by the societies' supporters (Griffiths, 1946).

Governance and regulation in pension provision

There are some parallels between the problems that have arisen in the provision of private pensions in Britain and the issues discussed in the last section, although there are also many differences. The key issue for the government is that there will continue to be a tax-financed pension for those with inadequately funded pensions, which gives the government an interest in ensuring that people contribute to funded pension schemes, and that these schemes provide adequate benefits. The government therefore promotes private pension provision through tax incentives that parallel the subsidies to interwar sickness insurance. At the same time, the government has an interest in limiting the cost of these incentives, to the extent that it can do so without triggering a rise in claims on tax-financed state pensions.

By the mid-1990s, several problems had emerged with the performance of the pension providers. Providers stood accused of marketing excessively complex products that allowed high administrative charges to be levied. The inflexibility of rules on stopping and starting contributions parallels the problems of lapsing in the insurance policies sold by industrial offices in the interwar years. The need for contributors to get advice parallels the desirability of 'sound but sympathetic' administration. Could problems of pension maladministration have been avoided if the governance structure of providers had been different? Would the aims and incentives of providers be better aligned with those of contributors in a mutual system of governance? At first sight, the answer would seem to be negative: mutuals were implicated in mis-selling pensions alongside commercial companies. However, if one looks in detail at the nature of mutual governance, the answer becomes more ambiguous.

The mutual providers that are engaged in pension provision alongside commercial companies are characterised by their pattern of shareholding. In a mutual, contributors are the shareholders, and managers must answer to them; in an externally-owned, commercial company, managers answer to outside shareholders. Why did shareholding fail to protect contributors' interests? In large companies with dispersed shareholdings, shareholder 'voice' is limited. In listed companies, managers respond to shareholders via their sensitivity to the share price: poor management lowers the price and increases the vulnerability of the firm to take-over. Managers' remuneration packages may also reflect the share price. To maximise the share price, managers can be expected to pursue profit-maximising strategies. In a mutual, there is no share price and no take-over threat. To some extent, managers are released from the demands of profit-maximisation. They have considerably more leeway to define and pursue a range of objectives than in a commercial company. One possible outcome is that managers pursue a quiet life, using the space they have to increase their own utility. This is by no means the only possible outcome. The managerial space may be filled by adopting a distinctive ethos; this may even be a customer service ethos. Accounts of modern mutuals and co-operatives suggest that managers may be attracted to ethical business practices (Birchall, 1998).

The key issue is whether the owners of a mutual have any more potential to influence the management of their company than outside shareholders. To exercise direct influence over management in any type of firm, shareholders must obtain information, have incentives to act on it, and have ways of exerting leverage over managers. Dispersion of ownership leads to corporate governance problems, as shareholders only obtain a fractional return for any effort they make to improve the management of the firm, and have difficulty in assembling a voting block to sanction or replace managers. These problems afflict mutual as well as commercial firms.

An illustration of the issues can be drawn from the mutual fund industry in the USA. The contributor-shareholders in mutual funds have various mutual corporate governance powers. Shareholders have voting rights, and certain management actions must be approved by a majority of share-holders, while other actions have to be taken by a board of directors which includes members who are independent of the fund management (Baumol *et al.*, 1989, p53). Despite these governance rules, there has been a lot of controversy about the administration charges levied on mutual funds. It has also been evident that investors do not exercise their voting rights with any enthusiasm, and tend to monitor little else than the current price of their shares. This is hardly surprising as, for a small investor, there is only a small reward for putting effort into monitoring and participating in the governance of a fund. The study by Baumol *et al.* concluded that competition between funds was the key to restraining administration charges. The authors proposed elimination of some of the corporate governance rules imposed upon funds, favouring instead a minimal regulatory structure and an emphasis on the promotion of competition. They argued that 'exit' (switching to another provider) would be more effective in protecting contributors' interests than 'voice' (discussing and voting on management decisions).

However, in the pensions field, the promotion of competition has had some perverse consequences. Ideally (from the government's point of view), providers would sell simple products that are cheap to administer, ensuring that pensions business is profitable even with low charges. However, simple products lack marketing 'angles'. Competition drives providers towards complexity (Mabbett, 1999, p17). Furthermore, competition is most effective when buyers are well-informed, but the complexity of pensions means that buyers often rely on advice, introducing problems about the incentives of advice-givers. Furthermore, the product involves long-term commitment, and the cost of switching between providers is high, which limits the efficacy of 'exit' for dissatisfied contributors.

In the policy debate in the late 1990s, two different responses to these problems emerged within the government. The Treasury view was that the industry should be regulated to promote the provision of simple, transparent pension products (Treasury, 1999). The Department of Social Security (DSS) took a more eclectic position, which included the possibility that pension scheme membership could be based around occupation, place of employment or other 'affinity organisations' (DSS, 1998, ch. 7, para. 66). This is essentially the pattern of the social insurance systems of Europe. While some schemes are managed by the 'social partners' (employers and unions) and resemble British occupational schemes, others, particularly in small business sectors and farming, have mutual constitutions that resemble those of the friendly societies. The key feature of affinity groups in this context is that they would divide up the market in a non-competitive, or less competitive, way. Contributors would belong to a scheme because of their affinity with other members, not on the basis of an appraisal of its costs, efficiency and performance. This distinguishes the proposed structure of mutuality from the existing pattern of mutual provision, where institutions owned by contributors compete with commercial institutions to attract members.

The idea of affinity groups was not well received. Many respondents to the government's consultation exercise had difficulty in imagining what the basis for affinity groups would be, apart from occupational groups. Since one purpose of stakeholder pensions is to expand coverage beyond existing occupational schemes, the concept of affinity did not address a major policy problem. Furthermore, it was clear that contractual approaches to the protection of contributor interests were much better understood by participants in the pension debate than governance-based approaches (Mabbett, 1999). It is interesting to note that the Treasury proposal, while apparently market-oriented and competition-promoting, is also 'statist' in its emphasis on regulation. The gist of the proposal is that the government designs and 'kitemarks' a very simple stakeholder pension product. It thereby represses competition over product features and fund management, while promoting competition over administration costs. It is arguable that the proposal is equivalent to franchising private companies to deliver what is, in effect, a funded state pension (Mabbett, 1999, pp22–23).

The DSS proposal, by contrast, could have had the effect of creating providers that enjoyed some legitimacy in public policy debates as representatives of contributors' interests. A commercial company is expected to pursue narrow private interests, leaving the 'public interest' to be defined by the state. A mutual association may be recognised as having wider interests that correspond to the interests of a collectivity. Representative internal governance arrangements (election of supervisory boards, etc.) could further enhance legitimacy. The effect would be to provide a check on government opportunism and enhance the representation of contributors' interests in public policy.

Conclusion: competition, regulation and opportunism

Earlier in this chapter, it was argued that commercial companies (industrial offices) won the competitive battle with the friendly societies, largely because they were less concerned about adverse selection, less scrupulous in their sales practices, and more expansionary in their policies. However, industrial offices lost the war, in so far as their sale of poor-value policies contributed to the development of state-run national insurance. If history were to repeat itself, there would be an expansion of state provision to substitute for the unsatisfactory outcomes of the competitive market in private pensions. This seems unlikely to happen, although it is salutary to note that the borderline between regulation and state provision is permeable. The more regulated providers are, the more they resemble mere agencies of the state.

This story implies that we can see the fate of mutual financial institutions as the product of two sets of processes. On one side, competition and the emphasis on consumer choice undermines the salience of mechanisms to give contributors a voice in the management of financial service providers. On the other, 'statism' in British public policy means that mutual associations do not have a significant role in policy formulation, despite the importance of government policy decisions for the protection of contributors' interests. Furthermore, we can note that competition and 'statism' are two sides of the same coin. They are part of a political culture which exhibits 'strong fetishism surrounding public/private sector differences' (Dunleavy, 1989, p260). While one may sympathise with Frank Field's view that 'statist solutions' have a 'numbing effect' on thinking about welfare provision (1996, p39), it turned out in the late 1990s that other solutions could not be devised.

The development of mutual financial institutions since the Second World War points to the conclusion that the competitiveness of the market structure is dominant over the institutional forms of its participants: in a competitive market, mutuals will tend to adopt similar strategies to commercial companies. Frank Field argued that the participation of new mutual associations in the provision of pensions would 'add yet a new cutting edge to ... competitive forces' (1996, p38). Certainly, having more providers is good for competition, but it is not clear why the mutual sector might be a promising source of providers, or that mutuals could or would adopt different competitive strategies to their commercial counterparts.

In the Labour government's attempts to find alternatives to Conservative pension policies, the language of 'stakeholding' and 'partnership' replaced that of privatisation and contract (*Financial Times*, 1998). It was argued that new forms of governance and different implementation structures were needed to grapple with the problems of opportunism and instability in regulatory arrangements. One purpose of developing less conflictual relationships ('partnerships') is to surmount these problems. 'Stakeholders' can be seen as groups with legitimate claims to have their interests represented in the policy process. However, the government proved unable to make this abstract vision concrete.

The declining salience of the concept of mutuality in the financial services sector can therefore be seen to reflect two features of the sector. One is the emphasis on the promotion of competition and consumer choice; the other is the 'statism' of British public policy. Both features undermine the value of *voice* in the governance of financial service providers. Given the nature of the market, it is questionable whether competition and exit really are superior to governance and voice. Equally, however, we can see that reliance on competitive models is deeply entrenched in the provision of insurance and pensions, and this is the fundamental reason why mutuals have not been able to maintain a distinctive identity in the financial services sector.

References

Baumol, W., Goldfield, S., Gordon, L. and Koehn, M. (1989) *The Economics of Mutual Fund Markets: Competition versus Regulation*, Boston, Mass., Kluwer.

Beveridge, W. (1942) *Social Insurance and Allied Services*, Cmd 6404, London, HMSO.

Beveridge, W. (1948) *Voluntary Action: A Report on Methods of Social Advance*, London, Allen & Unwin.

Birchall, J. (1998) 'The future of cooperative and mutual businesses', Unpublished paper, Uxbridge, Brunel University.

Department of Social Security (DSS) (1998) *A New Contract for Welfare: Partnership in Pensions*, CM 4179, London, The Stationery Office.

Dunleavy, P. (1989) 'The United Kingdom: paradoxes of an ungrounded statism', in Castles, F. (ed.), *The Comparative History of Public Policy*, Cambridge, Polity.

Field, F. (1996) *Stakeholder Welfare*, IEA Choice in Welfare Series No. 32, London, Institute of Economic Affairs.

Financial Times (1998) 'Field hints at limiting second-tier pensions to mutuals', 29 May; 'Minister moves to allay fears on pensions', 1 June; 'Sectors urged to join pension partnership', 3 June.

Goodrich, (1946) MP for Hackney North, in Debate on the National Insurance Bill, 22.5.46, quoted in *Beveridge Papers* VIII/53/(143), p. 48, LSE.

Griffiths, J. (1946) Minister of National Insurance, *Hansard*, vol. 423, cols 603–616, 23 May.

Mabbett, D. (1999) *Risk and Security in the Private Provision of Old Age Pensions: A Review of the Government's Stakeholder Pension Proposals*, Discussion Paper Series 99/4, Department of Government, Brunel University, Uxbridge.

Royal Commission on National Health Insurance (1928) *Report*, Cmd 2596, London, HMSO.

Treasury (1999) *Helping to Deliver Stakeholder Pensions*, Treasury, 3 February.

White Paper (1944) *Social Insurance, Part I*, Appendix II, Cmd 6550, London, HMSO.

Whiteside, N. (1983) 'Private agencies for public purposes: some new perspectives on policy making in health insurance between the wars', *Journal of Social Policy*, 12(2), pp. 165–193.

Yarrow, G. (1993) *Social Security and Friendly Societies: Options for the Future*, Regulatory Policy Research Centre, Hertford College, Oxford.

7 Farmer co-operatives

Organisational models and their business environment[1]

Jerker Nilsson

One of the most basic notions in business is that organisations must reflect the characteristics of their business environment in their own organisational structure, otherwise they will not be competitive (Kast and Rosenzweig, 1979). A successful firm is one that adjusts its product offerings to meet changing demand and that has the ability to adapt to a variety of demand changes, including large ones and rapid ones. Likewise, the efficient firm is able to incorporate the traits of the labour markets, the capital markets, and so on into its own structure. All in all, the attributes of the organisation should be a mirror of the attributes of its various markets.

Business people often assert that the intensity of competition is steadily increasing, even at an accelerating rate. Such claims may be correct as more and more markets are becoming more and more turbulent. Today, changes in the business environments are quicker and more comprehensive than ever before. Concerning the European agribusiness sector, the following may be mentioned:

Political changes

- A new Common Agricultural Policy is under way, though neither the contents nor the dates are yet known, only that a substantial liberalisation can be expected.
- Liberalisation can be expected also at the global level, following World Trade Organisation (General Agreement on Tariffs and Trade, GATT) negotiations.
- The enlargement of the European Union (EU) towards the East will mean both new demand and new competition by producers, though the consequences are yet unclear.
- As European Monetary Union is put into operation, a trend towards harmonisation of the economies of the member states can be expected, implying less difference in tax systems, more homogeneous product mixes and consumption patterns (Traill, 1997, 1998).

Technological changes

- The rapid development of information technology will bring about tremendous changes in all sections of business life.
- For many years the relative costs of transportation has fallen as a consequence of new technology, and this trend can be expected to continue, creating a global market for still more products.

Economic changes

- Retail chains are gaining considerable strength through mergers, acquisitions and alliances. Hence, retailing is increasingly an internationally operating industry, and the chains' private brands are ever more widespread (Grunert *et al.*, 1996; Steenkamp, 1997; Traill, 1997).
- Consumer demand is undergoing changes in many respects, the main trend being increased diversification towards convenience as well as ecological and ethical concerns (Grunert *et al.*, 1996, 1997).
- European consumers are changing in terms of demographics (Traill, 1997). There seems to be a trend towards a homogenisation of eating habits in the various parts of Europe (Angulo *et al.*, 1997; Steenkamp, 1997; Traill, 1997, p43). More important are the behavioural and attitudinal changes – the least common denominator is volatility (Grunert *et al.*, 1996, 1997; Steenkamp, 1997).
- Multinational food conglomerates function as so-called enterprise hunters, always interested in buying firms with strong brands and consumer appeal. Knowing that the leading brands are the most profitable, they tend to sell less profitable brands in the product portfolio. Owning brands with the strongest consumer appeal, they want to sell the same brands internationally, though production takes place in countries with the most favourable production conditions (Traill, 1997).

Agribusiness firms have responded in different ways. Large mergers and acquisitions have taken place, whereby the multinational firms have strengthened their positions. Technological developments have been made use of in different respects: information technology, logistics, transportation, production, and so on. Also, the part of the agribusiness industry that comprises agricultural co-operative firms has followed the paths of amalgamations, internationalisation and technological advancement. These changes within the co-operative sector are at present quite rapid (Cropp, 1997; Grunert *et al.*, 1997; Rogers, 1997; Lagnevik and Kola, 1998). Many co-operatives have, however, also done something else – made profound changes in their co-operative business form. It seems that the reorganisation processes are becoming more intense than ever before.

This chapter focuses on these changes concerning organisational models for agricultural marketing co-operatives. It seeks to suggest answers to some questions:

- How can the various co-operative organisational models be classified into categories from a market adaptation point of view, and which are the core attributes of each model? (Section 2)
- Which market conditions are the various organisational models suited to, and why? What is the business rationale behind each model? (Sections 3 and 4)
- What will the agricultural co-operatives look like in terms of organisational models a decade from now? (Section 5)

Organisational models for agricultural co-operatives

For many decades, a co-operative was a co-operative! With due respect to the requirements of the various industries, all agricultural co-operatives had almost the same organisational characteristics, generally expressed in terms of co-operative principles such as open membership, unallocated equity capital and governance on the basis of one member, one vote (Barton, 1989; Nilsson, 1996). Hence, there is good reason to use the label *traditionally organised co-operatives* for this organisational model – it has existed since the middle of the nineteenth century. Since the 1980s, a growing number of agricultural co-operatives with quite different attributes have come into being, both through new establishments and through transformation of existing traditional co-operatives. *Entrepreneurial co-operatives* is suggested as a generic label. This shift in organisational models for agricultural co-operatives is a one-way trend, from the traditional model to different entrepreneurial models. The reason is simple: the changes in the agribusiness environment described in the preceding section require new types of organisation that are adaptive and learning in relation to increasingly turbulent markets. Hence, it is understandable that the concept of co-operative models has now become quite popular (Hansmann, 1996; Cook and Tong, 1997; Torgerson *et al.*, 1997; van Dijk, 1997; Barton, 1989).

The characteristics of these new organisational models vary a lot, but the main difference is in ownership, whereby also a number of other factors are affected. Ownership in the new forms is no longer only collective. In some cases it may be purely individual, while in others there is a blend of collective and individual ownership. Table 7.1 suggests four main groups of entrepreneurial co-operative organisational models in addition to the traditional one. This classification is based on comprehensive empirical studies of agricultural co-operatives in the fifteen EU member states, conducted in 1997 (Agricultural Co-operatives, 1997: Table 7.1 deviates

Table 7.1 Main structural characteristics of EU agricultural co-operatives

Attributes	Co-operative organisational models				
	Traditional co-operative	Participation shares co-operative	Co-operative with subsidiary	Proportional tradable shares co-operative	plc co-operative
Entry	Free	Free	Variable	Restricted	Variable
Individualised equity	No	Only for investors	Only for investors	Yes	Yes
Assets appreciation	No	For investors	Yes	Yes	Yes
Voting scheme	Equality	Members: use Investors: share	Members: use Investors: share	Use/Share-based	Share-based
Majority of decision control	Members	Members	Members via the co-op	Members	Investors
External participation	No	Yes	Yes	Limited, or without voting	Yes
Members' equity contribution	Equal	Equal	Equal via the co-operative	Use-based	Shares
Return of income	Use-based	Members: use Investors: share	Members: use Investors: share	Use/Share-based	Share-based
Value added activities	Limited	Yes	Yes	Yes	Yes
Professional manager	No	Not always	Yes	Yes	Yes

Source: Bekkum and van Dijk (1997), p.171.

from the original in two respects: some rows have been moved and two columns have changed places).

Being very different from the traditional form of co-operatives, the entre-preneurial firms still deserve to be called co-operatives. Like the traditional co-operatives, the entrepreneurial ones are a type of vertical integration and hence they constitute an instrument for a group of businesspeople to ameliorate a badly functioning market. They accord with the definition that is generally recognised by researchers on agricultural co-operatives:

> First, the user-owner principle. Persons who own and finance the co-operative are those that use it. Second, the user-control principle. Control of the co-operative is by those who use the co-operative. Third, the user-benefits principle. Benefits of the co-operative are distributed to its users on the basis of their use. (Barton, 1989, p1)

Within these boundaries there are many ways of organising co-operatives, and a large variety of other characteristics can be added. Some of these follow from the legal and other institutional settings, others result from tradition. Hence, the various co-operative models, including the traditional one, should be regarded as special types.

Nevertheless, depending on how the constituent definitional elements are understood, there may be some uncertainties as to how the new organisational types adhere to the concept of co-operatives. Hence, if the ownership criterion is interpreted as full ownership, some of the new organisational models must be rejected as co-operatives, but if it is understood as majority ownership they are co-operative models. Exactly the same can be said for the control criterion. The benefit criterion, on the other hand, is not negotiable – all the co-operative models have the objective of providing best possible benefits to the members/patrons. Hence, the three criteria can be regarded as hierarchically ordered:

● the ultimate criterion is that the member shall have best possible *benefits* from the co-operative;
● if the benefits can be increased by allowing *ownership* to external parties (for example, by attaining economies of scale or scope through the partnership), this is an acceptable step for a co-operative, provided that the external partner does not get decisive control; and
● if the external partner is willing to invest only on the condition of being granted some *control* this may be an acceptable sacrifice, though that control must not impede the member benefits.

In the same manner, one could question whether traditional co-operatives, with their collective ownership, live up to the definition – they bear resemblance to foundations as the members' property rights are very restricted. If, however, collective ownership is accepted as real ownership, they are still co-operatives.

The four entrepreneurial organisation models mentioned in Table 7.1 express more and more radical deviations from the traditional type, as one continues from the left to the right. Concerning *legal form*, in the first three there are still co-operative societies with members. In the last one the entire co-operative is organised as a public limited company (plc) and hence, instead of being members, the patrons are shareholders. *Co-operative ideology* that is important to the traditional co-operatives loses more and more significance when moving right across the table, and current or *mainstream economic thinking* becomes increasingly applicable.

What unites the entrepreneurial models is that there are investors who are remunerated for their investments in the form of return on investment (ROI). This profitability component in the firms' objective function may explain the label 'entrepreneurial'. There are, however, different types of investor. In the participation shares co-operatives (hereafter only termed *participation co-operatives*) and the co-operatives with subsidiaries (hereafter *subsidiary co-operatives*), the investors consist of non-members while the proportional tradable shares co-operatives (hereafter *new generation co-operatives* or *NGCs*) and the *plc co-operatives* have members as investors. Hence, the first two can be called *external-investor co-operatives,* and the last two *member-investor co-operatives* (see Table 7.2). 'New generation co-operative' is the term used for the 200 or so proportional tradable share co-operatives that have been established in North America, mainly during the 1990s (Harris *et al.*, 1996; Nilsson, 1997).

The difference between the participation co-operative and the subsidiary co-operative is that the former has non-members as investors in the co-operative society itself, while the latter has non-members as co-owners of the plc subsidiary, though still having only members in the co-operative society that owns the remainder of the subsidiary. Hence it may be understood that the four entrepreneurial models can be grouped within a matrix (see Table 7.2, rows 'Core investors' and 'Business operations in . . .'): participation co-operatives and new generation co-operatives have their business operations conducted within a co-operative society, while subsidiary co-operatives and plc co-operatives have a plc for the businesses. For the sake of simplicity, the four entrepreneurial models are lumped into two categories when analysed in section 4 of this chapter (see head of Table 7.2). The participation co-operatives and the subsidiary co-operatives have much in common with each other, as do the tradable share co-operatives and the plc co-operatives. Talking about heterogeneity, it should also be noted that each category contains many sub-models that could vary to some extent; for example, there might be external owners to plc co-operatives and NGCs. Hence, the five co-operative models presented here should be interpreted as ideal types in a Weberian sense.

Table 7.2 Characteristics of agricultural co-operative models

Attributes	Co-operative organisational models				
	Traditional co-operative	Participation shares co-operative	Co-operative with subsidiary	Proportional tradable shares co-operative	Plc co-operative
		External-investor co-ops		Member-investor co-ops	
Main categories	Countervailing power co-ops	Entrepreneurial co-operatives			
Core investors	None	Non-members		Members	
Business operations in …	Society	Society	plc	Society	plc
Theoretical rationale for co-operative business	Neo-classical theory; Game theory; Transaction cost theory; Property rights theory	Neo-classical theory; Game theory; Transaction cost theory; Property rights theory; Agency theory		Transaction cost theory; Property rights theory; Agency theory	
Co-operative ideology	Yes	Less, and only in the co-operative society		No	
Success factor	Economies of scale	Economies of scale and scope		Economies of scope – streamlining	
Focus	Trade conditions	Patrons: trade conditions; Investors: ROI		ROI	
Mission	Defensive	Offensive		Offensive	
Best strategy (M. Porter)	Cost leadership	Product differentiation		Focus	
Member roles	Patron	Patron and eventually investor		Patron and investor	
Investments/product unit	Small investments/product unit	Large investments/product unit		Large investments/product unit	
Type of business operations	Low value-added; Primary processing; Domestic and exports; Member related	Also value-added; Diversified processing; Also international business; Also non-member business		Value-added; Advanced processing; Domestic and exports; Also non-member business	
Technology	Simple, well-known	Also advanced technology		Advanced technology	
Orientation	Production orientation	Market orientation with production restrictions		Market orientation	
Market type	A stable market	Turbulent markets		Turbulent markets	
Market signals	Product markets	Product market; Risk capital market		Risk capital market; Product market	

It is also important to note that it is possible to use more than one model in a specific co-operative organisation. For example, while some of the business operations are conducted in a traditional organisational framework, other businesses may be separated into a subsidiary owned together with others. Or, while the co-operative is basically traditionally organised, some of its activities may be in the hands of members who own tradable shares (e.g. Skånemejerier, see Nilsson and Bärnheim, 2000). Or a new generation co-operative may sell participation shares to persons who are supportive to the co-operative. Hence, the concept of co-operative organisational model does not necessarily apply to the entire co-operative enterprise but rather to its various strategic business units (SBUs). Each branch of business operations could have its own organisational model. On the other hand, it is not possible to mix the attributes from different co-operative models to create another model, as the different attributes of the models presented here together form a coherent whole. Any attempt to do so may result in a co-operative whose characteristics counteract each other. The consequence may be an inefficient organisation because of bad market adaptation.

The traditional co-operative model

The characteristics of the traditional co-operative model presented in Table 7.1 are some of the main so-called co-operative principles as well as some other features observed in actual co-operatives:

- Ownership is in the form of a co-operative society – not a plc or any other legal form – and this society is open; that is, there is a clause in the by-laws saying that new members may join the society. Hence, there is free entry.
- The enterprise is owned by the society; that is, collectively. There is often no individual ownership of equity or, if there is, this is limited and under collective control.
- Open membership, as well as (frequently) the lack of ownership shares, imply that there is no trading of shares, and hence, the members cannot realise changes in the value of the assets.
- The members' governance of the firm is equal, irrespective of their volume of trade with the co-operative or their volume of shares, if any. One member, one vote applies.
- Control is fully in the hands of the members.
- External partners have no influence either as shareholders or in governance.
- To the extent that the members have individual ownership of stock, this ownership is equal or otherwise based on administrative rules.
- The profit made by the co-operative is not reimbursed to the members as return on investment but as patronage refund; that is, allocated in proportion to the members' deliveries to the co-operative.

- Traditionally organised co-operatives tend to have no, or only limited, business activities that may be called value-added; they work with less advanced operations.
- Hence, it is understandable that these co-operatives mostly do not need top-qualified management.

The participation co-operative model

Participation share co-operatives have characteristics that deviate from the traditional co-operatives in a number of respects:

- The discriminating feature is that non-patrons may own shares in the co-operative society; for example, in the form of B-shares or certificates. The purchase of these shares is voluntary, though the co-operative may restrict it to a specific group of investors such as members (in an investor role), other co-operatives, staff or local citizens.
- The ownership of the investor shares is, of course, individualised.
- These shares are tradable and hence they may appreciate.
- The investors may have a voting right in the general assembly or the Board.
- The majority of the voting rights are, however, in the hands of the patrons; that is, the members of the co-operative society.
- While the members benefit from the co-operative in the form of good trading conditions as in a traditional co-operative, the investors get a remuneration for their capital, either at a fixed rate or depending on the profits attained.
- Given that the equity basis of the co-operative is extended through the external investors, there are more resources for research and development (R&D) and advanced products.
- Hence, there is also greater probability that there will be qualified management.

The subsidiary co-operative model

Co-operatives may run larger or smaller parts of their business operations within subsidiary firms owned together with outside partners. If a subsidiary is owned 100 per cent by a traditional co-operative firm, then the subsidiary should also be categorised as traditionally run. The core difference is whether there is an investor with ROI interests:

- Depending on what the co-operative decides, the external ownership may be open (the stock exchange) or closed (selected investor partners).
- The stock owned by the external investors is individual property.
- The investors' stock is subject to appreciation – on the day the shares are for sale, the investor hopes to get a good price.

- The external owners have seats in the general assembly and the Board.
- The co-operative holds the majority of seats on the Board.
- The profits are divided between the patron-members (via the co-operative society) and the external shareholders, each receiving remuneration in proportion to their ownership.
- This organisational model makes it possible to raise a much larger amount of capital than the preceding one, and hence, the chances for value-added business are larger.
- It follows that there is highly qualified management.

New generation co-operatives

As the proportional tradable shares co-operative model is more or less synonymous with the new generation co-operative, the name for the co-operatives that started in North Dakota and Minnesota during the 1990s, it is well described in the literature. Hence, the attributes are:

- The co-operative is run as a society but the membership is not open. Members are those who have bought delivery rights from the co-operative, and hence the membership is restricted.
- Delivery rights are tradable at a market rate, hence fully individualised and appreciable.
- Voting power is usually equally distributed but it is also possible to differentiate according to volume.
- The members are in power, though there may also be a minority of external investors.
- There is a strict proportionality between the member's investment in the co-operative and the volume of deliveries stated in the delivery contract.
- Members get their share of the profits as patronage refund, but because of the proportionality between deliveries and investments, the amount is equal to what they would get if the profits were allocated according to investments.
- Tradable delivery rights and fully individualised ownership have the effect that the business operations of the co-operative and the membership can be brought into perfect harmony. This model is therefore suitable for value-added activities, though of a very focused character.
- The co-operative has a highly qualified leadership and management.

The plc co-operative model

The plc co-operative organisational model is closely related to the NGC model, the difference being basically the choice of legal form. Hence, members become shareholders, though still remaining patrons of the co-operative. This has the effect that the voting power is according to investments, and that the profits are allocated to the shareholders as return on investments, not patronage refund. In practice, this may mean very little difference from the new generation co-operatives. Just like a NGC, a plc co-operative may have also external owners – the suppliers may feel tempted to grant even a fairly large portion of the stock to outside parties. However, if the external shareholders' share of the voting exceeds 50 per cent, the firm can no longer be called a co-operative.

The traditional co-operative organisational model

The traditional co-operative model has existed for well over a hundred years and is still the most widespread co-operative model in the agricultural sector. Hence, it has proven its viability in competitive markets (Sexton and Iskow, 1993; Søgaard, 1994; Gentzoglanis, 1997) in spite of the fact that it has been subjected to much criticism, accused of being inefficient, not least because of the vaguely defined property rights (e.g. Porter and Scully, 1987; Ferrier and Porter, 1991). There is, however, only limited understanding of why this co-operative model will lead to efficient firms, and under which conditions they are efficient. The most common economic theoretical tool for vertical integration is *transaction cost theory* (see Table 7.2). This is, of course, also relevant to traditional co-operatives (Bonus, 1986; Schrader, 1989; Staatz, 1987; Ollila, 1989; Staatz, 1989; Fahlbeck, 1996). It does not explain why the members choose to organise the co-operative traditionally. To understand this, *neo-classical economic theory* (LeVay, 1983; Tennbakk, 1996) combined with *game theory* is more instrumental (Sexton, 1986). Briefly explained, when the average cost curve of the processing activities is constantly declining and the price is independent of the volume supplied, the firm (or rather its owners) has an incentive to increase the volume as much as possible. Also a *property rights theoretical perspective* is appropriate; the best owners of a firm are those whose inputs to the firm's operations are the most uncertain ones (Fulton, 1995).

Looking at the core characteristics of the traditional model, a common pattern evolves: this type of co-operative will have the effect of raising the production volume of the co-operative (Nilsson, 1998). The unallocated capital as well as the gratis allocated capital means that the co-operative is able to raise the price paid to farmers for their raw product. The fact that the firms are organised as societies with open membership is further evidence for the volume maximisation goal. There is usually a special set of norms – a *co-operative ideology* – the effect of which is to ease the recruitment of suppliers (Hakelius, 1996). It is generally recognised that in the collection and the primary processing of agricultural commodities, the *economies of scale* are substantial. The larger the production, the lower will the costs be, and then, provided that the revenues are more or less independent of the sales volume of the individual co-operative, the larger will be the profits. Hence, a traditionally organised co-operative is able to pay a higher price to the farmers than would any other organisational type, or otherwise offer better *trade conditions*. So, it is no wonder that agricultural co-operatives have become dominant in most raw product markets. Thus, traditional co-operatives could be regarded as the farmers' way of defending their interests on the markets – they have, in the vocabulary of J. K. Galbraith (1993), the role of the farmers' *countervailing power* in relation to independent buyers. That is, the traditional co-operatives serve a *defensive* role.

An important proviso is that the co-operative should operate in markets where its sales volumes do not influence the price negatively. This is supported by empirical observations. The traditional type of agricultural co-operative has generally been successful in markets so huge that the co-operative's volume is only a very small fraction, and likewise in markets that are regulated by governmental agricultural policy. A quick look at the major markets in most countries reveal that very often, if not most often, co-operative firms dominate in selling unprocessed or slightly processed agricultural raw products. Traditional co-operatives simply constitute an exceptional tool for selling large quantities of commodities at low prices. Expressed in the words of Michael Porter (1980), these co-operatives constitute an excellent way of applying a *cost leadership strategy* (see Table 7.3).

An important element in the traditional organisational model is that the individually owned (allocated) capital should be small, and that the members do not receive any remuneration for their investment in the co-operative society. Because of the members' small investments, the gratis capital is an acceptable sacrifice for them. According to transaction cost theory, the member investments in the co-operative have the purpose of safeguarding their large investments in their farm enterprises, and so the amounts should be as small as possible – this is not meant to be risk capital but rather its opposite. Thus the members *are only patrons, not investors*. Any other policy would risk driving the members away and so the goal attainment of volume maximisation would be threatened. However, this policy also has another effect; the capital base for traditionally organised co-operatives tends to be quite weak when related to the volumes of raw product processed. Contributing to this is the fact that the collection of unallocated capital by the retention of net earnings may be problematic, as the farmers demand the best possible prices in order to produce large quantities and to remain members/suppliers.

However, the low amount of equity capital in traditionally organised co-operatives does not necessarily have to be a problem. The co--operatives are organised in order to market the members' raw products, either unprocessed or only moderately processed. Because of the *low degree of processing* and *limited business sophistication*, the *amount of investment* is small. Traditionally organised co-operatives do not need a

Table 7.3 Different co-operative organisational models' suitability for different strategic choice

Competitive strategy (Michael Porter)	Traditional co-operative	External-investor co-operative	Member-investor co-operative
Cost leadership	**Good prospects for successful business following from large volume**	External investors would hardly accept a volume maximisation objective	The co-operative cannot create enough volume to be competitive
Differentiation	The co-operative faces grave property rights problems (capital, involvement, control …)	**Good prospects for diversified business because of large capital and involved owners**	The co-operative cannot raise enough capital to work effectively in several markets
Focus	The co-operative faces grave property rights problems	Waste of resources if the co-operative focuses on one market only	**Good prospects for success in a specified market**

lot of capital in order to fulfil their mission for the members, because the tasks to be performed can apply a *simple, well-known technology*. As traditional co-operatives are fully owned by producers they are inherently *production oriented*. This is not necessarily a drawback, as they are working with low-processed, standard products on large markets that are also *stable markets* in the sense that the rate of product development is low. The average pricing principle used in relation to the members (as opposed to marginal pricing in all other business) does not harm the economy of the co-operative, as the markets are extremely large compared to the co-operative's outputs. Likewise, the fact that the *market signals* from the raw product market are dominating over market signals from the capital market has less significance because of the small investments.

During the latter part of the twentieth century, and especially in the 1990s, the competitive pressure on the commodity markets has increased so much that many traditional co-operatives have tried to earn more money by going value-added, reaching for new markets where the number of competitors is smaller, and the customers are less price sensitive and more attracted by various product attributes. In some cases they have also transformed their co-operative organisational model, but not always. For those co-operatives that have not adapted their organisational form, some problems are likely. Considering the current lively debate on governance structures and financial structures of co-operatives, these problems are evident in many cases.

These problems are related to the criticism that many scientists have directed towards co-operatives for being inefficient. Very often, the basis of this critique is the vaguely defined property rights in co-operatives (Furubotn and Pejovich, 1972; Jensen and Meckling, 1976, 1979; Fama, 1980; Fama and Jensen, 1983; Condon and Vitaliano, 1983; Vitaliano, 1983; Condon, 1990; Harte, 1997). When scholars use empirical illustrations, it seems that they choose traditionally organised co-operatives that are operating outside their business domain. These are firms that have collected a sizeable amount of capital, are investing this money in business operations far away from the members, work with highly processed products and so on, contrary to what was described above.

It is difficult to counter the allegations from these writers and it is easy for anybody to find further examples of co-operatives with considerable property rights problems. However, if traditionally organised co-operatives stick to the strategy of low investments, low value-added, low R&D, production orientation, and so on, delineated above, the critics' arguments do not hold true. Table 7.4 gives an overview of how these problems are connected to traditional co-operatives' choice of business strategy (Nilsson, forthcoming). It indicates that a traditional co-operative has good prospects to be successful when it comes to applying a cost-leadership strategy, while problems will become grave if

Table 7.4 Property rights and agency theoretical problems in traditional co-operatives with different business strategies

Property right/agency theoretical problems	Traditional co-operatives working in their proper domain	Traditional co-operatives working in entrepreneurial co-operatives' domains
Common property problem (free-rider problem)	As the membership is homogeneous and the assets are small, free-riding does not pay	Open membership combined with large assets mean that members have incentives to make use of the assets without contributing accordingly, reaping benefits at the expense of others
Portfolio problem	The business activities of the co-operative are so limited that all members benefit from all investments, especially as the membership is homogeneous because of the limited scope of the co-operative's business	As the investments are varied, many of them are not in accordance with the members' risk preferences, and it is impossible to judge whether the money would be better invested in the members' own firms
Horizon problem	As the investments are limited and the type of business is fairly stable over time, the investments are mainly reinvestments – hence, a member's share of the fortune of the co-op may amount to about the same as when that member entered the co-operative	Many investments may have a payback period longer than many members' remaining membership period; these members have reason to be opposed to such investments
Decision-making problem	As the business operations are so focused, the manager has no difficulty in judging what is in the interest of the members	As the co-operative develops a complex structure with business operations on turbulent markets, management has difficulties in seeing what is in the best interests of the members
Follow-up problem	The business is so simple and so production-related that the members are able to remain informed and to control it	Because of a lack of abilities and lacking motivation the inherently production-oriented members do not control all the co-operative's business branches appropriately, thereby giving management the possibility to acting autonomously

it tries to follow one of the other strategic classes that Michael Porter (1980) proposes – the differentiation or focus strategies. Similarly, one may, according to Table 7.3, find that these two strategies are the best ones for the external-investor and the member-investor co-operative forms, respectively.

Entrepreneurial co-operative models

External-investor co-operatives

External-investor co-operatives can vary a lot, depending on how large a share is owned by outside parties, and on the identity of the investors – *members in an investor role*, institutional investors, the stock exchange, and so on. The following applies mainly to firms where the investors own a relatively large share and have a clear interest in good returns on their investments. Hence, it is more applicable to subsidiary co-operatives than to participation co-operatives, because in the latter category the investors are most probably members who may have a propensity to look at their shares from the point of view of patrons rather than as investors, or are non-members with small investments. In external-investor co-operatives there is still a co-operative society as owner or co-owner of the enterprise, normally with a majority of the votes (Ketilson, 1997), and hence one may fear that the enterprise is monitored in pretty much the same way as are traditional co-operatives. Both the participation co-operative model and the subsidiary model involve co-operative societies that are owned collectively; there are no tradable shares in the co-operative society. So one may expect some property rights problems within the co-operative societies, especially as the type of business becomes larger and more advanced. Still, for several reasons, these problems are smaller than would be the case if a traditionally organised co-operative were to run the same type of business on its own:

- The co-operative society does not need to own the same large amount of assets as the investors are supplying money.
- External investors have an interest in keeping a close eye on the management in order to ensure that the firm is business-like, and there is also a chance that the co-operative is more thoroughly scrutinised by stock analysts and the mass media.
- It is also in the members' own interests that the firm is run efficiently, based on a *ROI objective*, as they must realise that the members and the investors are mutually dependent upon each other. The fact that external investors are involved creates a more business-oriented attitude within the co-operative society; there will be no cross-subsidisation between member groups, there will be strict cost-related pricing, and so on.

- Likewise, it is in the members' interest that the external-investor co-operative is run efficiently because then the investors are willing to pay more money for a small share of the firm, and so a larger share of the profits are allotted to the society to better the *members' trading conditions*. The investors are more willing to invest larger amounts of capital.
- The very fact that the co-operative society invites external co-owners may be an indication that the *co-operative ideology* has become weakened, and the fact that the society runs the firm together with others will suppress ideological considerations still further.
- Through the existence of external investors, the firm gets market *signals also from the capital market*. A variety of business decisions are based on that information: how much to invest, what to invest in, whether to issue new shares, and when. As the co-operative is working with market-oriented business activities, the society must welcome this information.

Hence the existence of external owners will lead to a different type of behaviour than in traditional co-operatives; a market-orientation, with ROI as the ultimate objective. The fact that there is still a co-operative society with producers as members does restrict the *range of market opportunities* looked at. For example, products whose contents contain none, or very few, of the farmers' commodities are not likely to be supported. The two main differences in comparison to a traditional co-operative are that an external-investor co-operative has more capital and a more profit-oriented attitude towards business. These two factors mean that the external-investor co-operative can invest in more advanced production and marketing, working with *highly processed and even value-added products* and reaching out for the often *turbulent consumer markets*. Expansion becomes an important goal; the strategy is offensive. In Michael Porter's (1980) terminology, the strategy chosen is *differentiation* (see Table 7.3).

The literature specifically regarding external-investor co-operatives is next to non-existent. Nevertheless, there are a large variety of theories to explain these co-operative models. *Property rights and agency theories* were hinted at above. The rationale behind these co-operative forms is partly the same as in the traditional co-operative case; to reap *economies of scale*. However, to explain forward integration, the *transaction cost theory* is more instrumental.

Member-investor co-operatives

In the two member-investor co-operative types, NGCs and plcs, the members' own shares that are tradable, negotiable and appreciable. This means that the property rights problems are small, provided that the market for shares can be made to function properly. No member has a chance of being a free-rider at the expense of the others. All investments are capitalised into the value of the shares, which solves the horizon problem.

The portfolio problem gets an effective solution as the co-operative's members become not only patrons but also investors. The decision-maker and the follow-up problems are less serious, as the members have an incentive to keep a close eye on management. The literature on NGCs has during the past few years become large and is expanding rapidly (e.g. Hackman and Cook, 1997; Zeuli, 1998), while literature on plc co-operatives is scarcer (Harte, 1997; Gunnarsson, 1999). Nevertheless, it is possible to discern some theoretical tools used to understand these organisational forms. Member-investor co-operatives are clear-cut examples of vertical integration, as so often in business life, and hence *transaction cost theory* is self-evident (Williamson, 1985). Property rights and agency theory have already been mentioned. As these co-operatives' competitive edge is not in creating large scale and low average costs, the *neo-classical and game-theoretical theories* cannot serve as economic-theoretical rationales as they do for traditional co-operatives. The member-investor co-operatives cannot ensure success through economies of scale but rather *economies of scope*, creating vertical chains where each processing stage is perfectly linked to all the others.

As the investors comprise (almost) exclusively members, the amount of capital is fairly limited, though larger than in a corresponding traditional co-operative. In member-investor co-operatives, the members' investments are truly risk capital, and hence they are willing to invest larger amounts. As the investments are made for a very specified purpose, a *focus strategy* is applied (see Table 7.3). Instead of volume, these co-operatives are heading for *highly processed, preferably unique products.* In order to reduce the high-risk exposure, these co-operatives have *highly professional managers* and use an *advanced technology.* The objective of the firm can be understood as to maximise the value of the members' combined assets in their own farm enterprise and their shares in the co-operative. Hence, the members' two roles as patrons and investors are of equal importance, whereby also the members forward *market signals* to the co-operative in both roles. In their investor role they have an interest in the co-operative to be *market-oriented, profitable, proactive and expanding.*

Agricultural co-operatives in the future

The future of European agricultural co-operatives will be varied, provided that the present trends continue towards still more open markets with still more intense competition (Cook, 1995; Ollila and Nilsson, 1997; Rogers, 1997). Of course, forecasts are always uncertain – the only certain forecast is that the present structure with a dominant group of traditional co-operatives will not continue:

> Existing farmers' co-operatives have a long tradition of treating their members equally, but this may hinder making certain arrangements for

subgroups of their members, such as Efficient Consumer Response Arrangements with retailers, in which only members with advanced facilities and superior production processes can participate ... Another drawback of co-operatives is that their locus of power (and perspective) even if they have integrated processing and distributing facilities, is close to primary production and far moved from the market. This does not make them very suitable to take the guiding role in an AVAP (Agrifood Value-Added Partnership) of which the very purpose is to derive competitive advantage from adding those values that consumers want. (Wierenga, 1997, pp52–53)

Various entrepreneurial co-operatives in the agribusiness sector are likely to be established in years to come. These will exhibit a still more heterogeneous pattern, working in a variety of industries and being organised in many different ways. In terms of turnover, the external-investor co-operatives will be highly dominant, though their number will not be very large. The member-investor co-operatives will become much larger in number, but as they are devoted to focused activities mainly in market niches their aggregate turnover will be limited. Even though the trend towards more entrepreneurial co-operatives can be expected to continue, the traditional co-operative model will not disappear. On the contrary, there will always be economic rationales for a business form that is constructed in order to attain considerable economies of scale in the collection and primary processing of agricultural raw products. The ongoing process of mergers and acquisitions will lead to extremely large co-operatives of the traditional type, resulting in pan-European enterprises.

It is, however, probable that the traditional co-operatives will increasingly establish subsidiaries together with external capital owners, thereby contributing to the growth of entrepreneurial co-operatives. These subsidiaries will take care of the value-added operations. To a lesser degree the traditional co-operatives may let some branches be run within firms that have resemblance to member-investor firms.

Not many of the existing agricultural co-operatives can be expected to transform themselves into a member-investor co-operative. The number of such co-operatives will increase markedly, but as the result of new establishments. Groups of non-members as well as members of existing co-operatives will find that they can make money by focusing on a specific market niche. The extent of such NGCs and plc co-operatives is highly contingent upon whether the existing co-operatives are able to exploit the market opportunities appropriately.

While the process of transition from traditional to entrepreneurial co-operatives may be rapid in these years, there is still considerable hesitation within many traditional co-operatives. A plausible explanation is the very characteristics of the traditional co-operative model – these may lead to some change resistance. To the extent that a traditionally organised co-operative has already tried to become value-added within its existing organisational model, the property rights problems may have become so grave that change initiatives have a poor outlook. Because of low member involvement, the members might regard the co-operative as an external trading partner, or management might have taken control and have an interest in maintaining the status quo. A strong ideological conviction may prohibit any change action; or, because they have little investment in the co-operative, the members may not feel any responsibility; or a large amount of unallocated capital may give a false sense of security.

Many traditional co-operatives may be too late in restructuring themselves and may run into economic difficulties. However, the outcome will seldom be the cessation of operations and dissolution of the co-operative, but rather a take-over by other co-operatives that *have* conducted their transformation on time. But take-over bids by investor-owned processors are also possible.

Note

1   This chapter has also been published as 'Co-operative organisational models as reflections of the business environment', *Finnish Journal of Business Economics*, 4, 1999 (Special Issue: 'The role of cooperative entrepreneurship in the modern market environment'), pp. 449–470.

References

Angulo, A. M., Gil, J. M. and Gracia, A. (1997) 'A test of differences in food demand among European consumers: a dynamic approach', in Wierenga, B. *et al.* (eds), *Agricultural Marketing and Consumer Behavior in a Changing World*, Boston Mass., Kluwer Academic Publishers.

Barton, D. (1989) 'Principles', in Cobia, D. (ed.), *Cooperatives in Agriculture*, Englewood Cliffs, NJ, Prentice-Hall, pp. 21–34.

Bekkum, O.-F. van and Dijk, Gert van (eds) (1997) *Agricultural Co-operatives in the European Union – Trends and Issues on the Eve of the 21st Century*, Assen, van Gorcum.

Bonus, H. (1986) 'The Cooperative Association as a business enterprise. A study in the economics of transaction', *Journal of Institutional and Theoretical Economics*, 142, pp. 310–339.

Condon, A. (1990) 'Property rights and the investment behavior of U.S. agricultural cooperatives', Unpublished Ph.D. thesis, Blacksburg, Va., Virginia Polytechnic Institute and State University.

—— and Vitaliano, P. (1983) *Agency Problems, Residual Claims, and Cooperative Enterprise*, Working paper, Blacksburg, Va., Virginia Polytechnic Institute and State University.

Cook, M. (1995) 'The future of U.S. agricultural cooperatives: a neo-institutional approach', *American Journal of Agricultural Economics*, 77, pp. 1153–1159.

—— (1997) 'Organizational structure and globalization: the case of user oriented firms', in Nilsson, J. and Dijk, G. van (eds), *Strategies and Structures in the Agro-Food Industries*, Assen, van Gorcum, pp. 77–93.

—— and Tong, L. (1997). 'Definitional and classification issues in analyzing cooperative organizational forms', in Cook, M. *et al.* (eds), *Cooperatives: Their Importance in the Future Food and Agricultural System*, Washington DC, The Food and Agricultural Marketing Consortium, pp. 113–118.

Cropp, R. (1997) 'Milk money. How dairy cooperatives impact farm-level milk prices', *Rural Cooperatives*, 64(6), November–December, pp. 4–10.

Dijk, G. van (1997) 'Implementing the sixth reason for co-operation: new generation co-operatives in the agribusiness, in Nilsson, J. and Dijk, G. van (eds), *Strategies and Structures in the Agro-Food Industries*, Assen, van Gorcum, pp. 94–110.

Fahlbeck, E. (1996) *Essays in Transaction Cost Economics*, Uppsala, Swedish University of Agricultural Sciences.

Fama, E. (1980) 'Agency problems and the theory of the firm', *Journal of Political Economy*, 88, pp. 288–307.

—— and Jensen, M. (1983) 'Separation of ownership and control', *Journal of Law and Economics,* 26, pp. 301–325.

Ferrier, G. D. and Porter, P. K. (1991) 'The productive efficiency of US milk processing co-operatives', *Journal of Agricultural Economics*, 42, pp. 161–173.

Fulton, M. (1995) 'The future of cooperatives in Canada: a property rights approach', *American Journal of Agricultural Economics*, 77, pp. 1144–1152.

Furubotn, E. and Pejovich, S. (1972) 'Property rights and economic theory', *Journal of Economic Literature*, 10, pp. 1137–1162.

Galbraith, J. K. (1993) *American Capitalism: The Concept of Countervailing Power*, New Brunswick, NJ, Transaction Publishers.

Gentzoglanis, A. (1997) 'Economic and financial performance of cooperatives and investor-owned firms: an empirical study', in Nilsson, J. and Dijk, G. van (eds), *Strategies and Structures in the Agro-Food Industries*, Assen, van Gorcum, pp. 171–182.

Grunert, K. G. *et al.* (1996) *Market Orientation in Food and Agriculture*, Boston, Mass., Kluwer Academic Publishers.

—— (1997) 'New areas of agricultural and food marketing', in Wierenga, B. *et al.* (eds), *Agricultural Marketing and Consumer Behavior in a Changing World*, Boston, Mass., Kluwer Academic Publishers.

Gunnarsson, P. (1999) 'Organisational models for agricultural co-operatives – a comparative analysis of the Irish dairy industry', Master's degree thesis, Uppsala, Swedish University of Agricultural Sciences.

Hackman, D. and Cook, M. (1997) 'The transition to new cooperative organizational forms: public policy issues', in Cook, M. *et al.* (eds), *Cooperatives: Their Importance in the Future Food and Agricultural System*, Washington DC, The Food and Agricultural Marketing Consortium, pp. 105–112.

Hakelius, K. (1996) *Cooperative Values. Farmer Cooperatives in the Minds of the Farmers*, Uppsala, Swedish University of Agricultural Sciences.

Hansmann, H. (1996) *The Ownership of Enterprise*, Cambridge, Mass., The Belknap Press.

Harris, A., Stefanson, B. and Fulton, M. (1996) 'New generation cooperatives and cooperative theory', *Journal of Cooperatives*, 11, pp. 15–29.

Harte, L. (1997) 'Creeping privatisation of the Irish co-operatives: a transaction cost explanation', in Nilsson, J. and Dijk, G. van (eds), *Strategies and Structures in the Agro-Food Industries*, Assen, van Gorcum, pp. 31–53.

Jensen, M. and Meckling, W. (1976) 'Theory of the firm: managerial behavior, agency costs and ownership structure', *Journal of Financial Economics*, 3, pp. 305–360.

—— (1979) 'Rights and production functions: an application to labor-managed firms and codetermination', *Journal of Business*, 52, pp. 469–506.

Kast, F. and Rosenzweig, J. (1979) *Organization and Management. A Systems and Contingency Approach*, 3rd edn, Auckland, McGraw-Hill.

Ketilson, L. H. (1997) 'The Saskatchewan Wheat Pool and the globalized food sector: can they remain true to their roots?', in Nilsson, J. and Dijk, G. van (eds), *Strategies and Structures in the Agro-Food Industries*, Assen, van Gorcum, pp. 54–74.

Lagnevik, M. and Kola, J. (1998) 'Are Porter's diamonds forever?', in Traill, B. and Grunert, K. (eds), *Product and Process Innovation in the Food Industry*, London, Blackie Academic & Professional.

LeVay, C. (1983) 'Agricultural co-operative theory: a review', *Journal of Agricultural Economics*, 34, pp. 1–44.

Nilsson, J. (1996) 'Co-operative principles and practices in Swedish agricultural co-operatives', in Monzón Campos, J. L. *et al.* (eds), *Co-operatives, Markets, Co-operative Principles*, Liège, CIRIEC, pp. 219–248.

—— (1997) 'New generation farmer co-ops', *Review of International Co-operation*, 90(1), pp. 32–38.

—— (1998) 'The emergence of new organizational models for agricultural cooperatives', *Swedish Journal of Agricultural Research*, 28, pp. 39–47.

—— (forthcoming) 'Organisational principles for co-operative firms', *Scandinavian Journal of Management*.

—— and Bärnheim, M. (2000) 'Remodelling a dairy producer co-operative', in Schwarzweller, H. and Davidson, A. (eds), *Research in Rural Sociology and Development, Volume 8: Dairy Industry Restructuration*, Elsevier/JAI Press, Amsterdam.

Ollila, P. (1989) 'Coordination of supply and demand in the dairy marketing system – with special emphasis on the potential role of farmer cooperatives as coordinating institutions', *Journal of Agricultural Science in Finland*, 61, pp. 137–321.

—— and Nilsson, J. (1997) 'The position of agricultural cooperatives in the changing food industry of Europe', in Nilsson, J. and Dijk, G. van (eds), *Strategies and Structures in the Agro-Food Industries*, Assen, van Gorcum.

Porter, M. (1980) *Competitive Strategy*, New York, Free Press.

Porter, P. K. and Scully, G. W. (1987) 'Economic efficiency in cooperatives', *The Journal of Law and Economics*, 30, pp. 489–512.

Rogers, R. E. (1997) 'The role of cooperatives in increasingly concentrated markets: reaction', in Cook, M. *et al.* (eds), *Cooperatives: Their Importance in the Future Food and Agricultural System*, Washington DC, The Food and Agricultural Marketing Consortium.

Schrader, L. (1989) 'Economic justification', in Cobia, D. (ed.), *Cooperatives in Agriculture*, Englewood Cliffs, NJ, Prentice-Hall, pp. 121–136.

Sexton, R. (1986) 'The formation of cooperatives: a game-theoretic approach with implications for cooperative finance, decision making, and stability', *American Journal of Agricultural Economics*, 68, pp. 423–433.

—— and Iskow, J. (1993) 'The competitive role of cooperatives in market-oriented economies: a policy analysis', in Csaki, C. and Kislev, Y. (eds), *Agricultural Cooperatives in Transition*, Boulder, Col., Westview Press, pp. 55–84.

Søgaard, V. (1994) *Farmers, Cooperatives, New Food Products*, Aarhus, Aarhus School of Economics/MAPP.

Staatz, J. (1987) 'The structural characteristics of farmer cooperatives and their behavioral consequences', in Royer, J. S. (ed.), *Cooperative Theory. New Approaches*, Washington DC, USDA, pp. 33–60.

—— (1989) *Farmer Cooperative Theory: Recent Developments*, ACS Research Report No. 84, Washington DC, USDA.

Steenkamp, J.-B. E. M. (1997) 'Dynamics in consumer behavior with respect to agricultural and food products', in Wierenga, B. *et al.* (eds), *Agricultural Marketing and Consumer Behavior in a Changing World*, Boston Mass., Kluwer Academic Publishers.

Tennbakk, B. (1996) 'Market Behavior of Agricultural Cooperatives', Dissertation, Bergen, Dept of Economics, University of Bergen.

Torgerson, R., Reynolds, B. and Gray, T. (1997) 'Evolution of cooperative thought, theory and purpose', in Cook, M. *et al.* (eds), *Cooperatives: Their Importance in the Future Food and Agricultural System*, Washington DC, National Council of Farmers Cooperatives/The Food and Agricultural Marketing Consortium, pp. 3–20.

Traill, B. (1997) 'Structural changes in the European food industry: consequences for innovation', in Traill, B. and Grunert, K. (eds), *Product and Process Innovation in the Food Industry*, London, Blackie Academic & Professional.

—— (1998) 'Structural changes in the European food industry: consequences for competitiveness', in Traill, B. and Pitts, E. (eds), *Competitiveness in the Food Industry*, London, Blackie Academic & Professional.

Wierenga, B. (1997) 'Competing for the future in the agricultural and food channel', in Wierenga, B. *et al.* (eds), *Agricultural Marketing and Consumer Behavior in a Changing World*, Boston, Mass., Kluwer Academic Publishers.

Williamson, O. (1985) *The Economic Institutions of Capitalism*, New York, The Free Press.

Vitaliano, P. (1983) 'Cooperative enterprise: an alternative conceptual basis for analyzing a complex institution', *American Journal of Agricultural Economics*, 65, pp. 1078–1083.

Zeuli, K. (1998) 'Value-added processing: an assessment of the risks and returns to farmers and communities', Unpublished Ph.D. thesis, St. Paul, Minn., University of Minnesota.

8 Mutuals in regional economic development

Mondragon and Desjardins

Race Mathews

Communities throughout the world are searching for ways to bring about local and regional economic development, in the face of pressures consequent in part on globalisation. Experience indicates that one answer is the use of credit unions to mobilise local and regional capital to expand existing businesses and create new ones. It is important to learn from success stories such as of Quebec's Desjardins credit union federation and the great complex of industrial, retail, financial, service and support co-operatives – now the Mondragon Co-operative Corporation (MCC) – at Mondragon in the Basque region of Spain. The challenge is to adapt what Mondragon and Desjardins have to offer in the light of local conditions and requirements. The danger is that the credit union movement will be overtaken by demutualisation before its capacity to foster local and regional economic development has begun to be properly understood or applied.

Mutualism

The strength of credit unions is in their character as mutualist bodies and their adherence to mutualist values and principles. Mutualism is about self-help – about people helping themselves by helping one another. What mutualist bodies – bodies such as mutual life assurance societies, permanent building societies, friendly societies and co-operatives – also have in common with one another is that they are almost always a response to urgent community needs. For example, the Rochdale Pioneers – the twenty-eight poor cotton weavers who established their co-operative in 1844 – were responding to an urgent community need for affordable household requisites such as food and fuel.

Credit co-operatives were a response to the need for affordable carry-on loans for smallholder farmers, and later for affordable consumer finance. Friendly societies were initially a response to the need for funeral benefits, and, later, for unemployment benefits, sickness benefits and medical and hospital care. Access to affordable life assurance was offered by mutual life assurance societies, as was access to affordable home loans by building societies. Agricultural processing and marketing co-operatives met a pressing need on the part of farmers to capture value-added on their produce beyond the farm gate. Worker co-operatives responded to the need on the part of workers for secure employment by enabling them to own their workplaces and jobs. Trade unions were originally mutualist bodies or co-operatives formed by employees in response to a pressing need to obtain a better working conditions and a just price for their labour. What is required now of credit unions and other mutualist bodies is an acceptance that they are not chained to the provision of services for which the original justification no longer exists, or has become less pressing. Rather, they should see themselves as pools of community capital that can be re-tasked in the face of new needs on the part of those for whose interests they are trustees.

That even radically root and branch reinvention is not beyond the will or wit of mutualist bodies is richly evident from the example of a notable US co-operative, Co-operative Services Inc. in Detroit. Co-operative Services Inc. was formed in the early 1940s in response to an urgent local need for affordable, hygienic household milk deliveries. When the corporate dairies moved in with a comparable service at a comparable price, the co-operative reinvented itself, and the community capital it had accumulated was re-tasked to meeting the need for affordable eye testing and spectacles. Following the arrival of the optometrical services corporations, the co-operative re-tasked its capital yet again, to meet the need for affordable accommodation and support services for older people. It now operates large apartment complexes – self-governing co-operatives within the overarching structure of the parent body – in several states.

A 'New Mutualism' is now likewise called for, enabling credit unions to reinvent and reposition themselves to respond as effectively in the future to their members' need for economic development and jobs as they did in the past to their need for personal loans for washing machines, refrigerators and cars. This does not mean that credit unions should give up their current role as providers of consumer and housing loans, but that they should widen their horizons to encompass activities in which in most instances they have not previously been involved. Is it asking too much of Australia's credit unions that they should show as much vision and vigour in reinventing themselves as a Co-operative Services Inc., a Mondragon or a Desjardins?

Desjardins

The Mouvement des Caisses Desjardins began in Lévis in Quebec in 1900, at the instigation of Alphonse Desjardins. A committed Catholic and advocate of social Catholicism, Desjardins was a *Hansard* reporter for the Quebec provincial parliament from 1879 to 1891, and later Clerk Reporting of the Canadian Parliament in Ottawa between 1892 and 1917 (Mathews, 1999). His conscience was aroused by the poverty and unemployment that were driving large numbers of his fellow citizens to the United States in search of work. He was appalled also by the inability of working people and farmers to borrow at interest rates that were within their means. His original *caisse* or credit union – La Caisse Populaire De Lévis – was seen by him as 'putting the savings of the people at the service of the people'. As in all credit unions, members pooled their savings, and took turns for affordable loans. The first transactions were conducted on 23 January, 1901 at Desjardins' home, which remained the nerve-centre of the movement until his death in 1920, and is now preserved in his memory as a museum by La Société Historique Alphonse-Desjardins. Credit union members, Desjardins believed, would be encouraged to practise thrift and financial responsibility. Christian and humane values would be fostered. Usury would be discouraged. In time, credit unions would form federations, and a great movement would emerge.

Desjardins' dream is now a reality. The movement which bears his name numbers some 1254 community credit unions (*caisses populaires*) and industrial credit unions (*caisses d'economie*), with 5.5 million members and assets totalling $C76.7 billion. The Desjardins credit unions are now the largest financial intermediary in Quebec and the sixth largest in Canada. Their collective market share within Quebec totals 41.2 per cent of all farm loans, 38.4 per cent of residential mortgage loans, 31.9 per cent of consumer loans and 21.1 per cent of loans for commercial and industrial purposes (Mouvement des Caisses Desjardins, 1999). The outstanding commercial success of the Desjardins credit unions reflects their commitment to continuous reinvention – to constantly adapting their objectives and structure in the face of changing needs and circumstances. As the long-serving former president of the Confédération, Claude Béland, puts it:

> The Mouvement des Caisses Desjardins is continuing to re-invent itself in order to remain the preferred financial institution of most Québecers, as well as their natural partner in collective projects at the local, regional and provincial levels. (Mouvement des Caisses Desjardins, 1998, p3)

Structurally, Desjardins community credit unions within Quebec are grouped at present on a regional basis, in ten federations. There is a separate federation for the industrial credit unions, and three auxiliary federations for credit unions outside Quebec. The functions of the federations are to promote the effectiveness, growth and development of their affiliated credit unions, and provide joint services such as communications, technical support, training and human resources management. The federations in their turn comprise La Confédération des Caisses Populaires et d'Economie du Québec. The Confédération sets objectives for the movement as a whole, after extensive consultation with the credit unions and their members. It is also a service provider for the credit unions and federations, in part through wholly-owned subsidiary companies. For example, credit unions are able to source their credit card and information technology services directly from the Confédération. Direct clearing within the Canadian payments system and at the Bank of Canada is made available through La Caisse Centrale Desjardins du Québec. The Desjardins-Laurentian Financial Corporation has majority holdings in four intermediary companies, with subsidiaries offering general insurance, life assurance, trust and investment management services, and corporate financing services. A liquidity and mutual aid fund is operated through Fonds de Sécurité Desjardins. A secure delivery service for cash and other valuables is provided indirectly from a Confédération subsidiary, Sécur, as is an automated system of authorisation and payment for pharmaceutical services by a subsidiary of the Desjardins-Laurentian Life Assurance Company (DLLA), Centre d'Autorisation at de Paiement des Services de Sante.

However, though the Mouvement's current structures are comprehensive and sophisticated, they have in no sense ceased to evolve. Nor is the Mouvement now resting on its laurels. On the contrary, further major changes in its structure are to take effect on 1 July, 2001. As from that date, the current regional federations will merge with the Confédération to form a single entity. At the same time, the service functions of the federations will transfer to eighteen regional service centres. Their political functions will transfer to a new regional assembly with a regional council member whose president will become a member of the board of the Confédération. At a grassroots level, mergers are expected to reduce the number of smaller credit unions to around 600.

Additionally, impressive as has been the capacity of the credit unions for structural change, what has been far more impressive is the continuous updating and expansion of their objectives. As the 1998 Annual Report affirms: 'Job creation and support are major concerns for Desjardins' (Mouvement des Caisses Desjardins, 1998, p30). What was conceived originally by Alphonse Desjardins as a means of combating usury and providing affordable consumer credit for working-class households is now also a driving force for regional and local economic development. The key elements of the Mouvement's involvement in economic development are plain. The development function is vested in part in a holding company, Investissement Desjardins (ID), that supports the development of industrial and commercial enterprises and participates actively in Quebec's economic growth. It is tasked:

- To support the development of Regional Investment Funds;
- To support high-tech businesses, in industries such as communications, electronics, health care and the environment;
- To assist businesses associated with the Desjardins movement in gaining access to international markets; and
- To act as a consultant to regional federations on investment in businesses within their regions.

Other ID objectives include, in the first instance, seeking out entrepreneurs who have proved they can make their businesses grow and become profitable, and who need additional strategic and financial support for acquisition, expansion or diversification projects; and, second, acquiring or maintaining majority or preponderant shareholdings in large companies that are actual or potential leaders in their sectors and should be owned in Quebec.

At the regional level, ID has so far established five of a projected ten wholly-owned regional investment funds. The funds reflect an explicit recognition by Desjardins that venture capital is often an essential ingredient for local businesses to succeed. For example, Investissement Desjardins recorded a first by joining forces with a federation, the Fédération du Saguenay-Lac-Saint-Jean, to launch a new venture capital fund with capitalisation in excess of C$6 million. Through this partnership, the region's companies are able to draw on the expertise of Investissement Desjardins advisers, have access to capital tailored to their requirements, and receive strategic support to ensure their growth. The Fonds d'Investissement Desjardins du Lac-St-Jean makes investments of C$50,000 to C$500,000 (Confédération des Caisses Populaires et d'Economie Desjardins du Québec, 1998, p33). In addition, many of the Mouvement's regional federations and their individual credit union affiliates participate in some 284 other local and regional investment funds with assets totalling C$3.5 billion. ID also supplements credit union capital and enhances development within Quebec from overseas sources. Its international thrust is seen as being 'to find foreign investors to become partners in Québec businesses, open foreign doors to Québec businesses and stimulate foreign investment in Québec'.

As of 1999, ID was associated, either directly or through its funds, with some seventy-four small and medium-sized businesses that were either starting up or expanding their activities, thereby helping to maintain or create close to 15,000 jobs in Quebec. Its strategy was to focus increasingly on the technology sector – on the computer software, telecommunications, health and multimedia industries – where its portfolio included some twenty businesses, many of which were said in the Annual Report to be 'just starting up and looked very promising' (Mouvement de Caisses Desjardins, 1999, p102). Nor, finally, is Desjardins indifferent to the uses of development along explicitly mutualist and co-operative lines. It also invests directly in the creation of new mutualist and co-operative businesses through both individual credit unions and Desjardins-Laurentian Life Assurance. A notable example is services for older people. As the 1998 Annual Report records: 'An aging population led several caisses to participate in setting up co-operatives offering home services, and DLLA is especially active in this field, giving financial support to the start-up and growth of co-operatives and the federation which groups them' (Mouvement de Caisses Desjardins, 1999, p32). That mutualist enterprises should be fostered along these lines is consistent with the Mouvement's overall unflinching adherence to mutualist values and principles. In Claude

Béland's eloquent and stirring statement:

> For the Desjardins credit unions, developing stronger business relationships with their members and promoting the co-operative way of life in the communities they serve will remain priority areas of involvement for many years to come (Confédération des Caisses Populaires et d'Economie Desjardins du Québec, 1998, p3) ... The social and economic disturbances currently affecting all societies around the world make the co-operative formula all the more relevant today, as communities seek ways to improve their lives in the midst of turmoil. In such an environment, our extensive network of financial co-operatives here in Québec is not only an invaluable asset for Québecers, but also a model for the world. (Mouvement de Caisses Desjardins, 1998, p5)

Mondragon

Mondragon is likewise a model for the world. The essentials of the Mondragon story are simple. Like the Desjardins credit unions, Mondragon was founded by a committed adherent of social Catholicism, the Basque priest Don Jose Maria Arizmendiarrieta. The Basques were on the losing side in the Spanish Civil War. In Arizmendiarrieta's words, 'We lost the Civil War, and became an occupied region' (Whyte and Whyte, 1991, p242). Appalled by the widespread destitution in the aftermath of the defeat, Arizmendiarrieta set out to rebuild the local economy in Mondragon, along with the confidence and self-esteem of his parishioners. His approach reflected a unique amalgam of ideas. Influenced as Arizmendiarrieta was primarily by his social Catholicism, he also drew freely on a rich and disparate range of other traditions including Rochdale co-operativism, Raiffeisenian credit unionism, social democracy, Christian socialism and Bellocian distributism. Mondragon co-operativism and the triumphant success of the co-operatives which embody it are his enduring memorial (see Azurmendi, 1991; MacLeod, 1997).

From a standing start in 1956, the Mondragon co-operatives have grown to the point where they are now the largest business group in the Basque region of Spain, the ninth largest business group in Spain, and a major competitor in European and global market places. What began forty-four years ago as a handful of workers in a disused factory, using hand tools and sheet to make oil-fired heaters and cookers, has now become a massive conglomerate of some 160 manufacturing, retail, financial, service and support co-operatives. Annual sales are now approaching – and will shortly exceed – US$7 billion.

The MCC report for 1998 shows that sales of manufactured goods were up on 1997 by 13.8 per cent, assets by 25.9 per cent and profits by 31.7 per cent. All told, the MCC provides jobs for roughly 3 per cent of the

Basque region's 1 million workers. While the region has lost 150,000 jobs since 1975, and the level of unemployment is currently around 20 per cent, employment in the co-operatives increased between 1997 and 1998 from 34,397 to 42,129. Export sales of MCC products in 1998 were up on 1997 by 18 per cent, to 47 per cent (Mondragon Corporations Cooperativa, 1998). The MCC is Spain's largest exporter of machine tools and largest manufacturer of white goods such as refrigerators, stoves, washing machines and dishwashers. It is also the third largest supplier of automotive components in Europe – designated by General Motors in 1992 as 'European Component Supplier of the Year' – and a leading supplier of components for domestic appliances.

Whole factories are designed and fabricated to order in Mondragon for buyers overseas. In addition, subsidiaries operated by the MCC in conjunction with overseas partners manufacture, for example, semi-conductors in Thailand, white goods components in Mexico, refrigerators in Morocco and luxury motor coach bodies in China. MCC construction co-operatives carry out major civil engineering and building projects at home and abroad, the building of key facilities for events such as the Barcelona Olympic Games. The steel structure for the Guggenheim Museum in Bilbao – a building comparable in stature to the Sydney Opera House – was fabricated by a Mondragon co-operative. The MCC also includes Spain's fastest-growing retail chain – Eroski – which currently operates 37 Eroski and Maxi hypermarkets, 211 Consum supermarkets, 419 self-service and franchise stores, and 333 travel agency branches. The MCC financial co-operatives – the Caja Laboral Popular (CLP) credit union and the Lagun-Aro social insurance co-operative – are among Spain's larger financial intermediaries.

The basic building blocks of the MCC are its manufacturing, retail, financial and service co-operatives, otherwise known as primary co-operatives. The primary co-operatives embody and exemplify the key values and principles of mutualism. Each primary co-operative is governed by a General Assembly, which meets at least annually to receive reports and determine policy. The Assembly in turn elects by and from its members a Governing Council, consisting of between three and twelve members. The Council steers the affairs of the co-operative between Assembly meetings. Governing Council members hold office for staggered four-year terms, with elections at two-year intervals. There is also an Audit or Watchdog Committee that monitors independently the co-operative's financial performance and its compliance with its formally established policies and procedures. The Governing Council holds regular consultative meetings with a Management Council consisting of the Chief Executive Officer and his/her senior executives. Independent of the Assembly and its offshoots, workplace groups within the co-operative elect a Social Council, which has a quasi-trade union function, with responsibility for areas such as job evaluation and industrial health and safety. Recent years have seen an increasing emphasis on industrial democracy – on participation and consultation at the shop-floor level – within many of the co-operatives.

Individual co-operatives are linked through groups. Originally, the groups had a geographical basis. However, with the establishment of the MCC in 1991 – with the replacing of Mondragon Mark I by the current Mark II model – they have been re-constituted along functional lines. There is a Financial Group, a Retail Group and an Industrial Group, with the Industrial Group in turn split into seven sub-groups. The aim is for the co-operatives within each group to engage in in-depth and continuous strategic planning, to identify and exploit economies of scale and business synergies, and to operate within an agreed overall strategy. A further and final level of linkage is afforded by the peak bodies of the MCC: the MCC Congress, the General Council and the Standing Committee. The key role of the Congress is to set the overall policy and direction of the co-operatives. The General Council is responsible for drawing up and applying overall corporate strategies and co-ordinating the activities of the co-operatives and co-operative groups. The Standing Committee monitors the performance of the Committee and the groups, and sees that the decisions of the Congress are implemented.

To what, then, are the achievements of the MCC attributable? First, the success of the co-operatives stems from the fact that every permanent worker is an equal co-owner of the co-operative where s/he is employed, with an equal say (on a one member, one vote basis) in the governance of the co-operative, and an equal proportionate share in its profits (or, on occasion, losses). Each worker has an individual capital account which is credited annually with his/her share of the co-operatives profits and enables him/her to maintain an ongoing appraisal of the performance of the co-operative and its management and his/her fellow members. In the words of a recent CEO of the MCC, Javier Mongelos, 'The workers who own these co-operatives know their future depends on making profits' (Parry, 1994, p12). The upshot is – among other things – a reduction in the agency costs the co-operatives incur, and a corresponding increase in their competitive advantage (see Mathews, 1999, pp10–12).

Second, the primary co-operatives are serviced on a mutualist basis by a unique system of secondary support co-operatives. Arizmendiarrieta became aware at an early stage of the co-operatives' development that they needed to be self-sufficient. The support co-operatives were his answer. Capital is now sourced by the primary co-operatives from a support co-operative, the Caja Laboral Popular (CLP) credit union, as are, for example, superannuation and other benefits from the Lagun-Aro social insurance co-operative, research and development services from the Ikerlan and Ideko research and development co-operatives, and technical skilling from the University of Technology co-operative. The structure of the support co-operatives differs from that of the primary co-operatives, in that they are owned and governed jointly by their workers, together with their primary co-operative clients. Profits distributed to workers in the secondary support co-operatives are linked to those of the primary co-operatives.

Third, and finally, the Mondragon credit union, the Caja Laboral Popular, has been much more than simply a source of capital for expanding current co-operatives or creating new ones. In the phase of rapid expansion that preceded the maturing of the co-operatives as signalled by the establishment of the MCC, what was then the Empresarial or Entrepreneurship Division of the CLP offered a uniquely comprehensive and effective service for incubating co-operatives and ensuring their success. Groups seeking to establish co-operatives were initially assigned a mentor or 'godfather' to work with them in the preparation of their application for a loan. Once loans were secured, the mentors remained with the co-operatives in order to assist them in the setting up of their business and enabling them to operate profitably. As a condition of its loan, a new business entered into a Contract of Association with the CLP that specified, among other things, the mutualist structure and processes it should adopt. It was likewise a condition of the contract that specified performance and financial data should be reported to the CLP on a regular basis. Thanks to regular and comprehensive reporting, the CLP could count on receiving an early warning where co-operatives experienced difficulties, and provide added specialist support through an Intervention Group within its Empresarial Division.

So effective was the Entrepreneurial Division that only a handful of the co-operatives failed to become going concerns. Consequent on the establishment of the MCC – on the move of the co-operatives from the Mark I to the Mark II stage of their development – the functions of the Empresarial Division have now been reassigned. Some elements have been incorporated within the MCC and others in new management consultancy support co-operatives. Mondragon's ongoing expansion is now much less through establishing new co-operatives, and more through strategic acquisitions and alliances.

Demutualisation

What, then, are the lessons of Desjardins and Mondragon for countries such as Australia, the USA and the UK? Where both the Desjardins and Mondragon credit unions differ most radically from other credit unions is in their constant reinventing of their structures and objectives in response to changing needs and circumstances. Credit unions and credit union movements other than Desjardins and Mondragon are mostly still offering much the same services as at their inception, and accordingly are referred to as 'frozen' co-operatives.

Australia is a case in point. While there have been financial co-operatives in Australia for more than a century, the credit union movement in its modern form had its inception in the early 1950s (see Lewis, 1996). Couples who were marrying at the time could get home loans at fixed interest rates of around 3 per cent over thirty-year periods. However, furniture and other consumer durables such as refrigerators and washing machines had to be bought on hire purchase at interest rates that were exorbitantly high. What followed was that families in outer-suburban Catholic parishes got together around card tables after Mass, pooled such savings as they had and took turns to borrow from the pool at interest rates they could afford. When their neighbours of other faiths (or none at all) saw what was going on and wanted to join in, what had initially been parish credit unions became community credit unions. Later again, trade unions recognised that the workplaces where their members were employed were also communities, and industrial credit unions began to be established. So much have Australia's credit unions been seen to be a good idea, that they currently have around three million members – one in every six of the nation's population – and assets of more than A$21billion.

Even so, for all the apparent strength of the credit unions, their position is precarious. Affordable personal loans are now available from a wide range of other financial intermediaries. By and large, the interest rates credit unions pay on members' deposits are no higher than those of other intermediaries, nor are their loan rates lower. In addition, research by the Credit Union Services Corporation of Australia (CUSCAL) – the peak body of the credit union movement – shows plainly that members of credit unions no longer understand or value their mutuality. They would for the most part readily acquiesce in their demutualisation if adequate inducements were to be offered. What follows from all this is that, if the prospect of new worlds to conquer is insufficiently attractive to prompt the credit unions to reinvent themselves, then the threat of demutualisation should do so. That the writing is on the wall is evident from the fact that, in recent years, most of Australia's permanent building societies and almost all its mutual assurance societies have succumbed to demutualisation. The latest victim has been the multi-billion-dollar mutualist insurance arm of the National Roads and Motorists' Association (NRMA). The demutualisation of NRMA Insurance was supported by 82 per cent of its members despite its outstanding success as a mutual, despite the disastrous consequences of earlier insurance mutual demutualisations, and despite expert advice against the proposed demutualisation from consultants engaged by the NRMA board.[1]

The cautionary message of the building and insurance society demutualisations experience is reinforced by Australia's first, and to date *only*, demutualisation of a credit union – the demutualisation of the Sunstate Credit Union in 1997. As at 30 June, 1997, Sunstate had 19,358 shareholders and a further 2725 depositing members without shares. The reserves of the credit union – its net assets – totalled A$8.036 million. The credit union's capital adequacy ratio of 12.9 per cent was comfortably above the minimum prudential requirement. Operating profit in 1998 was expected to increase over 1997 by 18 per cent or A$65,000, from A$371,000 to A$436,000 (First Provincial Building Society, 1997). Sunstate was a viable credit union, which could either have remained in business on its own, or preserved its mutualist character through a merger with another credit union. Alternatively, if the directors believed in good faith that the credit union was not viable, they could in a worst-case scenario have recommended that it be wound up, and its assets shared equally among its members in a conformity of sorts with mutualist principles.

Instead, the Sunstate directors made no attempt to defend the mutualist character of their credit union or retain the benefits of mutualism for its members. Far from recommending an amalgamation with another credit union, the Board's recommendation was that Sunstate should be merged with the First Provincial Building Society, which is a publicly-listed company. And far from ensuring that the assets of the credit union were distributed equally among its members, the Board recommended a grossly inequitable distribution. Of 4 million shares in the First Provincial Building Society offered to members of Sunstate, 200,000 were reserved for directors and 200,000 for employees. The effect was to make directors eligible for benefits roughly 300 times greater than those likely to be available to other members of the credit union. Employees were also made eligible for greater benefits than most members were likely to receive. Twenty-five thousand shares are reserved for the former General Manager of the credit union, who also has an entitlement to take up such further unreserved shares as may turn out to be available.

Most of all, members who did not wish, or could not afford, to take up their entitlement to shares – or were not qualifying members – were effectively denied their interest in the assets of the credit union, and received nothing whatever in return. Estimates at the time of the amalgamation suggest that 86 per cent of the members of Sunstate were unlikely to receive anything in exchange for forfeiting their entitlement to its reserves, and only 14 per cent were to benefit (Loughlin, 1997). That no regulatory objection to the merger was offered reflects poorly on the regulators; and that the court did not feel able to intervene reflects poorly on laws and the legislature (Federal Court of Australia, 1997). That individual directors instigated or were party to the merger brings into question whether they at any stage properly understood mutualism or were genuinely committed to mutualist principles. Given that six of the seven directors of Sunstate had held office for periods in excess of twenty years, and the seventh director for ten years, the question arises: on whom can credit unions rely to protect their mutualism?

Anecdotal evidence suggests that further credit unions are already in the sights of predatory demutualisers and the corporate law, accounting and public relations interests which benefit financially on so massive a scale from favouring and facilitating demutualisations.[2] As CUSCAL's general manager of movement development and business services, Graham Loughlin, sees the situation: 'I'd be surprised if some of Australia's regional banks weren't already identifying larger credit unions whose market niche aligned with their own development plans' (World Council of Credit Unions, 2000, p11).

Credit unions and government

What, then, is the remedy? How can Australia's credit unions be enabled to rise to the challenge of becoming drivers of local and regional economic development and the creation of jobs that so many of their members need so urgently? What pre-conditions are required to stir the credit unions out of their current torpor? How can they be enabled to fend off the unwelcome attentions of would-be demutualisers and move forward into a productive future that fully reflects the promise of their inception and the hopes of their founders?

In addressing these key questions, it is necessary first to consider the no less vital question of the role of government in regard to credit unions and credit unionism. What is needed is a recognition from government – preferably explicit – that credit unionism is about enabling ordinary people and communities to engage in self-help, and is thereby entitled to special consideration. It would be desirable for credit unions to have restored to them favourable tax treatment such as the Whitlam Labor government awarded to them in the 1970s in recognition of their not-for-profit status and contribution to community development and well-being. Such an argument has more recently been defended aggressively in the USA by the Clinton/Gore Administration (D'Amours, 2000, p2). However, the more pressing requirement, in the first instance, is for government to get out of the way of credit unions, get off their backs and allow them to carry on their work on behalf of the community with the least possible interference. This means getting rid as much as possible of the statutory and regulatory requirements that are blocking the establishment of new credit unions, cramping the development of current credit unions, or inhibiting them from striking out in new directions in response to new needs. Such requirements are obliging communities which have been deserted by the major commercial banks to establish community banks as a second-best substitute for credit unions.[3] It involves, among other things, recognising that one size does not fit all, and smaller credit unions differ in their regulatory requirements from larger ones. It involves striking off such legislative and regulatory shackles as might impede or discourage Australia's credit unions from involving themselves in local and regional economic development and job creation along similar lines to their Desjardins and Mondragon counterparts.

Second, legislation is needed urgently in order to protect credit unions against demutualisation, as much from within – as witness the Sunstate Credit Union or NRMA Insurance experiences – as by external predators. Ideally, legislation would be expressive of the fundamental characteristic of all mutuals, including credit unions: namely, that each generation of their members adds to their assets in the expectation that they will be retained for the benefit of others still to come. Current members are in effect trustees for the intentions of the dead and the inheritance of the unborn. At the very least there would be legislation such as has been enacted recently in Canada, requiring that directors, managers and staff of demutualising mutual assurance societies should not receive benefits other than those available to all policy-holders. Ideally, a definition of benefits for the purposes of the legislation would include overall remuneration increases (including stock option allocations) accruing to directors and senior managers for, say, a five-year period following any demutualisation. Meanwhile, pending proper statutory safeguards, credit unions could consider rule changes to guard themselves against demutualisation, such as have been adopted by some building societies in Britain. These societies now require, as a condition of admission, an undertaking from new members that any windfall gains to which they may become entitled consequent on a demutualisation will be paid to an agreed charity.

Options for change

What credit unions can do to help themselves can be summarised broadly as involving four options. These are a *'do-nothing' option* – untenable because effectively it betrays all that credit unions and credit unionism stand for, and thereby delivers them into the hands of the demutualisers – together with options respectively for minimum, intermediate and maximum change. None of these options require that credit unions should in any sense diminish their current role as consumer and housing loan providers. Each successive option retains the functions of those before it.

A *minimum change option* for credit unions would involve less embracing new policies than acting on one that has already been adopted but not yet put into effect. CUSCAL has for many years acknowledged that there needs to be a loan syndication mechanism whereby credit unions can participate in the larger commercial loans they are too small to fund individually. In this way, credit unions would be enabled to pull their weight fully in bringing about local and regional economic development – could adopt and be seen to adopt a strategic profile in the communities and environments in which they operate. What is now required in order for all this to happen is for CUSCAL to employ specialist staff with skills – including risk evaluation skills – that would enable them to properly assess and document commercial loans. Under a loan syndication programme, the lead credit union would do the preliminary analysis of the lending proposition, and then submit the documentation to CUSCAL for approval. The lead credit union would remain the interface with CUSCAL, but might itself commit to no more than, say, 10 per cent of the amount approved.

The rest of the loan would be offered by CUSCAL to other participating credit unions, so that the loan might ultimately be funded by nine or ten credit unions. A syndicated loan would have an allocated security, so that each credit union would own that proportion of the asset against which the loan was raised. In other words, if the overall loan was 10 per cent equity provided by the borrower and 90 per cent borrowed, each of the securities would retain the same ratio. Loans could in some instances be syndicated more widely, to involve, in addition to credit unions, other funding sources such as regional development authorities, pooled development funds, and perhaps industry superannuation funds. Syndicated loans are a regularly used mechanism within the Australian financial community, and most larger loans are funded through syndication. CUSCAL would simply be taking a sound concept and making it available for credit unions for loans of a much lesser magnitude, between, say, A$10 million and A$50 million. None the less, the facility would be profitable for credit unions and enable them to retain the loyalty of the members to whose most pressing current needs they would be seen to be responding (Fowler, 1998).

An *intermediate change option* for credit unions would be for CUSCAL to supplement an in-house facility for syndicated commercial lending, through the establishment of a subsidiary in the Investissement Desjardins (ID) mould, tasked specifically to undertake funding for local and regional economic development. The purpose of a CUSCAL subsidiary along these lines would be to enable credit unions to participate in the provision of equity as well as debt finance, as well as to more effectively partner the regional development funds and pooled development funds that focus so largely on equity. As has been seen, ID has already established no fewer than five of ten projected regional development funds of its own. There are also partnerships between individual Desjardins credit unions and federations and what is in all some 284 community investment funds currently operating in Quebec.

A *maximum change option* for credit unions would be one whereby, in addition to the functions already discussed, there was a specific commitment, as in Mondragon, to helping businesses that adopted mutualist or employee-ownership structures, with corresponding reductions in their agency costs and increases in their competitive advantage.[4] In this option, the CUSCAL subsidiary would have incubator and business support functions akin to those of the Empresarial Division of the Mondragon credit union, the Caja Laboral Popular, in the Mark I phase of Mondragon. There would be specific encouragement for co-operation between businesses along Mondragon lines, and perhaps secondary support entities as in Mondragon would be established. Alternatively, support services based on the model of those in the Emelia Romagna region of Italy might be preferred. None of this means that the credit unions should seek to replicate Mondragon, but rather that they should learn from Mondragon's example and apply the lessons in the light of their own needs and circumstances.[5] In Australia, as in Mondragon, the guiding principle should be, in Arizemendiarrieta's much-quoted phrase: 'We build the road as we travel' (Morrison, 1991).

Conclusion

What emerges from the foregoing is less a set of answers than a series of questions. Are Australians able to recognise in their credit unions a means of achieving local and regional economic development such as has been achieved by the Desjardins credit unions and the MCC? If so, will the currently silent majority of credit union members now speak out in favour of a reinvention of their credit unions that would enable them to respond to the need for local and regional economic development and jobs? Will others who do not currently belong to credit unions join them in order to see that a re-tasking of their capital to foster economic development now takes place. Is there within the community a genuine commitment to local and regional economic development that will enable a stand to be taken now against further demutualisation, and so ensure that the opportunity for reinventing mutualism and re-tasking mutualist capital is retained? Not least, do Australian political parties and legislators recognise the value of mutualist bodies and will they remove the legislative constraints that currently hold back mutualism from contributing to the well-being of the community on as large a scale as is within its capacity?

Notes

1   See Mathews, R. (1999), 'NRMA insurance demutualisation', *Journal of Australian Political Economy*, 44, December, p. 113. The demutualised Colonial Mutual Life Society has been acquired by the National Bank as has the demutualised National Mutual Life Society by the French insurance giant AXA. The demutualised Australian Mutual Provident Society (AMP) has incurred losses of around A\$1.5 billion through a botched take-over of the privatised New South Wales Government Insurance Office (GIO), with a corresponding precipitous fall in the price of its shares and speculation that it too is likely to be targeted for a take-over.

2   Fees for consultancies and other services for the demutualisation of NRMA Insurance are reported to have totalled A\$107 million, *Sydney Morning Herald* 19 February, 2000. The CEO of the Australian Mutual Provident Society (AMP) when it demutualised in 1997, Mr George Trumbull, is reported to have been allocated free shares to the value of A\$10 million over a three-year period following the demutualisation, together with a base yearly salary of A\$2.7 million. Subsequent reports have assessed the shares as having a substantially higher value, and Mr Trumbull received a severance package of A\$14 million when his contract was terminated prematurely in August 1999, *Age*, 8 October, 1997 and 15 April, 2000.

3   So restrictive has been the Australian Financial Institutions Commission legislation that only three new credit unions have been formed in the decade since its enactment. The Bendigo Bank – a former building society – has established community banks in conjunction with some nineteen local communities in Victoria, New South Wales, South Australia and Western Australia, and received inquiries from a further 500 communities. Participating communities are required to raise A\$250,000 in upfront capital and meet the branch running costs, and revenue is divided between the bank and the community on an agreed basis.

4   Ideally, the maximum option for change would be accompanied by further statutory measures to facilitate mutualist and proto-mutualist structures and practices. For example, changes are required in order to bring about uniform co-operative legislation throughout Australia, thereby enabling commercial co-operatives to raise capital and trade freely across state and territory borders. Proper employee share ownership legislation is required as a safeguard against – among other things – the abuse of Employee Share Ownership Plans (ESOPs) as a mechanism for tax avoidance, or extravagantly benefiting CEOs and other senior managers. Where employees are encouraged to accept share options in lieu of part of salary, there should be a statutory requirement for at least as full a disclosure of the conditions and risks as in other securities transactions.

5   Nor, for that matter, replicate the 'new Mondragon' – El Grup Empresarial Cooperativ Valencia (GECV) – which is currently expanding around Valencia in the Catalan region of Spain, thereby refuting those who argue that Mondragon is a one-off quirk of Basque history and culture. See MacLeod (1997), ch. 6.

References

Azurmendi, J. (1991) *El Hombre Cooperativo: Pensamiento do Arizmendiarrieta*, Mondragon, Otalora Institute.

Confederation des caisses populaires et d'economie Desjardins du Quebec (1998) *Desjardins 1998: The Co-operative Network of Financial Services*.

D'Amours, N. E. (2000) 'Credit unions, taxation and competition', *Credit Union Chronicle*, 3(11), Autumn.

Federal Court of Australia (1997) *Herbert Stanley Rolfe and Ors* v *Sunstate Credit Union Ltd*, 1109 FCA 23 October.

First Provincial Building Society Ltd (1997) *Amalgamation, Assessment and Financial Information and Reports*, Book 2, Toowong, Queensland.

Fowler, R. J. (1998) Letter to the author.

Lewis, G. (1996) *People before Profit: the Credit Union Movement in Australia*, Kent Town South Australia, Wakefield Press.

Loughlin, G. (1997) 'Sunstate Credit Union/First Provincial Building Society transfer of engagements', Credit *Union Services Corporation Bulletin*, 311.

MacLeod, G. (1997) *From Mondragon to America: Experiments in Community Economic Development*, Sidney, Nova Scotia, University of Cape Breton Press.

Mathews, R. (1999) *Jobs of Their Own: Building a Stakeholder Society*, Sydney, Pluto Press (Australia)/London, Comerford & Miller.

Mondragon Corporacion Cooperativa (1998) *Annual Report*.

Morrison, R. (1991) *We Build the Road As We Travel*, Philadelphia, New Society Press.

Mouvement des Caisses Desjardins (1998) *Annual Report*.

—— (1999) *Annual Report*.

Parry, J. M. (1994) 'Mondragon pushed to the peak of success', *The European*, 28 October.

Whyte, W. F. and Whyte, K. K. (1991) *Making Mondragon: The Growth and Dynamics of the Worker Co-operative Complex* (Revised 2nd edn), Ithaca, NY, ILR Press.

World Council of Credit Unions (2000) 'Demutualisation', *Credit Union World*, 2(1), March.

9 The competitive advantages of stakeholder mutuals

Shann Turnbull

This chapter compares the competitive advantages of a stakeholder mutual firm with those that are publicly traded, or family- or government-owned. A stakeholder mutual is owned and controlled by its employees, customers and suppliers. This creates *distributed* ownership among *diversified* stakeholders. Each stakeholder constituency elects its own board. These boards represent components of a 'compound board'. A compound board introduces distributed control but this does require a stakeholder mutual to have diversified accountability. In 'Anglo-Saxon' countries, publicly-traded, family and government firms typically have a unitary board with *homogeneous* ownership by investors. This form of governance is compared with distributed control provided by a compound board of a stakeholder mutual with diversified ownership.

Conventional mutuals also have homogenous ownership but it is with a single class of stakeholder. In Anglo-Saxon cultures, a conventional mutual is typically centrally controlled through a unitary board in a manner similar to investor firms. The differences in ownership and control between conventional mutuals, investor firms and stakeholder mutuals are shown in Table 9.1. The table also compares the forms of governance used by each type of firm. Hollingsworth and Lindberg (1985, pp221–222) state that there are 'four distinctive forms of governance . . . market, hierarchies, the clan or community and associations'. One type of associative governance is what Pound (1992, p83) describes as the 'political model'. Pound states that, 'this new form of governance based on politics rather than finance will provide a means of oversight that is both far more effective and far less expensive than the takeovers of the 1980s'.

No firm can exist without employees, customers and suppliers, including those providing infrastructure services in the host community. For this reason, these parties are referred to as 'strategic stakeholders'. The distinguishing characteristics of a stakeholder mutual are:

- Ownership is only with those people on whom the firm depends for its existence; and
- Control is distributed but not diversified through a compound board.

Table 9.1 Typology of firms discussed

Type of firm	Conventional mutual	Investor firm	Stakeholder mutual
Ownership	**Homogenous** For example: Workers OR Suppliers OR Customers	**Homogenous** For example: (a) Government OR (b) Family OR (c) Publicly-traded	**Diverse** With: Workers AND Suppliers AND Customers
Control	**Centralised** (Unitary board) △	**Centralised** (Unitary board) △	**Distributed** (Compound board) ⊖
Governance form	**Hierarchical, associative** and product **markets**	**Hierarchical** for government firms (a) **Markets** and **hierarchical** for private firms (b) and (c)	**Associative** plus **communities/clans** and internal political **markets** for influence and control with external product **markets**

Note: Heavy arrows indicate the two steps used in the analysis and for forming a stakeholder mutual.

Shareholders do not meet the test of being strategic stakeholders, as they are not required when a firm becomes viable. Viable firms are self-financing and do not need to raise funds from shareholders, as is the case for most publicly-traded firms. In some years, more money is distributed *to* shareholders in the USA from all listed companies through dividends, share buy-backs and management buy-outs than is raised by firms *from* shareholders.

Jensen (2000), Sternberg (1997) and Pejovich (1990) have noted the problem of firms being accountable to diversified stakeholders. However, their concern does not apply to a stakeholder mutual as it introduces distributed control *without* diversified control or accountability. Distributed control through a compound board is mandated in a number of continental European countries. Compound boards are found in all countries, as one company controlling another with outside shareholders creates constitutionally different components of a compound board. This is the predominant control architecture found throughout the world (as reported by La Porta *et al.*, 1999). The compound board within a firm is a feature of (non-trivial) employee-owned industrial firms throughout the world, even in Anglo-Saxon cultures where unitary boards are the dominant form (Bernstein, 1980). Venture capitalists and leverage buy-out associations

Table 9.2 Examples of the different types of firms discussed

Nature of ownership	Examples	Control architecture
Private/solitary	Family firm Government firm	Unitary in Anglo-Saxon countries, compound boards (CB) elsewhere
Distributed and homogeneous	Publicly-traded firm Conventional mutual Professional partnership Worker co-operative	Unitary and/or CB Unitary board Collective Distributed through a CB
Distributed and diverse	Firm in a Japanese *keiretsu*[a] Stakeholder mutual[b]	Distributed through a CB *but not* diverse
Redeemable equity	Mondragon primary coop	Distributed *but not* diverse (CB)
Limited redeemable	Mondragon secondary Coop	Distributed *and* diverse (CB)

Notes: [a]Publicly-traded; [b]Publicly-traded and/or redeemable.

who establish over-riding powers for a unitary board through a shareholders' agreement also create a compound board.

Ownership by diverse strategic stakeholders is not commonly found except in Japanese *keiretsu*. Conventional mutual firms, worker co-operatives and professional partnerships have distributed ownership but it is homogeneous within a single class of stakeholder (see Table 9.2). The analysis of a stakeholder mutual firm with distributed control and diversified ownership is undertaken in this chapter in two steps, as indicated by the two black arrows in Table 9.1. The first step is to compare centralised control with distributed control, and the second is to compare homogeneous investor ownership with diverse stakeholder ownership. The second section of this chapter considers the 'inherent problems from unitary control' in publicly-traded, family and government-owned firms. Unitary control introduces the corrupting influences of centralised power, the problems of information overload, and degraded information and control. This section identifies the need to recognise the limited ability of individuals to transact information, measured in bytes, on a reliable and consistent basis. In the third section, examples of distributed control are considered with a division of power, decomposition in decision-making labour, distributed information feedback, and elements of self-regulation. The examples include employee-owned firms, the stakeholder-controlled firms found in Japanese *keiretsu* and the stakeholder co-operatives located around the Basque town of Mondragon in Spain. The examples provide a basis on which to compare the competitive advantages of distributed control with centralised control to undertake the first step of the analysis.

The fourth section describes how a stakeholder mutual can be formed through privatisation or by the introduction of tax incentives for shareholders to convert their firms. The resulting information and control architecture of a stakeholder mutual is presented. This provides the basis for undertaking the second step of the analysis in comparing homogenous and diverse ownership. The concluding fifth section reviews the competitive advantages of stakeholder mutuals. It recommends the introduction of distributed stakeholder governance before any government enterprise is privatised. It also argues that unitary boards do not represent a competitive basis for convergence of the corporate governance regimes found in various countries. The argument continues: if governments wish to raise funds by selling their enterprises, this should be done on condition that diversified stakeholder ownership is introduced after the investors' time horizon to introduce the foundations for 'building a stakeholder democracy' (Turnbull, 1994a, 1994b).

Inherent problems from unitary control

This section considers the inherent problems of unitary control. First, there is the ability of centralised power to corrupt directors and firm performance because of their manifold conflicts of interest. Second, centralised control denies the ability of directors to obtain qualitative information about the business's strengths, weaknesses, opportunities and threats (SWOT), independently of management, who need to be a crucial element of any evaluation. Third, there is lack of information, independent of management, to monitor, control, direct, remunerate and retire management. Fourth, unitary control introduces information overload on decision-makers. Unitary control occurs when a single Board or control centre governs a firm. Many unitary Board firms overcome some of the problems of centralised control by having a supervisory Board such as is found in Japanese *keiretsu*, firms in continental Europe, and firms that have an influential shareholder who carries out the role of 'watchdog'.

Corruption of power

A unitary Board has absolute power to manage its own conflicts of interest. Table 9.3 explains how unitary Boards can lead to the corruption of both their members and the performance of the business by appropriating shareholder value. Section A of the Table lists the powers of directors to further their own interests or those of their nominees. Section B lists the powers of directors to maintain their Board position and benefits for themselves and/or their nominees. The natures of the eight conflicts of interest listed in section A can be, and have been, used to destroy the viability of many publicly-traded companies. This should not be unex-

Table 9.3 Corrupting powers of a unitary board

Directors have power to:

A. *Obtain private benefits for themselves (and/or control groups who appoint them) by:*

(a) Determining their own remuneration and payments to associates.
(b) Directing business to interests associated with themselves.
(c) Issuing shares or options at a discounted value to themselves and/or associates.
(d) Selling assets of the firm to one or more directors or their associates at a discount.
(e) Acquiring assets from one or more directors or their associates at inflated values.
(f) Trading on favoured terms with parties who provide directors with private benefits.
(g) Using firm resources and/or their status in other ways.

B. *Maintain their board positions and private benefits by:*

(a) Reporting on their own performance and influencing 'independent' advisers by:
    (i) Selecting auditors and other 'independent' advisers;
    (ii) Determining their fees;
    (iii) Controlling the process by which auditors are appointed by shareholders;
    (iv) Terminating the appointment of auditors and other 'independent' advisers;
    (v) Paying additional fees for work which is not required to be 'independent'; and
    (vi) Determining the terms of reference on which 'independent' advice is provided.

(b) Determining the level of profit reported to shareholders by:
    (i) Selecting the basis for valuing or writing off trading and fixed assets;
    (ii) Determining the life of assets and so the cost of depreciation;
    (iii) Selecting the basis for recognising revenues and costs in long term contracts;
    (iv) Selecting accounting policies within accepted accounting standards; and
    (v) Selecting, controlling and paying 'independent' valuers and determining the basis on which valuations are to be carried out.

(c) Not disclosing full pecuniary or non-pecuniary benefits even if required to do so.
(d) Determining how any conflicts of interest are managed.
(e) Filling casual board vacancies with people who support their own positions.
(f) Nominating new directors who support them at shareholder meetings.
(g) Controlling the nomination and election procedures and processes.
(h) Controlling the conduct of shareholder meetings.
(i) Appointing pension fund managers for the firm who also provide them proxies.
(j) Voting uncommitted proxies to support their own election.
(k) Not allowing the firm to compete with related parties who can vote for them.

pected as it is widely accepted that power corrupts and absolute power can corrupt absolutely.

The inherent conflicts of interest in unitary Boards are gradually being recognised by the growing practice of establishing sub-committees to consider the more contentious conflicts. However, while such sub-committees acknowledge the problem they are not a solution, as boards cannot contract out of their intrinsic conflicts of interest. The most common and contentious conflicts arise from directors determining (i) the accounting policies that determine how their performance will be assessed by investors; (ii) the remuneration paid to themselves; and (iii) their self-nomination for re-election. For these conflicts to be properly managed, a company requires a watchdog board or an active influential shareholder to carry out this role.

The appointment of a majority of non-executive directors (NEDs) to contentious Board sub-committees does not remove the intrinsic board conflicts even if the directors are described as 'independent'. The term independent is generally misleading 'double-speak'. This is because the information available to NEDs to make decisions is prepared by management and so is not independent of the self-interest of management. The information prepared for NEDs is commonly the principle source of information available to NEDs to direct, monitor, control, remunerate and change management. It should be considered misleading and deceptive conduct under the law to describe any director on a unitary Board as 'independent' unless they can meet three conditions. These are that the director has (i) information independent of management on which to act; (ii) the will to act; and (iii) the capability to act in the best interest of the company as a whole.

Lack of information

To obtain the *information to act*, directors not only need management's side of the story but also any opposing views that may be held by employees, customers, suppliers and other stakeholders. A 'loyal opposition' and a vigilant 'fourth estate' are commonly recognised as conditions precedent for good government. As the ability to sustain any business depends on its strategic stakeholders, it is simple good common sense for directors to establish processes for obtaining information from such people and to establish their long-term commitment, support and co-operation.

To obtain the *will to act*, directors need to hold their Board positions independently of those whose interest they may need to act against to further the interests of the company as a whole. The membership of Boards is commonly self-perpetuating. This makes it difficult for any one individual to act against the collective self-interest of the board to maintain their self-serving and self-perpetuating power, status and privileges.

The method of electing directors is commonly controlled by the directors or by the chairperson. This makes any individual director vulnerable to retirement if s/he is not a 'good team player'. The will to act independently can be encouraged by directors being elected by preferential voting. This also protects minority interests as it allows them to be represented to protect them from being exploited by any 'control group'. A form of preferential voting, which is mandated in some states in the USA, is described as 'cumulative voting' (Bhagat and Brickley, 1984; Dallas, 1992; Gordon, 1993). Under this system, all directors are elected each year, with each share obtaining as many votes as there are vacancies on the Board. Shareholders can then distribute their votes among the directors of their choosing. If there are ten positions to be filled, then each share has ten votes and a 10 per cent shareholder can accumulate sufficient votes to ensure that at least one director of their choice is elected. In this way, minority interests can obtain some protection from what Hailsham (1978; p125) described as 'elected dictatorship'. Cumulative voting avoids Boards becoming poorly accountable when they use the various powers (listed in section B of Table 9.3) to make themselves self-perpetuating.

To obtain the *capability to act*, directors need a process to prevent unethical and/or counter-productive practices before they occur. In Anglophile countries, directors are faced with the option of resigning and allowing undesirable activities to continue, or ignoring them, as a 'good team player'. Regulators are of little help in preventing a problem arising. Regulators normally take the position that they will only become involved once it is evident that 'the horse has bolted'. To close the stable door beforehand, a director needs to obtain either a board majority to support preventive or corrective action, or a watchdog Board to veto the matter. Watchdog Boards, described as 'Cour des Comptes' are mandated in France for government-owned firms (Analytica, 1992, p104). Financial institutions in France have watchdog Boards described as 'Censeurs' (Analytica, 1992, p107). Similar types of watchdog Boards are mandated for co-operatives in Spain as found in the Mondragon Corporacion Cooperativa (MCC) described by Turnbull (1995). The author has introduced watchdog Boards to Australia in two start-up enterprises he formed to reduce the cost of raising high-risk funds. They also protected his reputation as a professional company promoter (Turnbull, 1992b, 1993, 2000a).

Watchdog Boards have limited roles. Their main role is to avoid the situation of directors setting, marking and reporting on their own exam papers (Tricker, 1994; p246). This can occur because directors establish their own profit objectives and have considerable discretion under accepted accounting standards to determine the reported profit (Bazerman *et al.*, 1997). The watchdog Boards that were established by the author mediated any conflicts of interest, including those commonly managed by the audit, remuneration and nomination committees. In one situation, the watchdog Board also had the power to stop the author and his co-directors from over-borrowing by having the name of the watchdog Board chairman on the title deed of the land owned by the business.

Lack of independent feedback information on performance

A fundamental flaw in the Anglo-Saxon system of corporate governance is that directors can be given the 'mushroom' treatment by management. That is, they are kept in the dark and given informational manure. There are two reasons for this state of affairs. First, institutional investors, who in aggregate may typically hold a majority of the shares in publicly-traded companies, do not have any firm-specific knowledge or authority to provide meaningful oversight, alternative intelligence or assistance to the directors. Second, the unitary board structure means that directors become largely captive to the information provided by management. Compare this situation with that of a company in a Japanese *keiretsu*; Figure 9.1 illustrates Japanese diversified stakeholder ownership, which is created by firms issuing shares to their supplier and customer corporations to consolidate their relationships with them. The chief executive officers (CEOs) of these strategic stakeholder companies meet once a month, or even once a week to discuss operations.

The feedback information that these CEOs obtain from their subordinates provides the other side of the story of any operational problems in the

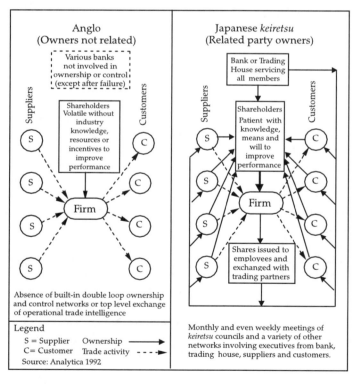

Figure 9.1 Anglo unitary *control* compared with Japanese distributed *control*. (Anglo investor *ownership* compared with Japanese diversified stakeholder ownership)

procurement or marketing of goods and services. The resolution of any problems or shortcomings in the quality or terms of trade can be crucial in obtaining competitive advantages. News of problems may not be reported, or be reported slowly, by subordinates, especially when they think management could regard the problems as reflecting on their own performance. It is a case of subordinates fearing that managers may 'shoot the messenger'. By providing access to both sides of the story, a *keiretsu* council is more likely to hear about problems that might not otherwise be identified. As a *keiretsu* council meets frequently, problems can be both identified and corrected expeditiously. Formal communication between suppliers and customers also allows both parties to contribute to resolving problems and developing co-operative relationships for increasing efficiencies.

Without self-correcting feedback information from informed and committed diversified stakeholders, a firm governed by a unitary board is subjected to jeopardy from a lack of information or self-serving biased information on its operational performance. This is a common problem in all public- and private-sector command and control hierarchies. Without independent qualitative and quantitative feedback information, directors of a unitary board do not have a creditable basis to direct, monitor, control, remunerate or change management or undertake a SWOT analysis of the business. In such situations there remain few operational reasons for a firm to possess a Board. In larger companies, the role of the Board becomes one of providing privileges of power, status and influence, and maintaining these by distributing such benefits to those that support the self-perpetuation of the practice. However, Bhaghat and Black (1998) provided evidence that the value of external directors was to influence or capture regulators, and to allow CEOs to spread the blame when performance declined.

Communications passing up and down any organisational hierarchy can suffer quite serious misunderstandings, mistakes and omissions when relayed through just three or four people, even when all individuals have the very best of intentions. When these people are in a management hierarchy, it is rarely in their own interest to report to a superior information that may reflect adversely on their own performance. This provides an incentive for biases, distortions and omissions in communication. The need to interpret information sent down a chain of command and condense information reported back up increases the problems of control and monitoring. These problems are common to hierarchies in both the private and public sectors (Downs, 1967, pp116–118).

Information overload

It was to avoid information errors and overload that, at the beginning of the twentieth century, large US firms changed from unitary (U) form structures to multi-divisional (M) form. Williamson states that, 'The problem of organization is precisely one of decomposing the enterprise in efficient information processing respects' (Williamson, 1985; p282). Williamson recognises the cybernetic significance of technical and temporal specialisation of organisational information by quoting the work of Ashby (1960) and Simon (1962), who were pioneering scholars in developing the science of information and control described as cybernetics. The science of cybernetics was established in the middle of the twentieth century when Weiner (1948) defined it as 'the study of information and control in animal and machine'. Beer (1959, 1995a, 1995b, 1995c) pioneered the extension of cybernetics to management and this author[1] has been extending the application of cybernetic principles to the governance of organisations (Turnbull, 1997a, 1997b, 2000c).

All information has some physical form, with its quanta measured in bits, with eight bits described as a byte (Kurzweil 1999; p299). The rate at which individuals can receive, process and transmit bytes is indicated in Table 9.4. The table shows that humans mainly receive information in the form of sight and sound. However, the fastest rate at which individuals can transmit bytes is limited to speech and movement, and so is around 10,000 times slower. In referring to the speed at which the human brain can process information, Kurzweil (1999; p103) states that, 'a profound weakness is the excruciatingly slow speed of neural circuitry, only 200 calculations per

Table 9.4 Human constraints in transacting bytes

Input channels Channel capacity in bytes/sec[a]	Smell <10	Taste <15	Touch <15	Sound 100 k	Sight 1000 m	Constraints in humans to transact bytes created by:
	1 **Reception** through organs					Physiology
	2 **Storage** through nervous system					Physiology
	3 **Perception/understanding** through the activation and strengthening of neural networks which correlate current patterns with previous ones					Neurology, experience, training, motivation and psychological status
Nature of transacting bytes in humans	4 **Insights/knowledge** through sequential processing in neo-cortex limited to around 200 calculations per second[b]					As above plus size and architecture of neo-cortex and psychological status
	5 **External responses** transmitted by movement and vocal chords					Proximity/distance, environmental conditions, culture, literacy and numeracy
Output channels	Touch	Signs	Writing	Sound	Speech	Information can be received 10,000 faster than the rate at which it can be transmitted
Channel capacity in bytes/sec	<15	<15	<15	<100k	<100k	

Notes: (k = kilobytes; m = megabytes)
[a]Sources of channel capacity: Cochrane (1997, 2000); [b](Kurzweil, 1999, p. 103).

second'. This compares with the hundreds of millions of sequential calculations per second (megahertz) of a desktop computer. The need to limit the 'span of control' of managers to between around five to ten people is a simple example of the need to design organisations to meet the limited ability of individuals to process bytes and manage complexity.

The limited ability of individuals to receive, internally transact and transmit bytes shown in Table 9.4 must necessarily limit the ability of individuals to communicate and process data, information, knowledge and wisdom. This is because data is composed of bytes. Information is meaningful data and so likewise is composed of bytes but requires more bytes to provide meaning. Knowledge is useful information and so is also composed of bytes and likewise requires more bytes to determine usefulness. Wisdom in turn depends upon how knowledge is applied and so requires many more bytes to relate present situations to those in the past, to compare how the application of knowledge may affect outcomes.

Besides the physiological limitations in transacting bytes, there are also neurological limits. These are described in the micro-economic literature as 'bounded rationality'. The term arises from Hayek (1945; p527) who noted that, 'The problem of a rational economic order is trivial in the absence of bounded rationality limits on human decision makers'. Williamson explains that:

> The physical limits take the form of rate and storage limits on the powers of individuals to receive, store, retrieve, and process information without error. Simon observes in this connection that 'it is only because individuals human beings are limited in knowledge, foresight, skill, and time that organizations are useful instruments for the achievement of human purpose' (1975; p21).

Williamson also noted that 'Imitation of the M-form innovation was at first rather slow' and that 'prior to 1968, most European companies administered their domestic operations through U-form or holding company internal structures' (1975; p140). However, there was less need for large European firms to adopt M-form architecture because decomposition in their decision-making was an inherent feature of their possessing multiple Boards.

Distributed control

This section outlines the presence of compound boards throughout the world and considers their operations. The ability of a compound board to decompose decision-making labour to allow ordinary people to achieve extraordinary results is examined by analysing the operation of an industrial cooperative in Mondragon.

Anglophone countries

Firms governed by more than one board are commonly found throughout the world, even in Anglophone countries, where a unitary board is almost universally adopted. Even in the USA, around 20 per cent of the Fortune 500 largest companies have a compound board. This is because they are controlled by a dominant shareholder/investor (Zey, 1999) who acts like a supervisory board. In some cases, such as Microsoft and News Limited, the dominant shareholder may also be on the operating board. The presence of an influential active shareholder can simplify decision-making labour by managing the most contentious decisions that involve the inherent conflicts of interest in a unitary board. However, if the influential shareholder has related-party dealings with the business, then some other types of decision-making may be simplified because the directors are not encouraged to consider any course of action that is not in the interest of the dominant shareholder. This reinforces the need for an independent watchdog board.

In many countries, the dominant shareholder is a multi-national corporation which has established a local publicly-traded affiliate. In emerging economies, the dominant shareholder is typically the founding entrepreneur. In the more developed economies, second or higher generation descendants and their families are the dominant shareholders. The Berle and Means (1932) stereotype of publicly-traded corporations being widely owned represents a minority in most countries of the world. This also applies to the most industrialised countries of continental Europe (ECGN, 1997; Bianchi *et al.*, 1999; Brecht and Roell, 1999) and in Japan (Analytica, 1992), where cross and block shareholdings predominate.

Compounds boards are also commonly found in firms not publicly traded in Anglophone countries. Non-trivial employee-owned firms have more than one board to create a division of power and checks and balances required to sustain them (Bernstein, 1980). However, the most common examples of compound boards in Anglophone countries are in start-up firms where a shareholder's agreement establishes supervisory powers for the venture capitalist. Compound boards are created with leverage management buy-outs (LBOs) when an association of investors supervises the operating board of employees. Jensen noted that such arrangement provided 'a proven model of governance structure' (1993; p869). However, the existence of compound boards is not generally recognised by scholars. The work of Kuhn suggests an explanation for this in terms of paradigms; 'normal science' does not 'call forth new sorts of phenomena: indeed those that will not fit the box are often not seen at all' (1970; p24).

Non-Anglophone countries

Unlike in England, where firms evolved under civil law in the seventeenth century, firms in continental Europe evolved under common law. To avoid personal liability to creditors, lead investors did not become involved in management. Instead, they formed a supervisory board who appointed the managers, who incurred personal liabilities through the purchase of goods and services. To protect managers from personal liability, the deed of formation specified that the firm would be dissolved if its equity were impaired by a specified amount. The managers formed an executive Board, who carried out the day-to-day operations, while the supervisory board concerned itself with what would be described today as strategic issues. The decomposition of decision-making labour was somewhat along the lines of the multi-divisional (M-form) firms which developed in the USA during the early twentieth century. The separation of many of the decision-making powers in European firms with a supervisory board was defined in the corporate charter and/or the law (Analytica, 1992; pp82, 86, 101).

Simple two-tiered supervisory board systems are found in the Netherlands and in some of its former colonies, such as Indonesia. In Germany, half the members of the supervisory board in the larger companies are employee representatives (Analytica, 1992; p87). German companies also establish a works council (Analytica, 1992; p82). In France, employees are not found on supervisory boards. However, there may be a third-tier board created to carry out 'watchdog' functions for shareholders. A third-tier watchdog board is also mandated for co-operatives in Spain (Whyte and Whyte, 1988; p37). The co-operatives located around the Basque town of Mondragon have introduced a fourth tier of control described as a 'Social Council' (Whyte and Whyte, 1988; p38); see Figure 9.2. The Social Council determines relative wage levels, safety, other working conditions and welfare issues. In this way it greatly simplifies the role of management and the CEO by removing one of the most important and contentious items from the function of managers.

The Social Council is made up of a delegate from each work group of 10–20 people and meets once a quarter. It reports to both the management board and the supervisory board. Mondragon firms limit their size to 500 employees,[2] which limits the size of the Social Council. All the employees meet once a year as a General Assembly to appoint members of the supervisory board who appoint the managers, who cannot be on the supervisory Board. The General Assembly also appoints a three-person Watchdog Council, which has wider powers than an audit committee, as it monitors the integrity of the governing processes. It may call for outside assistance from the Group banker who is owned by all the primary co-operatives in the Mondragon Corporacion Cooperativa (MCC) or from the management of the group in which the firm is a member (Turnbull, 1995). Thomas and Logan (1982; p109) have shown that 'the cooperatives are more efficient than many private enterprises' and 'have been more profitable than capitalist enterprises'. Mondragon demonstrates how the complexity of modern business can be decomposed into simpler units to

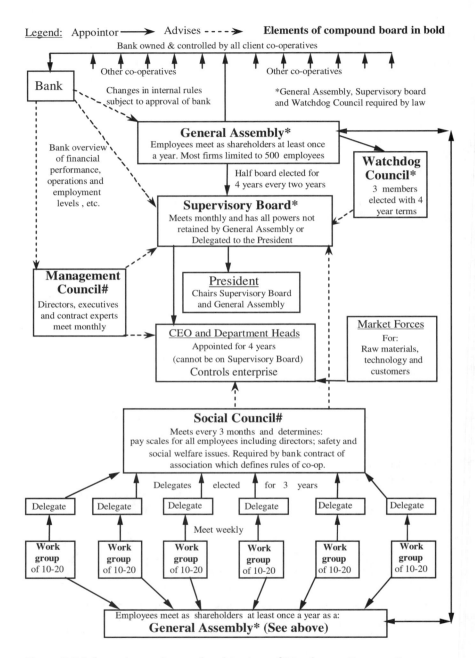

Legend: Appointor ⟶ Advises ----➤ **Elements of compound board in bold**

Bank owned & controlled by all client co-operatives

Other co-operatives   Other co-operatives

Bank

Changes in internal rules subject to approval of bank

*General Assembly, Supervisory board and Watchdog Council required by law

Bank overview of financial performance, operations and employment levels , etc.

General Assembly*
Employees meet as shareholders at least once a year. Most firms limited to 500 employees

Half board elected for 4 years every two years

Watchdog Council*
3 members elected with 4 year terms

Supervisory Board*
Meets monthly and has all powers not retained by General Assembly or Delegated to the President

Management Council#
Directors, executives and contract experts meet monthly

President
Chairs Supervisory Board and General Assembly

CEO and Department Heads
Appointed for 4 years (cannot be on Supervisory Board)
Controls enterprise

Market Forces
For:
Raw materials, technology and customers

Social Council#
Meets every 3 months and determines: pay scales for all employees including directors; safety and social welfare issues. Required by bank contract of association which defines rules of co-op.

Delegates   elected   for 3   years

| Delegate | Delegate | Delegate | Delegate | Delegate | Delegate |

Meet weekly

| Work group of 10-20 | Work group of 10-20 | Work group of 10-20 | Work group of 10-20 | Work group of 10-20 | Work group of 10-20 |

Employees meet as shareholders at least once a year as a:
General Assembly* (See above)

Figure 9.2 Information and control architecture of Mondragon Co-operatives

Source: Based on information from: Ellerman (1982); Whyte and Whyte (1988); Morrison (1991)

allow ordinary people with little or no management education to achieve extraordinary results.

A Japanese *keiretsu* also has elements of a stakeholder mutual in that there are formal channels of information feedback and control from strategic stakeholders. As indicated in Figure 9.1, a producer firm issues some of its shares to suppliers and customers to formalise its association with them. The CEOs of the supplier and customer firms, with those of the lead banker and/or the trading house servicing all members, meet as the *Keiretsu* council. While the suppliers and customers may each have only a minor equity interest, any concerns and suggestions they may have to improve operations are shared by the major shareholders such as the bank and/or the trading company. So while stakeholder constituencies may not have formal power to initiate change, they can play a pivotal role in improving operations *without* introducing the diverse accountability that concern the critics of stakeholder governance (such as Jensen, 2000; Sternberg, 1997; and Pejovitch, 1990). The involvement of stakeholders explains Porter's recommendation to corporations in the USA to include employees, customers, suppliers and members of their host community in their ownership and control (1992; pp16–17).

The competitiveness and even sustainability of a firm can be jeopardised by the loss and distortion of information in its command and control hierarchy (Downs, 1967; pp116–118). In a *keiretsu* firm, any operational deficiency that is not quickly, accurately or fully reported up its hierarchy may be reported up the chain of command in the supplier or customer firm. Employees in the supplier and customer chain of command have an incentive to report other people's problems, while employees in the producer firm have a disincentive to report problems in units under their control. Both chains of command could contribute to some problems, but in this situation separate reporting to the *keiretsu* council allows both sides of the story to be considered. In this way, a compound Board, representing separate constituencies, can facilitate the establishment of a 'loyal opposition' to management. It provides a basis for formal recognition of the symbiotic interdependency of suppliers, producers and customers, and their different needs and viewpoints.

Another advantage of a compound Board is that through sharing information, power is also shared. The sharing of power and the resulting need to establish 'power coalitions' (Dallas, 1988; p34) and so inter-dependency, provides a rational basis for developing trust to facilitate greater openness and 'richness' (Daft and Lengel, 1984) in communications. This explains the advantage of non-market and non-hierarchical systems of governance (identified by Hollingsworth and Lindberg, 1985; pp221–222), but neglected by economists and corporate governance scholars – an exception is Wruck and Jensen (1994). The development of trust in turn provides a way to reduce transaction costs (Akerlof, 1970). As pointed out by Dallas, 'It is better to have a number of constituencies present on the board rather than one, namely management. Each constituency can then keep the others in check' (1988; p80). This insight explains how a stakeholder mutual firm can introduce self-regulation to provide the basis for reducing the role of government regulation to protect employees, suppliers and consumers. It also provides criteria for designing the information and control architecture of a stakeholder mutual firm.

The stakeholder mutual firm

The introduction of feedback information and control from strategic stakeholders could be introduced for firms publicly traded, and family or government owned without changing their ownership. However, the analysis of this chapter is focused on distributed control with distributed and dispersed ownership. How this situation might be introduced to create stakeholder mutual firms is next considered.

Privatisation provides one way of introducing stakeholder mutual firms; property rights in the firm could be transferred from the government to the strategic stakeholders according to the value of their services and/or purchases. It could be achieved in somewhat a similar manner to coupon privatisation but where only strategic stakeholders obtain the coupons or property rights. However, this approach would deny revenues to the government from selling the business through the stock exchange or to a trade buyer. To avoid governments losing revenue, the conversion to a stake-holder mutual could occur after the investment time horizon for the initial investors. Private investors have financed many infrastructure projects on this basis through 'BOOT' schemes. A BOOT scheme requires a firm to (B)uild an infrastructure facility, (O)wn and (O)perate it for a stipulated period of time and then (T)ransfer it free of charge back to the government authority at the end of the period. However, to create a stakeholder mutual, the free transfer would be to the strategic stakeholders. The allocation of ownership and control rights could be on the basis of the market value of their contribution to the value of their services or custom. These arrangements create an ownership transfer corporation (OTC), described by Turnbull (1975, 1991, 1992a, 1994b, 1997a, 1998).

Strategic stakeholders replace investors and so can be described as 'deferred residual claimants'. In this way stakeholder mutuals meet the criteria of Jensen (2000, p16) for 'enlightened stakeholder theory' by adding 'the simple specification that the objective function of the firm is to maximize total long-term value'. However, as stakeholders are not required to invest any of their cashflow to acquire ownership they are not subjected to an 'opportunity cost' to provide them with a basis to discount the value of future ownership. This allows the present value of stakeholder residual claimants to be valued at ten or more times higher than that of the investors who are subjected to discounting over their time horizon.

The free transfer of equity to stakeholders of publicly-traded or family businesses could be encouraged with tax incentives that increase the present value of equity for owners who transfer long-term ownership to stakeholders. The size of the tax incentive for owners to increase their profits by giving away a small amount of ownership each year could be quite small (Turnbull, 1975, 1997a, 1998). This is because the value of money in the future discounted for risk and uncertainty diminishes at compounding rate. Equity discount rates are typically over 20 per cent and can exceed 40 per cent. The value of the one-time benefit that is required today for an investor give up 100 per cent ownership after 15 years is 6.5 per cent of current after tax profits with a 20 per cent discount rate. If investors have a 30 per cent opportunity rate, the one-time tax incentive to offset the value of all profits after 15 years needs only to increase profits by 2 per cent in the first year (Turnbull, 1997a, p19). No tax incentive was used by the UK government to attract investors to privatise water supply facilities with a 15-year operating licence, and the government retained the right to replace a licensee on ten years' notice without compensation (OFWAT, 1995).

The loss in government revenues from the tax incentive can be more than offset by increases in revenues from the tax base transferring from corporations to individual stakeholders who are likely to pay tax at a higher rate, and/or reduce welfare entitlements. In this regard it assumed that only resident individuals on the electoral rolls qualify for free equity in stakeholder mutual firms. Any free equity entitlements accruing to corporations as strategic stakeholders would need to pass through to their employees.

Many start-up companies dilute investors' ownership interests by share issues to employees, with or without a tax incentive. The introduction of stakeholder ownership and control interests can provide benefits to investors to offset the gradual dilution of the investor's equity without tax incentives. In a number of countries such as the USA, UK and Australia there are already tax incentives to encourage employee ownership, and as a result the degree of investor ownership is decreasing in even the largest publicly-traded companies. As a result, the aggregate of employee ownership is increasingly making them one of the largest shareholders. This illustrates how the process of ownership transfer is already taking place, but only to employees rather than being shared with other stakeholders.

Excess employee ownership can introduce counter-productive results with a unitary board, because of its absolute power to manage its own conflicts of interest. The experience with privatisation in Russia clearly demonstrates this problem (Black *et al.*, 1999; Fox and Heller, 1999; Megginson and Netter, 2000). The solution is a division of power (as suggested by Dallas, 1988, p80 and supported by the empirical evidence of Bernstein, 1980). Bernstein surveyed employee ownership around the world and did not find one firm that did not have a compound board. He identified six fundamental conditions for successful employee ownership:

1   Participation in decision-making;
2   Economic return to the participants based on the surplus they produce;
3   Sharing management-level information with employees;
4   Guaranteed individual rights;
5   An independent appeals system; and
6   A complex participatory/democratic consciousness (1980, p116)

Items 4 and 5 require a division of power, and so a compound board if external agents are not to become involved. As illustrated by Mondragon firms, a compound board provides a way to meet conditions 1 and 3. The above considerations support the view that a compound board is a condition precedent for employee control to be maintained on a sustainable competitive basis (Turnbull, 2000b).

The sharing of employee control with customers and suppliers, including the host community providing infrastructure services, introduces additional checks and balances on employee appropriation of value. Conversely, excessive appropriation of value by other stakeholders is countered by employee participation in control. A stakeholder mutual with at least three independent classes of strategic stakeholder provides a basis for introducing competition for corporate control through the board room, rather than the much more expensive and problematical competition for control through the stock market for publicly-traded companies.

An appropriate division of power can increase the welfare of all stakeholders (Persson *et al.*, 1996; Diermeier and Myerson, 1999). A stakeholder mutual with an appropriate division of power provides a firmer basis for introducing what Pound described as the 'political model of governance' than relying only on investors to create competition for corporate control (1993). Pound states, 'this new form of governance based on politics rather than finance will provide a means of oversight that is both far more effective and far less expensive than the takeovers of the 1980s' (1992, p83). The success of the political approach to corporate governance is illustrated by all the employee-owned firms surveyed by Bernstein, by Mondragon firms, and by VISA International. The founding CEO of VISA explains that it 'has multiple boards of directors within a single legal entity, none of which can be considered superior or inferior, as each has irrevocable authority and autonomy over geographic or functional area' (Hock, 1994, p7). None of the firms mentioned above is traded publicly and they all have compound boards.

However, this does not mean that a stakeholder mutual cannot be traded publicly. It just supports the view that firms do not have to be traded publicly to be efficient and internationally competitive. The conversion of a publicly-traded company to a stakeholder mutual would require the firm to be publicly traded during the transition period. Trading in stakeholder shares could also continue after the transition, which may involve ten or more years. There are various ways in which stakeholder mutual firms could be formed. A ten-year period could be practical for publicly-traded companies with appropriate tax incentives or for a privatisation process using a BOOT concept. If no tax incentive were provided, then a ten-year transfer holiday would provide investors with sufficient time to recover their costs and obtain competitive returns before

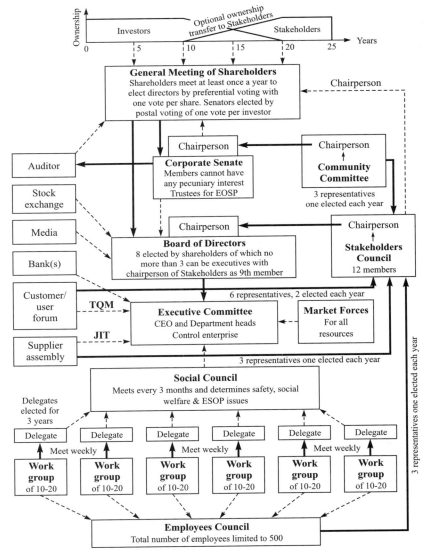

Figure 9.3 Stakeholder mutual information and control architecture

Notes

a Heavy lines indicate the power of appointment, light lines show information flows

b Elements of compound board shown in bold

their interest was diluted out over the following ten years. This longer transfer period is used in Figure 9.3, which illustrates how competition for corporate control can be introduced through a division of power introduced by a compound board.

The bottom section of Figure 9.3 replicates the architecture of a Mondragon firm. Participation by strategic stakeholders is introduced through customer forums and supplier assemblies. There may be a number of these, reflecting different goods and services and/or geographic locations. Larger firms such as the John Lewis Partnership in the UK, with over 40,000 employees, follow this practice for their employees by establishing branch councils in each location (*Gazette*, 1994). The customer forums provide a basis for developing and sustaining total quality management (TQM), while the supplier assemblies provide a basis for developing and sustaining just in time (JIT) delivery of goods or services. This provides another practical way in which stakeholder participation can add value to improve the competitive standing of a firm. Wruck and Jensen (1994, p248) define TQM 'as a science-based, non-hierarchical and non-market-oriented organizing technology that increases efficiency and quality'.

The customer/user forums, supplier assemblies, employees' council and community committee appoint delegates to a stakeholder council, shown on the right-hand side of Figure 9.3. The stakeholder council is in the position to carry out the role of a *keiretsu* council in providing feedback information to both management and shareholders on the operations of the business and the quality of management. A stakeholder council creates a systemic process to inform directors on the business SWOT independently of management (who may be part of the problem). The council can also provide an informed and knowledgeable evaluation to the directors on the quality of management. Likewise, stakeholder councils are in the best position to carry out director and board evaluation on behalf of the investors.

The self-interest and commitment to the business by stakeholders provides the incentive for them to contribute their services without payment. There are a number of examples cited by Givens (1991) of utility company customers in the USA donating money to improve the operations of their supplier. It is significant to note that such contributions, which fund the establishment of citizen utility boards (CUBs), may typically involve only 2 or 3 per cent of all customers. This provides a free ride for the other 97 per cent or so, providing an example of altruism, but not irrationality, as the benefit to all customers can be sufficient to repay those who do make a contribution. However, as deferred residual claimants, all strategic stakeholders obtain an incentive to contribute to maximising the long-term value of the enterprise to a greater extent than most investors, who are unlikely to have firm-specific knowledge unless they are also strategic stakeholders.

The establishment of a formal and rich feedback information system with clients also provides competitive advantages in developing new products and processes. Hippel (1986) reported that over 80 per cent of product innovations originate from users rather than the research and development department of the larger firms. Innovations developed by users reduce both risks and costs to producers in product development. Stakeholder councils provide a forum for identifying and collaborating with 'lead users'.

Stakeholders do not have the power to elect members of the watchdog committee (described in Figure 9.3 as a 'Corporate Senate' – Turnbull, 1992b, 1993) that protects the interest of all shareholders and mediates board conflicts of interest. This arrangement prevents stakeholders from compromising the duty of directors and senators to act in the best interest of shareholders as a whole, in ways that concern the critics of stakeholder governance. Pejovich (1990, p69) is concerned that 'co-determination' and 'industrial democracy' are 'code words for wealth transfers' which undermine the property rights of shareholders. However, wealth transfer could be an explicit objective of tax and other incentives used to introduce stakeholder mutuals.

The compound board created by the arrangements shown in Figure 9.3 meets the recommendation of Williamson (1985, p308) that if stakeholders are involved at all, they should be 'restricted to informational participation'. Figure 9.3 also illustrates Williamson's statement that the 'possibility is to invent a governance structure that holders of equity recognise as a safeguard against expropriation and egregious mismanagement' (1985, p305). A compound board introduces a new approach to corporate governance. It provides a constructive way to introduce Porter's recommendation to policy-makers to 'encourage board representation by significant customers, suppliers, financial advisers, employees, and community representatives'. Porter also recommended corporations to 'nominate significant owners, customers, suppliers, employees, and community representatives to the board directors' (1992, pp16, 17). However, as Williamson notes, Porter's recommendation would become counterproductive with a unitary board by introducing unacceptable conflicts of interests.

Porter made his recommendation after investigating the competitive advantages of firms in Japan and Germany. Both countries have institutional arrangements that provide rich feedback information from customers, suppliers and the host communities to improve the quality of goods, services, working conditions and health of the firm. In this way, directors obtain information independent of management. However, Porter's analysis neglects the compound board structure found in Japan and Germany. This further illustrates Kuhn's observation on phenomena that 'will not fit the box are often not seen at all' (1970, p24). However, once this shortcoming is understood, Porter's analysis still explains and supports the competitive advantage of a stakeholder mutual form of firm.

In Figure 9.3, provision is also made for community representatives to participate in the governance of a stakeholder mutual. Community representatives participate in the Stakeholder Council with those representing suppliers, employees and customers. The chair of the Stakeholder Council chairs the Board of Directors, and the chair of the Community Committee chairs the Corporate Senate. In each case, to protect the integrity of the property rights of investors, the chair does not have a deliberate vote, only a casting vote when the vote is tied. The presence of an independent chair also provides a basis for directors to be subject to creditable evaluation; self-evaluation by directors of themselves is just not creditable. However, unitary boards are increasingly undertaking self-evaluation to head off suggestions that there should be a shareholders' committee or some other board to undertake this task on a much more rigorous basis. This allows boards to claim that they are already subject to professional evaluation processes. Senator Murray (1998) proposed in the Australian Parliament that all publicly-traded companies be required to establish a corporate governance board (CGB) modelled on the Corporate Senate established by the author.

A Corporate Senate was established under the Anglophile Corporation's Law of Australia in 1987. It was created to reduce the cost of raising high-risk funds from investors in the USA and Australia while also protecting the reputations of the directors of a start-up business established by the author (Turnbull, 1992b, 1993, 2000a). It achieved its objective by obtaining veto rights over any proposals by the directors in which they had a conflict of interest, or any other conflicts as may be brought to the notice of Senators by board members elected by cumulative voting. The Senate had three members elected, with each shareholder having one vote no matter how many shares they held, as is the practice with co-operatives. In this way, the Senators could be elected independently of any parent company or control group to provide them with the *will to act*. Directors were elected by cumulative voting (Bhagat and Brickley, 1984; Gordon, 1993) with one vote per share for every board vacancy. This allowed minority shareholders to appoint a director to provide this person with the will to act against a control group. A director could act privately by reporting to the Senate any arrangements that favoured the control group over minority interests, and so became subject to the veto power of the Senate. In this way, directors obtained the *capability to act*.

Directors could overturn a Senate veto by calling a general meeting of stockholders and obtaining approval with a 50 per cent majority on a one vote per share basis. However, the public exposure of conflicts of interest, with both sides of the argument exposed to 'sunlight', would in itself inhibit the more blatant expropriation by a control group. The Senate had the power to report to shareholders independently of management. All its resolutions were made public in the annual report to shareholders, along with that of the auditor (whose professional independence was protected by being under the control and direction of the Senate).

Stakeholder councils provide directors with the information to act. Cumulative voting for directors can provide directors with the will to act. A corporate senate elected on a one vote per investor basis provides directors with the power to act. In this way, a stakeholder mutual with the architecture described in Figure 9.3 can meet the three tests described earlier, to avoid the corruption of people and performance. It would be unusual for any government, family or publicly-traded firms in Anglophile countries to be in a position to meet these tests.

Competitive advantages of stakeholder mutuals

The distinctive feature of a stakeholder mutual is its *diversified* ownership with *distributed* but not *diverse* control involving its strategic stakeholders. Diversified ownership among strategic stakeholders represents a 'reinvention' of the concept of a mutual firm. Distributed ownership is a common characteristic with publicly-traded companies, but it is not generally diversified through the involvement of stakeholders. When a firm matures and becomes self-financing, it no longer needs investors, so shareholders no longer represent strategic stakeholders. This situation is illustrated with management buy-outs that can eliminate investors who are not operational stakeholders.

There are many ways of designing the information and control architecture of a firm with diversified ownership to provide distributed control. Various ways of distributing control in employee firms are presented and analysed by Bernstein (1980). This chapter has only considered the arrangements illustrated in Figure 9.3. These are best suited for a firm located at a single location. When many locations are involved, matching branch stakeholder information and control architecture would become desirable (as in the John Lewis Partnership – *Gazette*, 1994). The architecture of Figure 9.3 would allow distributed control to be introduced to government, family and publicly-traded firms without jeopardising the property rights that provide a basis for concerns about stakeholder involvement in corporate governance. Nor would the architecture complicate the fiduciary duties of company directors. Instead, it would simplify the roles and duties of directors and so reduce their exposure to personal liability while providing processes to protect their reputations by managing their conflicts of interest. Besides protecting the interest of shareholders, the arrangement could reduce risk and enhance shareholder value from the participation and commitment of strategic stakeholders and the feedback of competitive intelligence that might not otherwise be available to a unitary Board.

A fundamental problem of a unitary board is to obtain access to information that identifies problems. External directors who have been selected because of their independence from the firm are likely to have little knowledge, authority or experience with its detailed operations. As shown in Figure 9.1, for Anglo-Saxon firms, shareholders may be short-term and without industry knowledge, resources or the ability to improve performance. Institutional investors have little incentive to incur costs in becoming involved in corporate control, as it is their beneficiaries who obtain the most benefit from increases in performance. In a Japanese *keiretsu* the Board is accountable to long-term, patient shareholders with the information, will and capability to improve performance. To summarise, the competitive advantages of a stakeholder mutual are:

1   Decomposition in decision-making labour to reduce bounded rationality.
2   Distributed power to:

    i facilitate competitive viewpoints;
   ii mediate conflicts of interest of decision-makers;
   iii control expropriation of shareholder value;
   iv control stakeholder exploitation;
   v facilitate interdependency, trust and co-operation;
   vi facilitate self-regulation;
   vii increase numbers of decision-makers; and
   viii increase sharing of information.

3   Distributed intelligence to:

    i reduce errors in decision-making (Neumann, 1947);
   ii increase communication channels and reduce errors (Shannon, 1949);
   iii increase the variety of control to improve management of complexity (Ashby, 1968); and
   iv facilitate different levels of organisational learning (Mathews, 1996).

4   Introduce elements of self-regulation to reduce the complexity of government regulation
5) Enrich democracy by allowing more citizens, acting as stakeholders, to participate in the ownership and control of organisations that affect them.

Many of the advantages of distributed control identified in this chapter could also be made available to government, family and publicly-traded companies. The higher level of investor protection of having a watchdog board, and the higher level of continuous improvement information from strategic stakeholders, provide a compelling basis for enhancing the share price of an initial public offering (IPO). The introduction of distributed control, with its competitive advantages, would maximise the revenues obtained by governments from privatisation even without immediate diversified ownership. This is why distributed control is recommended as a condition precedent for privatisation.

    Even if governments privatise firms through a trade sale, distributed control also provides a way to privatise the significant costs of regulation.

By empowering stakeholders to look after their own interests, the need for prescriptive detailed regulations can be minimised. Even natural monopolies would not require a regulator, provided that customers obtained effective power to control management. Even without formal power imprinted into the constitutions. In US utilities, CUBs have been effective in moderating price increases (Givens, 1991).

The contrary characteristics of people require rich interpersonal communication. Market prices cannot provide the richness of information required. Price is what Ashby (1968) describes as 'second order information' because it is only a number containing a few bytes. Numbers have no meaning unless there is qualitative information describing the goods or services and the process of exchange, including the trustworthiness of the parties involved (Akerlof, 1970). The use of a hierarchy to govern activities creates problems through excessive power, and poor trust and communication. It also inhibits the ability of organisations either to manage complexity or to become self-regulating. Management practices such as JIT and TQM require associative relationships between suppliers, employees and customers to establish trust, with rich and frequent exchange of information.

Conclusion

This chapter has presented arguments that the conversion of family, government or publicly-traded firms in Anglophile countries into stakeholder mutuals would improve their efficiency and competitiveness. It has also noted that a stakeholder mutual introduces more sociable relationships and develops various constructive forms of social capital. The discussion has identified the lack of information feedback and so competitive advantages in family- and government-owned firms and those traded publicly in Anglophile countries. A number of the inherent conflicts of interest in unitary-governed firms were identified, that can corrupt both people and performance. This provided the basis for recommending that convergence of corporate governance practices not be based on unitary boards, and that all government-owned firms adopt stakeholder governance, whether or not they are being privatised. When government firms are being privatised it is recommended that they also introduce 'boomerang' ownership, which transfers ownership back from investors to stakeholders in a manner similar to BOOT projects.

Boomerang ownership prevents excessive profits being paid to investors that causes the growing inequality in wealth. This situation is largely created by property rights, which allow investors to capture profits in excess of the incentive required to invest (which I described as 'surplus profits'; Turnbull, 1992a). Stakeholder mutuals provide a way of distributing surplus profits to the people who create them. These are the employees, customers and suppliers whom all firms need to sustain their existence. Conventional corporations with government-sanctioned rights of perpetual succession provide investors with unlimited, unknown and uncontrollable surplus profits. This is inequitable, inefficient and unsustainable, without increasing government transfers to those who are made worse off. It is also inconsistent with the assumption of a market economy that competition will allocate resources efficiently. It allows firms owned outside a country, region or community to extract economic values, that are 'unlimited, unknown and uncontrollable' (Penrose, 1956).

A stakeholder mutual creates a democratic basis for distributing surplus profits because, by definition, all strategic stakeholders participate in its ownership and governance. Additional stakeholders can be included. Participation is an integrated political, social and economic activity. It provides a way of enriching democracy by allowing those affected by a firm to have some influence over its operations, and to share in its risks and returns. Tax incentives are recommended to encourage all firms to convert to being stakeholder mutuals (Turnbull, 1975, 1992a, 1997a).

The inclusive nature of the governance of a stakeholder mutual allows many elements of government regulation to be taken over, thus reducing the frustration and costs of bureaucratic and legal interventions. The ability of a stakeholder mutual to displace the role of government arises from its providing micro political power to stakeholders to govern themselves. This is currently denied in family, government and publicly-traded firms. As a result, many citizens: 'are demoralised by unemployment, alienated by insensitive bureaucracies, exploited by business, depressed by environmental degeneration, powerless to take control of their lives and cynical about the interest or the ability of politicians to make things better' (Turnbull, 1994a, p85). Stakeholder mutuals provide a building block for citizens and their politicians to make things better. They provide a way of creating a much more equitable, efficient, democratic and sustainable stakeholder society.

Notes

1   Stafford Beer is a past president of the World Organization of General Systems and Cybernetics and a pioneering practitioner of management cybernetics. In Toronto, 3 August, 1996 he reviewed Turnbull (1997a) and advised the author that he was not aware of cybernetics being applied to corporate governance. Beer's work involved communications and control *within* firms or bureaucracies, and was also based on information rather than bytes. President Allende retained Beer in 1971 to assist him in managing the Chilean economy. http://members.newsguy.com/~mayday/crypto/crypto6d.html and http://pespmc1.vub.ac.be/:/CSTHINK.html. Cybernetic scholars interested in applying cybernetics to the governance of organisations were invited by the author on 13 February, 2000 to publish their interest at http://pespmc1.vub.ac.be/Annotations/SOCINT.0.html

2   Evolutionary biologist, Robin Dunbar, has identified important limitations of the human brain. Dunbar (1993, p685) reports that the capacity of the human neocortex limits the maximum number of people with whom an individual can

establish social bonds and trust to around 150. He also reported research which suggested that 500 people represents a 'critical threshold beyond which social cohesion can be maintained only if there is an appropriate number of authoritarian officials' (Dunbar, 1993, p687). These findings provide another reason why firms have diminishing return to scale in addition to the three identified by Coase (1937, p87). These were the diminishing returns to management from (i) additional costs of 'organising' within the firm; (ii) the inability 'to make best use of factors of production' and 'because the "other advantages" of small firms are greater than those of a large firm'. The limited ability of individuals to process bytes and the loss of information in hierarchies shown in Table 9.4 provide an explanation of 'diminishing returns to management'.

References

Analytica (1992) *Board Directors and Corporate Governance: Trends in the G7 Countries Over the Next Ten Years*, Oxford Analytica Ltd, England.

Akerlof, G. A. (1970) 'The market for "lemons": qualitative uncertainty and the market mechanism', *Quarterly Journal of Economics*, 84, pp. 488–500.

Ashby, W. R. (1960) *Design for the Brain: The Origin of Adaptive Behaviour*, (2nd edn), London, Chapman & Hall.

—— (1968) *An Introduction to Cybernetics*, London, University Paperback.

Bazerman, M. H., Morgan, K. P. and Loewenstein, G. F. (1997) 'The impossibility of auditor independence', *Sloan Management Review*, 38(4), Summer.

Beer, S. (1959) *Cybernetics and Management*, London, English University Press.

—— (1995a) *Brain of the Firm*, (2nd edn), Chichester, John Wiley & Sons.

—— (1995b) *Decision and Control: The Meaning of Operational Research and Management Cybernetics*, Chichester, John Wiley & Sons.

—— (1995c) *The Heart of the Enterprise*, Chichester, John Wiley & Sons.

Berle, A. A. Jr. and Means, G. C. (1932) *The Modern Corporation and Private Property*, New York, Macmillan.

Bernstein, P. (1980) *Workplace Democratization: Its Internal Dynamics*, New Brunswick, NJ, Transaction Books.

Bhagat, S. and Black, B. (1998) 'The uncertain relationship between board composition and firm performance', in Hopt, K., Roe, M. and Wymeersch, E. (eds), *Corporate Governance: The State of the Art and Emerging Research*, Oxford University Press.

Bhagat, S. and Brickley, J. A. (1984) 'Cumulative voting: the value of minority shareholder voting rights', *Journal of Law & Economics*, 27 (October), pp. 339–365.

Bianchi, M., Bianco, M. and Enriques, L. (1999) 'Pyramidal groups and the separation between ownership and control in Italy', Working paper, Commissione Nazionale per le Societa e la Borsa (CONSOB), http://papers.ssrn.com/paper.taf?abstract_id=168208

Black, B. S., Kraakman, R. and Tarassova, T. (2000) 'A Russian privatization and corporate governance: What went wrong?', *Stanford Law Review*, 52, pp. 1731–1808. http://papers.ssrn.com/paper.taf?ABSTRACT_ID=181348

Brecht, M. and Roell, A. (1999) 'Blockholdings in Europe: An international comparison', *European Economic Review*, 43(4–6), pp. 1049–1056.

Coase, R. H. (1937) 'The nature of the firm', *Economica*, 4, pp. 386–405, reproduced in Barney J. B. and Ouchi, W. G. (eds) (1986) *Organisational Economics*, San Francisco, pp. 80–98.

Cochrane, P. (1997) Private e-mail communication to the author dated December 21 from Peter Cochrane, Head of Research, British Telecom, UK. http://www/labs.bt.com/people/cochrap/

—— (2000) 'Hard drive: bandwidth and brandwidth', *Daily Telegraph*, 6 April, London, http://www.telegraph.co.uk:80/et?ac=002781235701807&rtmo=wA0eAK5b&atmo=99999999&pg=/et/00/4/6/ecrhard06.html

Daft, R. L. and Lengel, R. H. (1984) 'Information richness: a new approach to managerial behaviour and organization design', *Research in Organizational Behaviour*, 6, pp. 191–233.

Dallas, L. L. (1988) 'Two models of corporate governance: beyond Berle & Means', *Journal of Law Reform*, University of Michigan, Fall, 22(1), pp. 19–116.

—— (1992) 'The control and conflicts of interest voting systems', *North Carolina Law Review*, November, 71(1).

Diermeier, D. and Myerson, R. B. (1999) 'Bicameralism and its consequences for the internal organisation of legislatures', *The American Economic Review*, 89(5), pp. 1182–1196.

Downs, A. (1967) *Inside Bureaucracy*, Boston, Mass., Little Brown.

Dunbar, R. I. M. (1993) 'Coevolution of neocortical size, group size and language in humans', *Behavioral and Brain Sciences*, 16, pp. 681–735.

ECGN (1997) 'The separation of ownership and control: a survey of 7 European countries', *Preliminary Report, Volume 1*, European Corporate Governance Network, 25 October, Brussels, http://www.ecgn.ulb.ac.be/ecgn/docs/pdf/eu97report.pdf

Ellerman, D. P. (1982) *The Socialization of Entrepreneurship: The Empresarial Division of the Caja Laboral Popular*, Sommerville, Mass., Industrial Co-operative Association.

Fox, M. B. and Heller, M. A. (1999) 'Lessons from fiascos in Russian corporate governance', Working paper No. 99-012, University of Michigan Law School; forthcoming in *New York University Law Review*, 2000, http://papers.ssrn.com/paper.taf?ABSTRACT_ID=203368

Gazette (1994) 'John Lewis Partnership', 76(38), pp. 956–958, 22 October, London.

Geanakpolos, J. and Milgrom, P. (1984) *Information, Planning and Control in Hierarchies*, Unpublished paper, March.

Givens, B. (1991) *Citizens' Utility Boards: Because Utilities Bear Watching*, Centre for Public Interest Law, University of San Diego School of Law, California.

Gordon, J. (1993) 'What is relational investing and how cumulative voting can play a role', Paper presented to Columbia University Law School's Centre for Law and Economic Studies' Conference on 'Relationship Investing: Possibilities, Patterns and Problems', New York Hilton, 6–7 May.

Hailsham, Lord (1978) *The Dilemma of Democracy: Diagnosis and Prescription*, London, Collins.

Hayek, F. H. A. (1945) 'The use of knowledge in society', *American Economic Review*, 35 (September), pp. 519–530.

Hippel, E. (1986) 'Lead users: a source of novel product concepts', *Management Science*, 32(7), July.

Hock, D. W. (1994) 'Institutions in the age of mindcrafting', Bionomics Annual Conference, October 22, San Francisco, California, http://www.cascadepolicy.org/dee_hock.htm

Hollingsworth, J. R. and Lindberg, L. N. (1985) 'The governance of the American economy: the role of markets, clans, hierarchies, and associative behaviour', in Streeck, W. and Schmitter, P. C. (eds), *Private Interest Government: Beyond Market and State*, pp. 221–267, London, Sage.

Jensen, M. C. (1993) 'The modern industrial revolution, exit, and the failure of internal control systems', *The Journal of Finance*, 48(3), July, pp. 831–880, http://papers.ssrn.com/paper.taf?abstract_id=93988

—— (2000) 'Value maximization, stakeholder theory, and the corporate objective function', forthcoming in Beer, M. and Norhia N. (eds), *Breaking the Code of Change*, Harvard Busines School Press.
http://papers.ssrn.com/paper.taf?abstract_id=220671

Kuhn, T. S. (1970) *The Structure of Scientific Revolutions* (2nd edn), University of Chicago Press.

Kurzwiel, R. (1999) *The Age of Spiritual Machines: When Computers Exceed Human Intelligence*, New York, Viking.

La Porta, R., Lopez-de-Silanes, R. F. and Schleifer, A. (1999) 'Corporate ownership around the world', *Journal of Finance*, 54, pp. 471–517.

Marschak, J. and Radner, R. (1972) *The Theory of Teams*, New Haven, Conn., Yale University Press.

Mathews, J. (1996) 'Organizational foundations of economic learning', *Human Systems Management*, 15, pp. 113–124.

Megginson, W. L. and Netter, J. M. (2000) 'From state to market: A survey of empirical studies on privatization', New York Stock Exchange Working Paper No. 98–05, http://papers.ssrn.com/paper.taf?ABSTRACT_ID=158313

Morrison, R. (1991) *We Build the Road As We Travel*, Philadelphia, New Society Press.

Murray, A. (1998) *Minority Report, Report on the Company Law Review Bill, 1997*, Parliamentary Joint Committee on Corporations and Securities, March, The Parliament of the Commonwealth of Australia, http://www.aph.gov.au/senate/committee/corp_sec_ctte/companylaw/minreport.htm

Neumann, J. von (1947) *Theory of Games and Economic Behaviour*, New Haven, Conn., Yale University Press.

OFWAT (1995) 'What's in the water companies' Operating Licences', http://www.open.gov.uk/ofwat/infonotes/appt.htm

Pejovich, S. (1990) *The Economics of Property Rights: Towards a Theory of Comparative Systems*, Netherlands, Kluwer.

Persson, T., Roland, G. and Tabellini, G. (1996) *Separation of Powers and Accountability: Towards a Formal Approach to Comparative Politics*, Working Paper, No. 100, Innocenzo Gasparini Institute for Economic Research (IGIER), July, Milan.

Penrose, E. (1956) 'Foreign investment and the growth of the firm', *Economic Journal*, LXVI, June, pp. 220–235.

Porter, M. E. (1992) *Capital Choices: Changing the Way America Invests in Industry*, Research report presented to the Council on Competitiveness and co-sponsored by The Harvard Business School, Boston, Mass.

Pound, J. (1992) 'Beyond takeovers: politics comes to corporate control', *Harvard Business Review*, March–April, pp. 83–93.

—— (1993) 'The rise of the political model of corporate governance and corporate control', *New York University Law Review*, 68(5), November, pp. 1003–1071.

Shannon, C. E. (1949), *The Mathematical Theory of Communications*, Urbana, Ill., University of Illinois Press.

Simon, H. A., (1957) *Models of Man*, New York, John Wiley.

—— (1962) 'The architecture of complexity', *Proceedings of the American Philosophical Society*, 106, December, pp. 467–482.

Sternberg, E. (1997) 'The defects of stakeholder theory', *Corporate Governance: An International Review*, 5(1), January, pp. 3–10.

Thomas, H. and Logan, C. (1982) *Mondragon: An Economic Analysis*, London, George Allen & Unwin.

Tricker, R. I. (1994) *International Corporate Governance*, Singapore, Simon & Schuster.

Turnbull, C. S. S. (1975) *Democratising the Wealth of Nations*, Sydney, The Company Directors' Association, http://cog.kent.edu/lib/TurnbullBook/TurnbullBook.htm

Turnbull, S. (1991) 'Re-inventing corporations', *Human Systems Management*, 10(3), pp. 169–186.

—— (1992a) 'New strategies for structuring society from a cashflow paradigm', paper presented to the Fourth Annual Conference of the Society for the Advancement of Socio-Economics held at the Graduate School of Management, University of California, Irvine, Calif. in a 'track' on the Third Way, 27 March, http://cog.kent.edu/lib/turnbull1/turnbull1.html

—— (1992b) 'Positions vacant, wanted: corporate whistle-blowers', *JASSA The Journal of the Securities Institute of Australia*, 4, pp. 2–6, December, Sydney.

—— (1993) 'Improving corporate structure and ethics: a case for corporate "Senates"', *Director's Monthly*, Washington DC, National Association of Company Directors, 17(5), May, pp. 1–4.

—— (1994a) 'Building a stakeholder democracy', in Economic Planning Advisory Commission, *Ambitions for our Future: Australian Views*, Canberra, Australian Government Publishing Service, October, pp. 83–90.

—— (1994b) 'Stakeholder democracy: redesigning the governance of firms and bureaucracies', *Journal of Socio-Economics*, 23(3), Fall, pp. 321–360.

—— (1995) 'Innovations in corporate governance: the Mondragon experience', *Corporate Governance: An International Review*, 3(3), July, pp. 167–180. http://cog.kent.edu/lib/Turnbull6.htm

—— (1997a) 'Stakeholder governance: a cybernetic and property rights analysis', *Corporate Governance: An International Review*, 5(1), January, pp. 11–23, http://cog.kent.edu/lib/turnbull6/turnbull6.html

—— (1997b) 'The application of cybernetic knowledge in governing society', International conference on 'Knowledge, Economy and Society', University of Montreal, Quebec, 3 July.

—— (1998) 'Should ownership last forever?', *Journal of Socio–Economics*, 27(3), pp. 341–363, http://papers.ssrn.com/paper.taf?abstract_id=137382

—— (2000a) 'Corporate charters with competitive advantages', *St. Johns Law Review*, New York, St. Johns University, 74(44), pp. 101–159.

—— (2000b) 'Democratizing employee ownership', *Director's Monthly*, Washington, DC, National Association of Corporate Directors, 24(5), p. 13. Full text listed as 'Employee governance' at http://cog.kent.edu/lib/turnbull3.html

—— (2000c) 'Gouvernement d'entreprise: Théories, enjeux et paradigmes' (Corporate governance: theories, challenges and paradigms), *Gouvernance: Revenue Internationale*, 1(1), pp. 11–43, Montreal. English text at http://papers.ssrn.com/paper.taf?abstract_id=221350

Weiner, N. (1948) *Cybernetics*, New York, John Wiley.

Whyte, W. F. and Whyte, K. K. (1988) *Making Mondragon: The Growth and Dynamics of the Worker Co-operative Complex*, Ithaca, NY, ILR Press.

Williamson, O. E. (1975) *Markets and Hierarchies: Analysis and Anti-trust Implications*, New York, Free Press.

—— (1985) *The Economic Institutions of Capitalism*, New York, Free Press.

Wruck, K. H. and Jensen, M. C. (1994) 'Science, specific knowledge, and total quality management', *Journal of Accounting and Economics*, 18, pp. 247–287, http://papers.ssrn.com/paper.taf?abstract_id=47731

Zey, M. (1999) 'Major changes in corporate strategy and structure of the Fortune 500 in the 1990s', Paper presented to the 11th Annual Meeting of the Society for the Advancement of Socio-Economics, University of Wisconsin, Madison, 11 July. (Working paper available from author at Texas A&M University.)

10 Member participation in mutuals

A theoretical model

Johnston Birchall and Richard Simmons

On 27 June, 2000, the members of Europe's biggest mutual – Standard Life – voted to retain its mutual status, turning down the prospect of windfalls of between £2000 and £6000 in favour of member ownership. But what does member ownership mean in practice? How involved should customer-members be in the running of a mutual? What are the obligations of a board of directors towards their members? It is difficult to defend the record of mutuals in their relations with members. Standard Life is fairly typical. In the aftermath of the demutualisation vote, one analyst pointed out how the 'pathetic turnouts at mutual annual general meetings' indicated that there was much less pressure on a mutual board than on one that answered to shareholders (Steel, 2000). Another pointed to the decision of the Board to give £5 million to sponsor a golf tournament, 'without so much as mentioning it to policyholders' (Paul, 2000a). The £10 million spent by the Board on defending its mutual status included an advertising campaign that explained that mutuality meant not having shareholders, but did not stress its democratic accountability to members. The Board was criticised by its opponents for being less than honest in its estimates of what the windfall payouts would be if it did demutualise, and in failing to admit that current policy-holders' policies would be protected in any case. It was also criticised by its supporters for refusing to disclose the full cost of the television advertising campaign and for the decision not to tell endowment mortgage holders about potential shortfalls in their profits before the vote (Paul, 2000b).

These kinds of questions were being raised immediately, on the morning after the announcement of the vote. A leader in one of the major Scottish newspapers commented that it was a 'wake-up call, to communicate better with, and take more account of, its members' (*The Herald*, 2000). The Chief Executive of the trade body, Scottish Financial Enterprise, said Standard Life 'had realised it had to improve its communications with its policy-holders. Standard Life has rightly learned its lessons about how they communicate'. The Chief Executive of the mutual agreed, saying 'the company has got to better sell the benefits of mutuality to members' (Flanagan, 2000). The Chairman commented, 'We have learned a number of lessons. Over the coming months, we will be reviewing all the ways the company interacts with its members' (McConnell, 2000).

In theory, there are two principles that should be guiding a mutual's member relations strategy. Derived from the Rochdale co-operative principles, these are democratic control and member benefits (Birchall, 1997). All people who are users of the business should be able to become members, and members should ultimately be in control of the business. They delegate day-to-day decisions to an elected board, but should have the final say about important decisions at annual and special general meetings or, if a constitutional change is proposed, in a postal ballot. Members should, in return, receive benefits proportional to their dealings with the mutual. In order for these two principles to be put into practice, a certain minimum of member participation is required.

Staying with the example of Standard Life, let us now examine the practical implications of these points. First, Standard Life has 4.5 million policy-holders, but only the 2.3 million who have with-profits policies are allowed to be members. Already, the democratic control principle has been compromised. Then it is hard to see how the 2.3 million members are exercising control, since the board will be elected at annual general meetings where there is a very small turnout; even the special general meeting at which the recent vote was announced was attended by only 800 people. Some mutuals, such as the Nationwide Building Society, do now give their members a postal ballot for electing the Board. However, in the absence of any member organisation, it is difficult for ordinary members to get elected. In 'normal times' most mutual boards will be self-selected and will not face much serious opposition. Only when they face a demutualisation ballot or very poor trading results will members become organized independently. Second, the decision to reward members in proportion to their business is up to the board; in the case of Standard Life, the chief executive announced straight after the ballot that there would not be a loyalty payment to members. Some building societies (notably Britannia) have introduced loyalty bonuses based on the number of years people have been members. However, this is part of a business strategy decided by the board, rather than the democratic decision of all the members to award a 'dividend on purchases' that used to be the practice in consumer co-ops.

One reason for this 'democratic deficit' in mutuals is that a board has very little incentive to foster democracy. The 'tendency to oligarchy' noticed by Michels (1949) is an almost universal phenomenon, and can only be countered by either an outside force (such as a social movement or interest group) or, more unusually, by a commitment to democratic values within the board itself. In the UK, mutuals have not been part of a social movement since terminating building societies gave way to permanent societies in the late nineteenth century. It seems that it has been too much to expect that, in the absence of outside pressures such as the threat of demutualisation, a board will be much concerned with democratic renewal. Another reason for the democratic deficit is that it is very difficult to communicate with, and organise, large numbers of members. There are three issues here. First, there is the high cost and administrative challenge of contacting and eliciting a response from literally millions of people; the 2.3 million members of Standard Life are not untypical, and some building societies have many more. Second, there is the problem of member apathy. Turnout at AGMs is traditionally low, and even in the extreme circumstances of a vote to demutualise, less than half the Standard Life members (1.1 million) bothered to vote. Third, there is a wider problem about the lack of appreciation of the nature of mutual businesses. According to Llewellyn and Holmes (1991) it is not evident that the public any longer understands or cares about mutuality.

In the rest of this chapter, we shall be considering this problem, asking what makes members of large-scale mutuals and co-operatives participate, and whether it is feasible for a Board to have a strategy for ensuring participation. If the answer to these questions is 'No', then debate becomes limited to a purely economic discussion, and a serious question is raised about whether mutuals should demutualise in order to gain the disciplines of the market. These include scrutiny by shareholders, the signals given by a floating share price, and the threat of a hostile take-over if the business is over-capitalised or under-performing. Indeed, it seems that some mutuals have already found these arguments compelling in moving voluntarily towards shareholder ownership. In order to answer the questions concerning participation, we shall first present a theoretical model of what makes people participate, and then apply this to the situation of large-scale mutuals.

What makes members participate?

Before identifying theories of motivation, it is important to understand what we mean by participation. In a study of the social psychology of co-operation, Argyle defines it as: 'acting together in a co-ordinated way at work, leisure, or in social relationships, in the pursuit of shared goals, the enjoyment of the joint activity, or simply furthering the relationship' (1991, p4). If we substitute for 'at work, leisure, or in social relationships' the phrase 'in a mutual form of organisation', we get a useful definition of participation. We also get a distinction between three different types of participation. Argyle clarifies these as co-operation towards material rewards; communal relationships; and co-ordination. These are quite similar to three types found in one of the authors' research studies into housing co-operatives:

- Taking part in decision-making in the co-operative;
- Carrying out tasks that further the co-operative's aims; and
- Taking part in the social life associated with the co-operative.

Taking part in decision-making includes all the democratic aspects of a co-operative or mutual: attendance at general meetings, becoming a committee member, forming sub-committees and so on. This is usually treated as the crucial type, because without it decision-making is not democratic, and managers and directors are not called to account. Carrying out tasks includes all unpaid activities for which members volunteer. In small co-operatives that cannot afford to hire paid workers, it is crucial to the organisation's survival. Even in larger ones it can be important as a supplement to paid work that increases the quality and effectiveness of the organisation. It provides an alternative for those who wish to express their commitment but find participation in formal meetings difficult. Then there is participation in the social life associated with the organisation. Co-operatives and mutuals vary in the extent to which they offer more than just the meeting of instrumental goals. Some have social activities as a by-product, others use them consciously to create a wider sense of community. In these cases, participation also has the attraction of being accessible to those who find meetings difficult or unattractive, and it utilises skills that members often already have in organising cultural and fund-raising events. The propositions developed by theories of motivation ought to take into account all three of these types of participation (Birchall, 1988a). While in mutuals it is the first – taking part in decision-making – that is crucial to ensuring that the organisation remains democratic and accountable, we argue later in the chapter that the other types are also important. In particular, they underpin participation in decision-making with a mobilisation of 'latent' member potential around core values, and a building-up of institutional networks.

There is a hierarchy of participation in decision-making, beginning with the giving out of information, moving up through receiving of information, consultation, member involvement towards genuine member control (see Figure 10.1). The higher the lêvel reached, the more genuine the attempt on the part of the boards of mutuals to be in practice what they are in principle – member-controlled businesses. This does not mean necessarily that members will always want to be at the top of the hierarchy. They will appreciate good communications and consultation as well. The level reached depends on the issues being discussed, and on a prior agreement or understanding as to what should be decided by the members, and what should be delegated to their representatives on the Board, or to top managers. Mutuals that ask members to vote on important issues can, and should, also do market research among members and send them information regularly via a newsletter. They can go further, and follow the example of the Oxford, Swindon & Gloucester Co-operative Society, that has produced a series of 'clarity guides' for members. These guides seek to make the annual report, the implications of corporate governance, and the way members can make their voice heard clear for everyone (Walker, 1997).

Member control
Involvement of menbers in decision-making
Consultation with members
Receiving information from members
Giving out information to members

Figure 10.1 A hierarchy of member involvement

It all depends what can be expected from participation. In large-scale co-ops and mutuals, participation has traditionally been seen as 'non-accelerating'; a few elected officers attempt to serve the mass membership. This makes sense in terms of the fact that there are 'diminishing marginal returns' (Oliver, 1984) for active participation in decision-making and corporate governance, so that beyond a certain point new contributions produce smaller – or even zero – increments in the collective good. Once the various 'jobs' are being done, there is little marginal pay-off for participation, and free-riding becomes likely. However, where this situation becomes acute and oligarchy sets in, there is the danger of losing touch with the 'masses'. Later in the chapter we shall be suggesting a strategy for maximising member participation through realising the 'mobilisation potential' (Klandermans and Oegema, 1987) of members, and making their membership meaningful.

There are very few studies of participation in large-scale mutuals. We might expect the literature on consumer co-ops to be helpful, because in this sector the level of participation has been an issue for a very long time. A study published in 1965 found that participation in British consumer co-ops varied between 1 and 5 per cent of members, but was highest in those co-ops where political parties or other oppositional groups of members were active (Ostergaard and Halsey, 1965). A more recent study, an International Joint Project on Co-operative Democracy, asked how member democracy could be made meaningful in large consumer co-ops. The project presents several interesting case studies about how this can be done. However, it does not ask the underlying question concerning what makes people participate (International Joint Project, 1995). The conventional wisdom is that participation correlates strongly with social class and status. A study by Pestoff, drawing on data from a 1971 survey in Sweden, found the opposite, that participation in farmer and consumer co-operatives was correlated with a lower than average education level, low income, and manual work. However, he also found that these correlated with an intervening variable, which was age. Older people were more likely to be active, and to have a lower income, education level and so on (Pestoff, 1991). This study did not tackle the question of why individuals decide to participate (though Pestoff developed an interactive model of participation and organisational development, which we shall be incorporating into our model below).

If we want to know why people participate, there is no alternative to the application of some fresh thinking on the subject. First, we summarise the literature on the pre-conditions for participation, and on what makes people participate for the first time. Then we present two contrasting theories of motivation, one individualistic and one mutualistic. We summarise five different attitudes to participation that explain why some people build up a commitment and others do not. In each case, we apply the theories to the situation of large-scale mutuals and attempt to generalise about what the elements of a participation strategy might be. Finally, we suggest a strategy for participation based on a dynamic model of mobilisation and making membership meaningful.

Pre-conditions for participation

Ever since Almond and Verba's seminal work on 'civic culture' (1963) there has been a general awareness that participation is necessary to safeguard democracy, but that it is difficult to promote. It is dependent not only on a cognitive orientation that can be affected by the general level of education, but also on affective and evaluative attitudes that are deeply rooted in the experiences of nations, groups and individuals (Almond and Verba, 1989). There is a need for a detailed theory of motivation. Existing theories have identified correlations between participation levels and pre-conditions (such as the level of education, income group, and personal characteristics such as age and gender), outcomes (such as self-confidence and enhanced knowledge), and the immediate context (issues that are likely to trigger action). These still leave an explanatory gap concerning why a person will, in a particular instance, choose to participate. Theories identifying immediate causes, such as a rational calculation of the costs and benefits involved, or a desire to defend one's community or to express deeply held beliefs, get closer to a full explanation. Yet in focusing on instrumental, communitarian or expressive aspects (as summed up by Parry *et al.*, 1992), they tend to provide only partial explanations.

Figure 10.2 summarises the literature on the pre-conditions for participation. In deciding to participate, people who have experience of participation and are aware of the opportunities are advantaged, although if this previous experience was bad it can lead to disillusionment and resistance to further involvement in similar organisations. The people most likely to participate will be those who have the *time and energy*. However, busy people can often make time for more commitments, and the link between employment status and family commitments and willingness to participate is not strong. Mutuals will not, in any case, be asking members to put in a great deal of time. *Personal resources* are important. There is a correlation between income, educational level and participation. Those mutuals whose members are middle to high earners and have a higher than

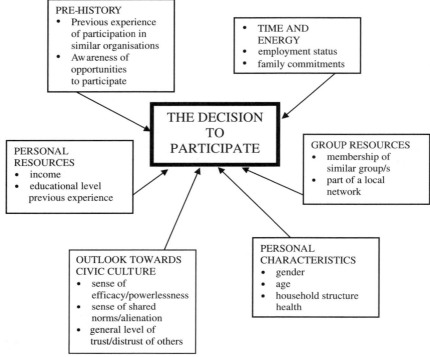

Figure 10.2 Pre-conditions for participation (derived from the literature).

average educational level will find it easier to foster participation, but again the association is weak. Consumer co-ops that have traditionally appealed to lower-income people have a better record of participation, and capitalise on the previous experience of people who have participated in trade unions and political parties. Such '*group resources*' are important, and it is likely that participants will be found from among those for whom 'joining in' is a familiar activity. A person's *outlook on civic culture* is important for two main reasons. First, those who feel a sense of powerlessness or alienation from mainstream society are less likely to participate. This might affect, for instance, credit unions working among people who are socially excluded, but one would assume that this is less of a problem for financial mutuals whose members are from the middle classes. The latter assumption might be over-optimistic, however; for example, increasing societal individualism and atomisation may affect the outlook on civic culture of those from the middle classes, despite the fact that they may be better resourced to act. Second, it should also be noted that a distrust of the 'system' and a sense that powerful people are making decisions on our behalf can also lead to participation, but of a more oppositional sort.

Finally, Pestoff's finding, noted above, that members of co-operatives had lower incomes than average and were more likely to be manual workers, reminds us that these generalisations about the pre-conditions for participation may hold more generally, but are not a very accurate predictor of who participates in co-ops. One of the main purposes of co-operatives has always been to provide organisational expression for the needs of low-income people, and so it is not surprising that they contradict the more general picture.

An individualistic theory of participation

In choosing an explanatory model, we have to consider the question of whether people are inherently individualistic or co-operative. This is a controversial question in social psychology (Argyle, 1991) and in epistemology between methodological individualists and communitarians (Avineri and De-Shalit, 1992). In the 1970s and 1980s, the debate was dominated by a paradigm in evolutionary biology that most behaviour could be explained in terms of 'selfish' genes. It was thought that, even though co-operation was often a more rewarding strategy, it was hindered by a 'prisoners' dilemma' in which lack of trust led individuals to 'defect' (Dawkins, 1976). This viewpoint has been modified by insights from game theory which suggest that, given time (and certain other specifiable conditions), self-seeking individuals can learn to co-operate (Axelrod, 1984; Dawkins, 1989). Sociologists emphasise the importance of habitual behaviour, the growth of social solidarity, and resulting high-trust relationships, in modifying the individual's calculation of utility (Birchall, 1989). In their study of participation by political party members, Whiteley and Seyd combine rational choice and social psychological theories, in what they call a hybrid 'incentives' model (1998). We propose something similar in choosing two approaches, one individualistic, and the other communitarian. However, rather than merging them into one theory, we intend to keep them separate, using what Denzin calls 'theoretical triangulation' – using multiple perspectives in relation to the same set of objects. As Denzin suggests, they may also lead to a more comprehensive understanding – 'a final interpretive network might combine features from interpretations that were initially contradictory' (1989, p243).

The individualist approach we examine was developed by George Homans in the late 1950s. It is a blend of behaviourist psychology and 'elementary economics' (Homans, 1974) which assumes that people are motivated by individual rewards and punishments, and provides a set of quite simple generalisations about how they interact. The mutual approach was developed by a sociologist, P. I. Sorokin, who assumed that people can be motivated by collective goals, a sense of community and co-operative values (Sorokin, 1954).

Homans assumes that human behaviour is motivated by payoffs – it depends on the amount of reward and punishment it fetches. Figure 10.3

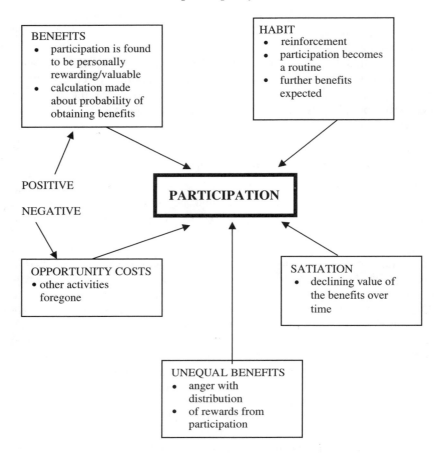

Figure 10.3 Individualistic variables affecting participation
Source: Derived from Homans (1974).

summarises his generalisations. First, people will continue to participate if they find it personally beneficial. What they see as a benefit can be anything from money, through personal status to opportunities to meet others, or to gain greater understanding or confidence. Those wishing to promote participation will have to ask themselves how it can be made beneficial for members. Because people vary in what makes them interested, a broad approach is needed, providing a mixture of 'rewards'. Take, for example, an appeal to members to vote for the Board. Some may vote because they are pleased to be asked, others because they are curious to find out what type of person is standing for election, and others because it makes them feel personally important. Some may only respond if their voting form is entered into a 'prize draw'.

Second, people make a rational calculation about the probability of obtaining the benefits they value. The strategy has to be consistent and not disappoint people. If members are promised a chance to take part, for instance, in the testing of a product, the promised incentives should meet their expectations. Third, the more members who value the benefits, the more likely they are to participate. This is a key finding for mutuals, because they provide long-term products such as mortgages and pensions that are valued highly by members; if they do not participate actively, it will not be because of apathy. When people do participate, they do not make these calculations about benefits every time; that would in itself be a costly exercise. Once they have been induced to take part the first time, they may get into a habit of participation that keeps them going to meetings, or filling in voting forms. In general, this is good news for those promoting participation, provided that a positive 'affirmation' of their motivation to participate continues to be provided.

Turning now to the negative side of the equation (see Figure 10.3), we note that participation will eventually drop off if the benefits cease to match expectations, or if their value to the participants declines over time. If people find participation less rewarding than they used to, a 'modification' of their motivations to participate becomes likely, and new incentives have to be found. Every so often, members will want to calculate or recalculate the opportunity costs of participation. The nature of these costs varies from individual to individual as much as do the benefits. They vary depending on what else a person wants to do with his or her time. Homans says *'for an activity to incur cost, an alternative and rewarding activity must be there to be foregone'* (1961, p59). Unemployed people will find participation less costly than those with a full-time job. Women who have to look after children will find direct costs in arranging child care, either in paying a babysitter, or indirectly in incurring an obligation to do the same for someone else. More generally, there are a wide variety of personal costs associated with participating. These may include the degree of interest or boredom felt in a meeting, the degree of discomfort at having to sit for a long time, feelings of inadequacy at not being able to understand what is going on, and so on. They have the effect – other things being equal – of lowering participation in the long run. A strategy that minimises costs – by providing comfortable rooms to meet in, child care arrangements, transport to meetings, easy ways to send back a voting card or a questionnaire – will succeed better.

Members will have views on how the benefits from participation should be distributed. Those who take part at cost to themselves may get angry or frustrated if others get the same benefits without participating – this is the familiar 'free-rider' problem. If those who participate can receive benefits conditional on their participation, so much the better. As co-operative promoters observe, once people have been disappointed in the results of their efforts, it becomes much harder to interest them in new initiatives (see Levi, 1998). One failure can have repercussions well into the future.

There are, of course, severe limitations to Homans' approach. It is reductionist, deriving propositions about human behaviour from experiments on animals and on human subjects in experimental conditions. It is individualist, assuming that if we know about individual behaviour we can generalise about social behaviour, and this does not taken into account the effects of belonging to a group. It is heavily dependent on American sources, and other cultures might not value individual rewards so highly (Homans, 1961, p7). Most important for our purposes is the fact that when applied to mutuals and co-operatives it only works well where respondents really do have an instrumental view. In a study of six housing co-ops, for instance, it only illuminated one case study where the co-op was dominated by an instrumental attitude among members (Birchall, 1984). When participants themselves express more mutual sentiments, it seems unethical to distort their worldview by converting expressions of collective sentiment and purpose into the language of individual benefit. We need a theory that can take at face value the views of participants who explain their motivation in mutual terms. For this we can turn to Sorokin.

A mutual theory of participation

Sorokin identifies five key independent variables that have direct effects on levels of participation – duration, extensity, adequacy, intensity and purity, and he treats participation as a dependent variable. Together they make up a quite comprehensive theory of what makes people participate (see Figure 10.4), but with one limitation; Sorokin was concerned with people joining together in groups, and did not consider the intervening effects of participation being mediated through a formal organisation. For this we add a sixth variable derived from Pestoff (1991), which we call 'organisational strategy'. Three of the variables, adequacy, intensity and purity, are internal to the experiences of participants, and they vary positively with participation; the more there are of them, the greater the participation. The other three are external factors that have a more complex relationship with participation, varying negatively or positively depending on the strategy, or lack of it, taken by the organisation to promote participation.

Adequacy refers to whether an organisation is succeeding in its aims – the greater the adequacy, the greater the participation. This is obvious, since people will not take part if they think an organisation will fail, and if it succeeds will be encouraged to see their contribution as important. This is a communitarian restatement of Homans' first proposition about reward, though in terms of common goals. Co-operative promoters are well aware of this generalisation. For instance, in an important book on the running of agricultural co-ops, Parnell says 'The degree of member participation within any co-operative depends largely on the impact which the co-operative

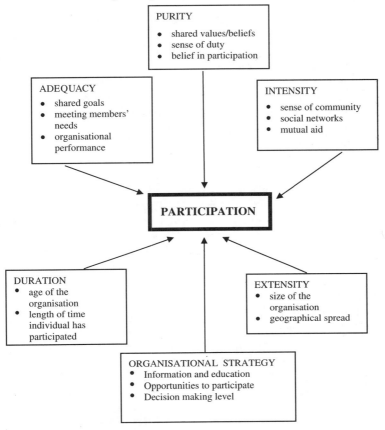

Figure 10.4 Mutualistic variables affecting participation
Source: Derived from Sorokin (1954).

has on the daily lives of its individual members' (1995, p105). He draws from this the lesson that co-operatives have to focus on providing goods and services that meet their needs. There is beginning to be a general realisation among promoters that, unless mutuals and co-operatives identify what the members need and are good at delivering it, members will not participate.

Intensity concerns the sense of community among members – the greater the intensity, the greater the participation. This is because if people have emotional ties to each other they will care about each other's welfare, be more committed to improving their economy and environment, and will put a higher value on any improvements they make. It is no accident that some of the most successful co-operative movements in the world are expressions of regional identity – for instance, the Mondragon co-operatives in the Basque region of Spain and the credit union movement in the

French-speaking region of Quebec in Canada. Unfortunately, from the point of view of a promoter of member participation, the successive mergers of co-ops and mutuals into large-scale national or even transnational companies makes such regional identification less likely. However, there can be a small 'loyalty effect' in the region in which the head offices of mutuals are based; Standard Life, in its campaign to stay mutual, emphasised the contribution it makes to the Scottish economy. Another small effect is the loyalty and sense of attachment members feel towards their mutual's brand name.

Purity concerns the values underlying the motivation to participate; the greater the purity, the greater the participation. In any organisation some members will derive satisfaction from knowing that the organisation is working according to certain deeply held principles, and so, in Homans' terms, they will find it rewarding to participate – the greater the purity, the greater the participation. The demutualisation debate has stimulated some members to set up defence organisations, both at the level of an individual mutual such as Standard Life, and a whole industry, as in the 'Save Our Building Societies' association. This is a very important development, as it shows that there is a small minority of members who can be called upon to represent the majority and who derive personal satisfaction from doing so. There is also a minority who have an internalised sense of duty or obligation to participate when asked. The reason why some people feel a sense of duty and others do not is something we are still working on, but we know that it can be strengthened by both formal and informal education in co-operative values and principles. Particularly valuable is the kind of learning that occurs naturally in a co-operative in which the business side and the democratic side of the co-op are well integrated (Jakobsen, 1995).

Sometimes commitment to co-operation alone is enough to foster participation, but when co-operatives are seen as part of a wider social movement, this can have a marked impact on participation. For instance, participation in European consumer co-operatives was high when co-operative women's guilds were campaigning more generally on behalf of women. Participation in the wholefood co-operatives of the USA and the UK during the 1970s derived from a wider sense of mission. When consumer co-operatives see their role not primarily as a retailer but as a consumer movement – in the UK in the last century, in Japan in the post-war period – high levels of participation follow. As the UK Co-operative Bank and, more recently, the co-operative insurance society (CIS) have demonstrated, mutuals that set out to meet members' desire for an ethical or environmentally aware business policy will have no trouble in fostering loyalty among people who share their declared values (though they have yet to build on this by encouraging active participation).

These three factors – intensity, adequacy and purity – are internal to the members' own reasoning about why they participate. Then there are three factors that are external to the members' own motivations. First, *duration*. It is tempting to use the analogy of human ageing, and to say that organisations are young, become middle-aged and then grow old. Over time, democracy is likely to turn into oligarchy, and participation declines (Michels, 1949). This happens because participation becomes routinised, fewer important decisions need to be made, these can be left to trusted leaders, and so oligarchy sets in (in Oliver's (1984) interpretation, participation increasingly provides diminishing marginal returns and free-riding becomes more likely). *Extensity* is the size of an organisation and the nature of its geographical base. Other things being equal, the greater the extensity, the lower the participation. There are good reasons for this. First, there is a limit to the amount of territory with which people identify. In Western Europe, members of consumer co-operatives have resisted amalgamation into larger units partly because they can only identify with their own village or town (Birchall, 1994). Second, there are limits to effective participatory democracy. These can be seen quite easily in meetings; there are natural limits such as the extent to which a voice will carry, the length of time a meeting would need to take if all wish to be heard, and so on (Dahl and Tufte, 1973). The generalisation holds: the larger the organisation, the lower the level of participation.

In Sorokin's model, duration and extensity are fixed entities that always vary negatively with participation. However, organisational strategies can make a difference. For instance, it is not necessarily true that the older the organisation, the more likely it is to lose its sense of purpose or to deform. The UK Co-operative Bank was already a hundred years old when it embarked on an expansion plan based on an ethical policy that has become a model for other co-operatives and financial service mutuals (Birchall, 1998). In this case, good leadership, backed up by directors committed to serving the interests of consumers, infused the business with a new sense of purpose. Nor is size always a predictor of low participation. Some large consumer co-ops have developed methods by which participation can be promoted; the creation of regional democratic structures, the use of newsletters and other media to increase people's knowledge, the mobilisation of large numbers behind consumer campaigns, and so on. Also, large size can be combined with decentralisation, as in the Japanese *han* system of large co-operatives that have within them hundreds of small consumer groups (Nomura, 1993).

This is why we have added to Sorokin's model a sixth factor identified by Pestoff, which we call *organisational strategy*. Pestoff insists that: 'Membership activity is not just an expression of individual preferences or predisposition to participate, but also, in part, a response by members to the options for participation offered by the organisation through its structures' (1991, p63).

Membership activity is explainable in terms of the interaction between members and their organisations, and is primarily the product of decisions made by its leaders rather than by its members. Structural differences between organisations explain a major part of the differences in member participation. We have already noted one of these structural factors – size – but add here the number of opportunities to participate, the information and education policy of the organisation, and the levels at which decisions are made. The more the leaders – elected representatives and managers – provide opportunities for participation, inform and educate the members, and enable them to make genuine decisions at a low level in the organisational structure, the higher the level of participation is likely to be.

Feedback and synergic effects

In practice, each of these six variables makes its own contribution to making membership meaningful and is present in varying strengths, fluctuating in quite complex but reasonably predictable ways. Depending on how they work together, they set up either a virtuous or a vicious cycle; strengths or weaknesses in each independent variable tend to reinforce each other, and to have a cumulative impact on levels of participation. Once a virtuous cycle is entrained, the effect is 'synergic'; that is, the combined strength of several variables all working in the same direction is greater than if they were working separately (see Figure 10.5). For this reason, interventions to improve a mutual or co-operative in one area will usually have knock-on effects in others.

For instance, it is generally thought that (following Michels, 1949) duration also varies negatively with purity; over time, we might expect commitment to the organisation to decline, and oligarchy to set in. In mutuals, this is what has happened. On the other hand, sometimes duration works the other way, in that over time habits build up, and commitment to the organisation and participation in its structures may be taken for granted. This explains the great tenacity of some active consumer co-op members, who have continued to participate on boards despite continual economic setbacks going back decades. Duration varies positively with intensity; the sense of community builds up over time. Adequacy has quite a strong relationship with intensity; the greater the sense of community, the greater the value placed on the effective management of a mutual or co-operative (though it does not guarantee the means to do so). Conversely, a well-managed organisation usually leads to a strengthening of community. Similarly, the sense of commitment to self-managing (purity) produces a drive to succeed, while success reinforces commitment. A sense of community usually produces a felt commitment to the values of democracy and co-operation, and it makes it easier for members to agree common goals.

In practice, these three positive variables are so intertwined that it is often difficult to separate them. Certainly, when asked about their

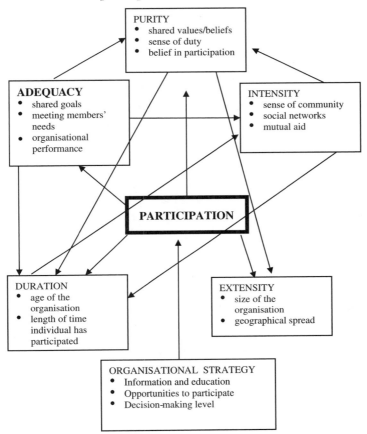

Figure 10.5 Feedback between mutualistic variables and participation, and synergy between each other

motivations, active members may switch from one justification to another, even within the same sentence, without feeling the need to unravel them. Improvements in the organisation's performance on one variable should affect the others, and so, if improvement in one area is difficult, attention to another where change is easier may be a good strategy. However, it is possible to run a successful mutual without much intensity or purity, provided the members really desire what it has to offer; in this case, Homans' theory becomes more applicable.

Just because participation is classed as a dependent variable, it does not mean that it has no effects. There is feedback of a direct kind on the variables analysed above. The quality of the participation experience is important in itself. Members may want tangible benefits, have some sense of community and some embryonic commitment to working together, but be put off by the high personal opportunity-costs of taking part. This may be because meetings are too long, exhausting, difficult to understand, held in a stuffy or uncomfortable meeting hall, or because the costs in child care or lost wages are too expensive. For this reason, it is important for the organisation's strategy to recognise what can reasonably be expected of, and by, members in the participation process. If participation is enjoyable, informative, and enhances the self-image of the participants, it acts on the other variables to strengthen and confirm them. Whatever else they do, promoters must cut down the opportunity costs as much as possible: here Homans and Sorokin are in agreement.

Attitudes to participation

What do we know about attitudes to participation? In a later edition of his work, Homans provides a five-fold categorisation of responses to the demand for participation (1974 – see Figure 10.6). First, there are the *true believers*, who are prepared to participate in order to achieve common goals. Second, there are the *freeloaders*, who want to obtain the benefits without sharing in the opportunity costs of participation. Third, there are the *sceptical conformers*, who do not expect participation to work, do not participate, but otherwise tend not to cause trouble. Fourth, there are the *holdouts*, who refuse to conform but stay in the participation structures and withhold approval, often spreading gossip and misinformation, but always injecting a note of cynicism and suspicion into the proceedings. Last, there are the *escapees*, who are so disenchanted that, given a chance, they will leave the process altogether; in the case of tenant-controlled housing (ownership and management co-ops) this desire to escape may be literal and involve a move of home.

The consequences from different mixes of these types are quite easy to predict. There are at least four different scenarios. In the first, there is a substantial minority of true believers willing to participate in order to represent members in general. They have a 'pool' of supporters from whom replacement committee members can be drawn when current members get tired or 'burn-out'. True believers may carp about the freeloaders, even worry that the latter will destabilise the organisation, but usually their worries are exaggerated (see Birchall, 1988a). In the second scenario, there is a small pool of true believers, and a large majority of freeloaders. Unless some freeloaders can be persuaded to become true believers, disillusion and 'burn-out' will occur sooner, and there will be no replenishment of the participatory group. In the third scenario, there are some true believers, and some freeloaders, but a substantial minority are skeptics, who are suspicious, and holdouts, who are actively wanting to demutualise the organisation, given the chance. A participation strategy needs to aim at the conversion of holdouts and sceptics into at the very least freeloaders, or to find ways of expelling them from membership (in our terms, making them 'escapees') as some building societies have done with active

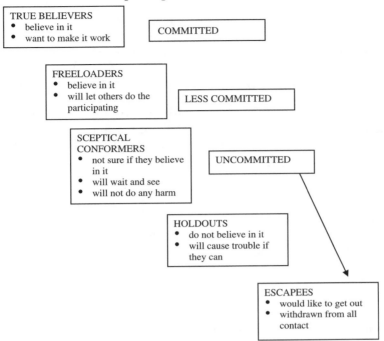

Figure 10.6 Individual attitudes to participation
Source: Derived from Homans (1974).

campaigners for demutualisation. This expulsion of members has caused some controversy, because it looks on the surface to be unfair. However, a closer examination of the co-operative principle of open membership shows that, while co-ops and mutuals should offer membership to all those who can make use of the organisation's products or services, they should also apply a test of 'co-operativeness' (Birchall, 1997). This means they are not just within their rights to exclude people who do not share a belief in the principles, but it is their duty to do so. In this case, the observation that 'people no longer understand or care about mutuality' has potentially serious repercussions – mutuals could be faced with a 'death wish' scenario of expelling large sections of the membership! The only other options are demutualisation or the development of a strategy that mobilises the potential of members and maximises their active participation.

Towards a strategy for member participation

The distinction between true believers and freeloaders can be used to develop a quite sophisticated member participation strategy. Some consumer co-ops are now targeting three types of member:

1. Those 'true believers' who can be persuaded to train as potential board members;
2. Those who can be formed into a kind of 'supporters club' who believe in the aims of the organisation and will participate through voting or attending annual meetings or social events; and
3. Those who believe vaguely in the ethos of the organisation, will not participate, but want to be kept informed and to have their views canvassed occasionally.

This points to a strategy of three levels, with the aims and methods used to promote participation being different for each type of potential participant. The argument is that large-scale co-ops and mutuals do not need mass participation. They need a small group of a few hundred active members who emerge from the membership, are prepared to interest themselves in the business, to stand for elections to boards, and to represent members in general. They need a much larger group to be knowledgeable about the organisation, to develop some loyalty and pride in it, to have some appreciation of its distinctive values, and to vote intelligently for their representatives. They need to keep in touch with the mass of members through market-research type methods, but also through asking them to endorse important decisions.

The problem with this approach is that it too easily becomes static. The traditional mutual approach has been shown to quickly become non-accelerating; that is, where a few office-bearers and 'true believers' attempt to serve the mass membership. This type of approach underestimates the potential for member involvement, and does not plan to enable members to move from one level to another over time. A more dynamic approach is to identify stages in the development of a strategy. Drawing on the literature on mobilisation, we present in Figure 10.7 a four-stage model.

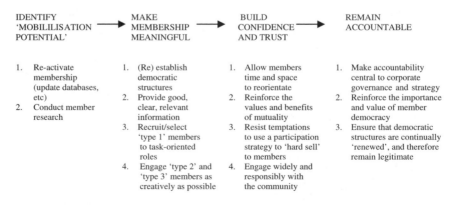

IDENTIFY 'MOBILILISATION POTENTIAL'	→	MAKE MEMBERSHIP MEANINGFUL	→	BUILD CONFIDENCE AND TRUST	→	REMAIN ACCOUNTABLE
1. Re-activate membership (update databases, etc) 2. Conduct member research		1. (Re) establish democratic structures 2. Provide good, clear, relevant information 3. Recruit/select 'type 1' members to task-oriented roles 4. Engage 'type 2' and 'type 3' members as creatively as possible		1. Allow members time and space to reorientate 2. Reinforce the values and benefits of mutuality 3. Resist temptations to use a participation strategy to 'hard sell' to members 4. Engage widely and responsibly with the community		1. Make accountability central to corporate governance and strategy 2. Reinforce the importance and value of member democracy 3. Ensure that democratic structures are continually 'renewed', and therefore remain legitimate

Figure 10.7 A four stage model of mobilisation of members

Identifying the actual 'mobilisation potential' may not be entirely straightforward, and in no large mutual is it likely to be approached in these specific terms. However, similar processes appear to be under way in several large mutuals, which have recently restated their commitment to mutuality. Hence, according to Mertens (1997), as one part of the strategy at the Rabobank in the Netherlands, compulsory membership has been abolished in favour of membership based on freedom of choice. New members would be 'any customer who maintains a significant relationship with the bank'. Heaps (1998) also details how, as part of the members' bonus loyalty scheme at the Britannia, requiring members to register has allowed the society to 'clean up our members' database considerably', and gain 'a clearer understanding of the nature of our relationship with each of our members'.

Identifying the mobilisation potential of the organisation is the first stage. A new, 'accelerating' approach becomes possible, with the relative mass mobilisation of the (in Homans' terms) 'free-riding' membership around core values, and the rebuilding of institutional networks. This can be achieved both by extending the reach of current networks, and forming new, possibly inter-sectoral coalitions (see Coles, 1997). A key challenge will be to increase opportunities for face-to-face interaction between the corporate body and its members, and between members themselves. This may run counter to current business strategies in the world of finance, where increasing numbers of transactions are being encouraged to take place over the internet. However, face-to-face communication has been emphasised by a number of commentators as being important. It increases members' awareness of issues, attitudes and opportunities for action (Parry *et al.*, 1992), and reduces uncertainty and encourages trust (Whiteley and Seyd, 1997). If Llewellyn and Holmes (1991) are right about the extent to which the public no longer understands or cares about mutuality, such a strategy might even prove to be essential. Advertising, public relations and other marketing communications to support member mobilisation, it may be argued, would not have the same effect as face-to-face interaction. As Popkin says, 'campaigns and the media only send the initial messages; until these have been checked with others and validated, their full effects are not felt' (Popkin, 1994, p46). It may be further argued that face-to-face interaction may help to work against the growing form of atomisation and individualisation in society. At present, people are more likely to 'cash in' an identifiable share of something for themselves than feel the desire to share in something much larger but much less tangible with others (e.g. by taking 'windfalls').

The second stage is to make membership meaningful. This involves those methods discussed above of democratic involvement and the provision of better information (clarity guides, etc.), but developed further to involve adding some form of tangibility to membership through face-to face interaction. Hence, the latent potential of the membership might be mobilised through such methods as social and promotional events, open debates and discussions, secondments of staff to community organisations, ensuring a corporate presence at community and other events which help to (re)build networks, and other forms of involvement decided by members (such as sponsorship) with the aim of re-presenting the organisation's association with the values and benefits of mutuality.

The next stage is to build confidence and trust in the membership, to allow members to 'internalise' the message, and to reinforce that message through an emphasis on the (unique?) advantages of mutuality, or the 'co-operative difference'. This includes better deals on mortgages and savings rates, support for fair trade, ethical investment, and so on. The fourth and final stage is then to remain accountable to members through democratic structures, which are reinvigorated and sustained by all of the 'earlier' stages.

For Llewellyn and Holmes (1991, p321) this might represent a 'missionary' approach, or 'a romantic case for "democracy" and "consumer involvement" about which considerable scepticism is warranted'. However, while it may represent an ideal-type scenario, it is not, perhaps, an unattainable one; in all elements of the above there are clear examples to be followed of good practice currently working in co-operative and mutual organisations. Even from an economic viewpoint, the case being made is not based on 'romanticism'. As Heaps (1998) points out, the powerful (often global) corporations which have come increasingly to dominate the business world are beginning to hijack some of the characteristics of mutual institutions. Hence, in the world of finance one may become an American Express Card 'member', or, in retailing, a Tesco Club Card 'member'. Similarly, many such companies are becoming aware of the need to consult with and involve a range of stakeholders over their activities (Turnbull, 1997; Freeman, 1984). However, these initiatives can often amount to little more than a marketing or public relations 'gloss'. 'Members of a mutual need to be reminded that membership gives them something different and something extra and that this is available only because they own the organisation' (Heaps, 1998, p6). In many ways this is an apt message for consumers in the new millennium, for it seems to be saying that style – good products, ethical trading and investment (and substance), genuine democratic accountability and control, involvement with the community – *can* be combined in the large-scale consumer businesses of today.

Conclusion

Large-scale mutuals and co-ops may never become mass-participation organisations, but they can do far more than they are doing at present to promote member participation. They are facing a crisis of legitimacy, and have to demonstrate their right to exist in the mutual form. They have to show that they are in practice what they are in principle – member-owned and member-controlled organisations. They need to integrate into their business planning the needs and priorities of members. There are important lessons to be learned here from the experience of member development in consumer co-operatives. In order to succeed, the participation strategy has to be integrated into the wider business planning of the organisation, and not be seen as a separate activity. There is a need for specialist participation managers, but they have to be located high enough up in the hierarchy to make the strategy count. The strategy has to include staff and member training that stimulates a wide sense of ownership of the strategy. Managers have to be 'value-driven', because it is their job also to identify and seek to meet the needs of people who are not yet members (Davis, 1996).

The spectre of demutualisation is haunting the boardrooms of many insurance mutuals, building societies, co-operative banks and consumer co-operatives around the world. There is a danger that those with a will to survive as mutuals will try to enlist members by superficial attempts to communicate that only confirm what many analysts suspect: they had become arrogant, inward-looking organisations whose managers and boards were accountable to no one but themselves. There is a kind of 'dynamic conservatism' that motivates organisations threatened with take-over to embrace quite radical reform if it means avoiding other changes forced on them from outside. In a study of schools, hospitals and public-sector housing departments, one of the authors of this chapter found that managers were willing to transfer wholesale to a new organisational form in order to safeguard jobs, working practices, and the public service ethos of the organisation. They changed, fundamentally, in order to stay the same (Pollitt and Birchall, 1998). In the short run, mutuals will become better at communicating with their members, but they may not have the technical knowledge or the political will to go beyond the first two levels on the hierarchy suggested above in Figure 10.1. They will change in order to stay the same. However, in the long run, the above analysis suggests that only by embracing an ongoing, radical participation strategy that acknowledges their original nature as member-owned and member-controlled businesses can mutuals convince members and the wider public that they have the right to exist.

References

Almond, G. A. and Verba, S. (1963) *The Civic Culture: Political Attitudes and Democracy in Five Nations*, Princeton, NJ, Princeton University Press.
—— (1989) *The Civic Culture Revisited*, London, Sage.
Argyle, M. (1991) *Co-operation: The Basis of Sociability*, London, Routledge.
Avineri, S. and De-Shalit, A. (eds) (1992) *Communitarianism and Individualism*, Oxford University Press.

Axelrod, R. (1984) *The Evolution of Co-operation*, New York, Basic Books.

Birchall, J. (1984) 'Why should people participate?', *Journal of Co-operative Studies*, 51.

—— (1988a) *What Makes People Co-operate?*, Oxford, Headington Press.

—— (1988b) *Building Communities: The Co-operative Way*, London, Routledge & Kegan Paul.

—— (1989) 'Time, habit and the fraternal impulse', in Young, M. (ed.), *The Rhythms of Society*, London, Routledge.

—— (1994) *Co-op: The People's Business*, Manchester, Manchester University Press.

—— (1997) *The International Co-operative Movement*, Manchester, Manchester University Press.

—— (1998) *A Short History of the UK Co-operative Bank*, Meiji University Guest Lecture Series No. 3, Tokyo.

Coles, A. (1997) *'Building Societies: Why Stay Mutual?'*, Paper to Building Societies Association Conference, 10 September, London.

Dahl, R. A. and Tufte, E. R. (1973) *Size and Democracy*, Palo Alto, Calif., Stanford University Press.

Davis, P. (1996) 'Towards a value-based management culture for membership-based organisations', *Journal of Co-operative Studies*, 29(1), pp. 93–111.

Dawkins, R. (1976; 2nd edn, 1989) *The Selfish Gene*, Oxford, Oxford University Press.

Denzin, H. K. (1989) *The Research Act*, Englewood Cliffs, NJ, Prentice Hall.

Flanagan, M. (2000) 'Mutual friends praise victory vote', *The Scotsman*, 28 June.

Freeman, R. (1984) *Strategic Planning – A Stakeholder Approach*, Boston, Mass., Pitman.

Heaps, J. (1998) 'Making mutuality matter', Paper to Building Societies Association Conference, 3 September, London.

Herald, The (2000) 'A sense of greater good', Leader, 28 June.

Homans, G. (1961) *Social Behaviour: its Elementary Forms*, New York, Harcourt Brace Jovanovich.

Homans, G. (1974) *Social Behaviour: Its Elementary Forms* (second edition), New York, Harcourt Brace Jovanovich.

International Joint Project on Co-operative Democracy (1995) *Making Membership Meaningful: Participatory Democracy in Co-operatives*, Saskatoon, Centre for Study of Co-operatives.

Jakobsen, G. (1995) 'When education for co-operation leads to development in co-operatives: a study of educational processes', *Journal of Rural Co-operation*, 23(2), pp. 119–150.

Klandermans, B. and Oegema, D. (1987) 'Potentials, networks, motivations and barriers: steps towards participation in social movements', *American Sociological Review*, 52, pp. 519–531.

Levi, Y. (1998) 'Local development and co-operatives: none, only one, more than one in the same village', *Journal of Co-operative Studies*, 31(1), pp. 50–77.

Llewellyn, D. and Holmes, M. (1991) 'In defence of mutuality: a redress to an emerging conventional wisdom', *Annals of Public and Co-operative Economics*, 63(3), pp. 319–348.

McConnell, I. (2000) 'Standard Life stays mutual', *The Herald*, 28 June.

Mertens, B. (1997) 'Mutuals in Europe', Paper to Building Societies Association Conference, 10 September, London.

Michels, R. (1949) *Political Parties*, Chicago, Free Press.

Nomura, H. (ed.) (1993) *Seikyo: A Comprehensive Analysis of Consumer Co-operatives in Japan*, Tokyo, Otsuki Shoten.

Oliver, P. (1984) ' "If you don't do it, somebody else will": active and token contributors to local collective action', *American Sociological Review*, 49, pp. 601–610.

Ostergaard, G. and Halsey, A (1965) *Power in Co-operatives*, Oxford; Basil Blackwell.

Parnell, E. (1995) *Reinventing the Co-operative: Enterprises for the Twenty-first Century*, Oxford, Plunkett Foundation.

Parry, G., Moyser, G. and Day, G. (1992) *Political Participation and Democracy in Britain*, Cambridge University Press.

Paul, G. (2000a) 'Standard's life-threatening status', *The Scotsman*, 28 June.

—— (2000b) 'Standard Life will change despite victory', *The Scotsman*, 28 June.

Pestoff, V. (1991) *Between Markets and Politics*, Boulder, Col., Westview Press.

Pollitt, C. and Birchall, J. (1998) *Decentralising Public Service Management*, Basingstoke, Macmillan.

Popkin, S. (1994) *The Reasoning Voter: Communication and Persuasion in Presidential Campaigns*, University of Chicago Press.

Sorokin, P. I. (1954) *The Ways and Power of Love*, Boston, Mass., Beacon Press.

Steel, A. (2000) 'It was all very well for the 1800s but now it simply doesn't pay', *The Scotsman*, 28 June.

Turnbull, S. (1997) 'Stakeholder co-operation', *Journal of Co-operative Studies*, 29(3), pp. 18–52.

Walker, P. (1997) 'The future of UK co-operatives', Paper to Building Societies Association Conference, 10 September, London.

Whiteley, P. and Seyd, P. (1998) 'New Labour, new party? The effects of organisational and constitutional changes on participation in the British Labour Party', Paper given to the Annual Meeting of the American Political Science Association, Boston, Mass.

11 The new mutualism and Labour's Third Way

Stephen Yeo

This chapter examines what the New Labour government might learn from the past and present of co-operative and mutual enterprise in Britain. Until recently, 'co-operation' and the 'co-operative movement' have meant more in Britain than 'mutuality' and mutuals. This may be significant; the strength and continuity of 'the co-op' as quantity in this culture may have weakened 'mutuality' as quality. Large organisations, like tall trees, have consequences for the undergrowth. Boundaries between co-ops and mutuals are imprecise. Some retail co-operative societies have 'mutual' in their title. Co-ops are mutually owned and democratically governed forms of enterprise; participation in them depends on members' humanity, not on the size of their financial stake.'Our humanity is our title deed' said an English Chartist in the 1830s, following Tom Paine in the struggle to detach voting rights from property ownership. Some co-ops trade with, and find ways of sharing surplus with, non-members. Mutuals tend not to do so. Full mutuality implies reciprocity between members rather than anyone else. But hard definitions of co-ops and mutuals, and the alleged differences between them, often stem from the outside – from law and from competitors – as much as from internal practice.

'Mutuality' re-entered national conversation during the late 1990s. Even at the height of working people's co-operative and mutual enterprises in nineteenth-century Britain, 'mutual' was never as familiar a label as 'co-op', 'friendly society', 'union', 'club', or 'industrial and provident society'. The mutual insurance industry provided a possible exception, perhaps because insurance has a built-in element of mutuality to it. Interest in mutuality, mutuals and the 'new mutualism' among policy-makers has, however, been a feature since the mid-1990s. It provides the occasion for this chapter. In a 1999 'audit' of mutuality in Britain, Charles Leadbeater and Ian Christie suggested an inclusive definition of 'a mutual organisation':

> A mutual organisation is owned by its members, who also have a say – usually a vote – in the corporate governance of the organisation ... The distinguishing feature of a mutual is that the member-owners are more than investors. They usually have another relationship

with the mutual, either as consumers, producers or suppliers. The members create and own the organisation either to consume its services or to come together as joint-producers.

(Leadbeater and Christie, 1999, pp15–16)

The roots of New Labour

The Labour Party in Britain has exceptionally deep and strong roots in pre-Party, pre-statist social movements, and co-operative and mutual enterprises. These roots distinguish the Labour Party in Britain from many of its equivalents elsewhere in Europe. New Labour could learn from these pre-1900, roots, provided seven necessary conditions are met.

The first condition is that New Labour continues to get over its initial impatience with the past. If there is to be a New Britain (the title of a 1964 Labour election manifesto), its energies must come from what is, after all, an old set of countries. There has been a young, ugly dismissal of the past in New Labour. 'Baggage' has been deplored. The past itself has been seen as such, by contrast with the 'new'. People without baggage have been preferred. The second condition is that New Labour continues to search for a new politics, with a small 'p', which promotes voluntary, associational activity. Association, and *associationism*, in this context, is used to contrast with *statism*. Statism is by now a familiar label for politics which abstract 'the state', and then give it the definite article, as though 'it' is a thing rather than a set of (changing) relations. In another way of putting it, statist politics reify and enlarge 'the state', while being incapable of re-forming its relations in qualitative, as opposed to quantitative ways. Because statist politics cannot see the state as a changing set of relations, such politics cannot produce wholly new, and more social, relations.

Associationism is also used here, in order to make a contrast with *collectivism*, in a particular sense of rule by professional and managerial experts. 'Collectivism', in this specialised sense, was epitomised in Britain within the Fabianism of Sidney and Beatrice Webb. It informed the Soviet Union, which the Webbs loved (during the 1930s) as a 'new civilisation'. Collectivists also enlarge the state. But they see the state more clearly than as statists. Their project is to re-form the state in the interests of a *nouvelle couche sociale* (an emergent – latterly dominant – class of professionals and managers, during the nineteenth and twentieth centuries).

Associationism, statism and collectivism have been three quite different tendencies within the 'socialist' inheritance. They may be said to represent three socialisms, of which only one, associationism, now offers a democratic, inclusive way forward. Statism and collectivism cannot be 'for all' (see Yeo, 1987a, 1987b; and Hirst, 1994, 2000). Associationism is the way forward, towards which point the 'third sector', the third way and 'social' as the ubiquitous adjective it has now become (social enterprise, the social economy, social investment, social finance, social audit etc.). Its most powerful vehicle will be co-operative and mutual enterprise.

The third condition is that New Labour continues to distance itself, explicitly, from the statist dimensions of its own, twentieth-century, socialist and social democratic inheritance, while also remaining open, as Tony Blair is, to earlier, nineteenth-century, less statist components of liberalism and socialism. In a speech to the National Council of Voluntary Organisations in 1999, the Prime Minister suggested that, while the nineteenth century saw the apotheosis of the individual, and the twentieth that of the state, the twenty-first century could be the age of the voluntary association. The fourth condition is that New Labour becomes more critical of technical, professional and managerial solutions, delivered from above, to problems of anti-social exclusion. And that, correspondingly, New Labour sets about enabling excluded people to include themselves in our own, genuinely social, voluntary, associational solutions to the problems of inequality in the distribution of resources and power.

We *need* to do it ourselves. To the extent that we are enabled to do it ourselves, we shall come, more and more, to *want* to do so. 'They' and 'them', as objects of political policy, will become 'we' and 'us' as subjects of social activity. Redistribution becomes something we do, rather than something they do for, or to, us. One site of struggle here will be over whether and how current government policies on social exclusion are ever implemented in genuinely inclusive, more than piecemeal ways, paying attention to process as well as to output. 'The community' can either be abstracted, like 'the state', or it can materialise, in a multiplicity of forms. Some of these forms will be cussed and full of awkward elbows. They cannot all be streamlined and made smoothly grateful to 'the centre'. Community champions may champion things that politics finds awkward, new or old.

The fifth condition is that New Labour continues its ambition for culture change as well as electoral victories, *power* in civil society as well as governmental *office*. In the three years following May 1997, there was an insistence upon a cultural change (even a cultural revolution) in areas such as lifelong learning. There was also a commitment to the most culturally radical word of all: 'everyone'. Repetition of phrases such as 'the many, not the few' risked ridicule during the first years of New Labour government. Such phrases do not deserve ridicule. 'The many not the few' has not yet become rhetoric, any more than lifelong learning has yet been attenuated into policy targets for specific age-groups. The single word 'everyone' remains the largest difference between New Labour and former New Right politics. 'Social inclusion', 'the many, not the few', 'for all', 'everyone' … remain valuable markers of the sea change in politics that became evident during the late 1990s. The tide remains to be taken.

The sixth condition is that New Labour continues its interest in co-operative and mutual enterprises (CMEs). This is no matter whether CMEs are described as such, or as self-help organisations, social enterprises, community enterprises, the social economy, or the 'third sector'. The numerous recent ways of describing the field of co-operative and mutual enterprise are themselves indicators of powerful developments during the late 1990s. These developments include a Labour Party/Co-operative movement Co-operative Commission. This will report to the Co-operative Congress in May 2001. To put it mildly, such *potential* had not been evident during the previous twenty years. CMEs had become residual, even to themselves. An anti-social condition diagnosed early by Raymond Williams as 'mobile privatisation' had become dominant (Williams, 1964, 1974, 1983). The final condition is that New Labour continues its commitment to lifelong learning, including its own capacity to learn from defeat as well as from victory. Defeat is not the same as failure. Its conditions provide essential clues to subsequent success, in government as well as in opposition. Learning from defeat in opposition was a strength in New Labour. Learning from defeat in government, and thus avoiding failure, was perhaps less evident in New Labour's first term of office.

Old Labour

By *Old Labour* is meant the state-focused political party that was formed in 1900 in Britain. The Labour Party quite quickly adopted the modern, or machine, form of the political party that had been developed by Liberals and Conservatives in Britain since the 1870s. In a word, it aged into Old Labour. During the twentieth century, similarities in organisational form across parties became more striking than differences, in spite of the pre-1900 roots of the Labour Party in co-operative and mutual enterprise. By the time such similarities were discovered by academics in the 1950s, they had become too set to be dissolved. Indeed, the title 'the Labour Party' came to refer to a parliamentary formation rather than a social movement. The productive activity behind the label, however, remained that of independent affiliates. These were societies, federations and unions that formed electoral and other, federal, committees for specific purposes. Labour Representation in Parliament was one of these. Such societies saw association and 'society' as their principal product. Their presence coloured the Labour Party throughout the twentieth century, even while becoming more residual, and less dominant. It is these societies, federations and unions that will be referred to here as 'old, old labour', in contrast to Old Labour. Old Labour is the statist formation, the political party, which gathered strength as the Labour Party, with ups and downs, from 1900 until New Labour. As New Labour pointed out, the downs in terms of electoral victories, exceeded the ups.

'Society' was a real term for future social relations for old, old labour's societies, federations and unions. It was not just an abstract term for present anti-social relations. Social relations were already constituted, as they saw it, by co-operatives, friendly societies, clubs, unions and the like; societies which produced things for themselves rather than policies and representation for other people. Their utopia did not consist of general election victories. Social relations would be extended through the multiplication and federation of CMEs. The Party was not their be all and end all. It was their Political (with a big 'P') umbrella. The umbrella was intended to protect their political (with a small 'p') or associational activity. The much reviled Ramsey Macdonald realised this more than any subsequent Labour Party leader until Tony Blair.

It was through this social activity that the future was to be made – not by Acts of Parliament. The Labour Party (Old Labour) became like other political parties under protest from below. There were battles over organisational form, not over *whether* democracy but *what kind* of democracy: what power should leaders have? How should Conference behave? Who was the 'constituency' of whom? A great deal of cultural creativity 'from below' went into old, old labour's forms and their traces in those of the Labour Party. They were intended to make democracy as direct as it could be on a large scale.

Throughout the twentieth century, Old Labour as a political party retained traces of old, old labour's associational, co-operative and mutual forms. Labour Party branch life – and its ward associations – were not easily obliterated as *social* formations by governmental and political purposes. The realism of delegation was preferred to the abstraction of representation. Subscriptions were collected person to person. Road stewards complemented shop stewards. Ward association meetings retained authority over general management committees, constituency associations over 'agents', political and organisational, rather than ceding such authority to the central Party machine. Devices such as 'affiliation' and 'the block vote' were self-conscious inventions, designed to give very large numbers of *members* of societies, federations and unions power to constitute the body politic, in a way which the idea of 'the individual' and his or her 'access' never could. Membership meant more than votes and subscriptions. The machine-like aspects of the work of the Parliamentary Political Party form, with its large 'P's, were intended to be subordinate to and to serve democratic associations affiliated to it. They were not intended to be the main performance indicator that they became by the end of the twentieth century. The Labour Party could be said to have been 'demutualised' during the twentieth century.

There was no *individual* membership of the Labour Party until 1918. But, far from being in the pocket of trades unions, the Labour Party's alliance, even with them as its main source of affiliated membership, was and remains 'contentious' (Minkin, 1991). Parliament and its programmatic, policy demands, were powerful inhibitors of other democracies in Britain, until New Labour began to disturb the settlement in 1997. All power to Parliament in this Kingdom was the cry, with parliamentary absolutism replacing royal absolutism. The sovereignty of the sovereign transferred swiftly to the Executive in Britain: 'Ministers are Kings in this country', as Hardwicke once remarked. But, in the contentious alliance between unions and Party, there remained the sense from the union side that 'going into union' (as it was known in the early nineteenth century before *trade* unions had differentiated from other forms of union) was a product in and for itself. For co-ops, friendly societies, building societies, clubs, educational societies and associations, going into *their* unions always had been, and remained, their scope and purpose. For trade unions, even at their most structurally differentiated and specialised, 'industrial' relations would not continue in perpetuity, without becoming more social, by means of their unions. It was only from the political side that 'confusing' industrial and political relations became such a sin. For unions, such confusion is a prerequisite of either sets of relations – the industrial and the political – being social-ised. 'Union', in many federal forms, was capable of forming a new, more moral world. This world would be characterised by a new kind of politics, rather than by the old kind run by a different team. The task, as co-operators saw it, was to bring co-operation into politics, and not politics into co-operation.

The new kind of politics would be constituted by CMEs: 'We shall have an association, in which the free development of each is the condition for the free development of all.' Such a vision was never completely rubbed out by politics. Even after all his work towards a welfare state, the Liberal collectivist Willliam Beveridge (a member of the Shepherds' Friendly Society) expressed the vision, at the conclusion of his final major Report (Beveridge, 1948):

> So at last human society may become a friendly society – an Affiliated Order of branches, some large and many small, each with its own life, in freedom, each linked to all the rest by common purpose and by bonds to serve that purpose. So the night's insane dream of power over other men, without limit and without mercy, shall fade. So mankind in brotherhood shall bring back the day.

For much of its life between 1900 and 2000, the statist, parliamentary, 'representational' Labour Party tended to substitute itself – its own parliamentary representatives and their legislative programmes – for voluntary self-activity among its supporting associations, or affiliated organisations. Less and less did Old Labour support the self-activity of old, old labour which had been its matrix. It did not ask its own 'great tradition' to undertake the work it had in hand: the friendly societies to constitute the welfare state, the co-op to constitute associated consumption (or even a consumers' association), clubs to be the limbs of a democratic, and learning, leisure 'industry' (sport as well as drink), the mutual improvement tradition to inspire modern learning centres, unions to socialise 'industrial' relations, building societies to tackle 'the housing problem', and so on. It was a peculiarity of British socio-political development compared to that of other countries, how powerful such self-activity on behalf of labour (with a small 'l') had been during the nineteenth century. And for how long and with what creative strength it preceded the political party formation. After 1900 the division of labour between association and politics slowly became sharper.

The sad results for working people's ideals by the third quarter of the twentieth century were chronicled in the interviews that comprised Jeremy Seabrook's classic, *What Went Wrong?* (Seabrook, 1978*)*. The fact that things *had* gone wrong provided the space into which the New Labour project moved during the 1990s. It continues to provide the space in which to reintroduce that project to its predecessors, as more than baggage. Rather than baggage, we may be dealing with substances that have elective affinity in Goethe's sense, in that they have the potential to 'most decidedly seek and embrace one another, modify one another, and together form a new substance'.

Old, Old Labour

By *old, old labour* is meant collective self-activity by large numbers of working people in large-scale associations mostly created during the nineteenth century. These organisations were trade unions, co-operative societies, and an array of movements including friendly societies, clubs, educational associations and building societies. They were co-operative and mutual in a number of overlapping ways. Doing more than one thing at the same time, rather than 'delivering' a single 'output' is part of what mutuality *is*. They valued *membership*, and sought to give it material, fully corporate, meaning. They valued *democracy*, within and between their own organisations as well as more widely. They sought to give democracy meaning for the many, and to run it through many channels, beyond any single, professional/managerial, political conduit. One of the early impulses behind building societies, for example, was not only equitable allocation of property between members, but also for disenfranchised working people to acquire property at a time when having a vote depended on it. One of the impulses behind the Workers Educational Association (WEA) was to learn in democratic ways, through classes, branches and districts of an association. But it was also to educate for democracy, by means of an appropriate curriculum. Hence struggles between the WEA and other educational associations, for example the Plebs League, over what a democratic curriculum might consist of – a curriculum capable of realising the full potential of working people as the class they had been made into. The form and the content were not divided. If it were only groceries, or insurance, or better-waged work, or houses, or instruction that was delivered, rather than these things in association with each other, as a method of social advance, co-operation and mutuality would not have been the product. A recent revival of interest among co-operators in 'co-operation among co-operators', and in the 'bundling of services', is a sign of renewed interest in mutuality.

The forms of governance and management in these enterprises emphasised equal *ownership*, in material ways, so that members could 'own' their own collective decision-making processes. A sense of owner-ship was being developed which was critical of ownership as the individual, exclusive right to use and to sell. Indeed, the idea that if I own something, no one else has any rights over its use, and I can alienate it when I like, to whom I like, and at the highest price I can get, had a long struggle before it became capitalist common sense. Process was integral to product in co-operative and mutual enterprises. *Divisions of labour* were a social problem to be tackled as well as an economic opportunity to be embraced. The division of labour as the sharing of work was one thing. That was what *co-operation* between large numbers of human beings meant. The division of labour as structured, more or less permanent, differentiation between human beings was quite another thing, leading to deformations of *competition* and *class*. Co-operation and mutuality was about *resisting* class as an excluding category, and *employing* class only for the purposes of moving out of the other side of it, into a commonwealth. Competitive class deformations were to be replaced by social relations described as co-operative, a commonwealth, a friendly society, 'the democracy', 'the nation', and so on.

These enterprises were strong for more than half a century before 1900. They remain strong in the year 2000, and they will probably remain strong during the twenty-first century, regardless of the fate of the fragile political formation, 'New Labour'. It may be important for politicians to perceive that association *takes place*; co-operation and mutuality *happen*. Such even-tuation is human. It does not wait for patrons or for politics. It survives prohibition. The question for New Labour is: can it draw on such strength, historical and modern? The project of old, old labour's associations – called here 'co-operative and mutual enterprises' – has been, broadly speaking, liberal and labour with a small 'l'. Labour refers here to working people. 'Socialist' has not been their preferred self-description. The terms 'social', 'associational' – even 'associationism' – were ones they developed from the early nineteenth century onwards. The terms 'social science', a 'social eco-nomy' and 'the social movement' referred to the working-class movement as the futurity (to use John Stuart Mill's word) of society.

By the end of the nineteenth century, the magnet of an enlarging state, its professionals and managers, had pulled 'socialism' powerfully towards itself, try though some labour activists did to pull it back to their own 'leagues', 'unions', 'federations', and associations. The most important thing to realise about twentieth-century 'socialism' is that the struggle between rival clusters of real potential (class struggle in its real sense) took place within it, at least as much as between it and other '-isms' such as capitalism. Partly for this very reason, old old labour and its enterprises stood apart from this scramble for 'socialism'. Now that New Labour no longer needs to do so it can innovate more boldly. Old old labour, at its strongest and popular best, preferred the practice of possibilities *now*, rather than their postponement until after something else had happened (an election victory, a revolution, the 'downfall of capitalism', the next 'stage of history'). Progress was something they made: not something someone else decreed. It is up to us, all over again.

Co-operative and mutual enterprises (CMEs)

The term 'co-operative and mutual enterprises' is used here to describe old, old labour's associations, their past and their present. This is in the hope that 'CMEs' will become as familiar to practitioners and to policy makers in the early twenty-first century as the term SME (small and medium-sized enterprises) became during the last fifteen years of the twentieth century. New Labour can learn a great deal from CMEs, their past as well as their present. The multiplication of related terms near to policy-making circles – social economy organisations (SEOs), self-help organisations (SHOs), social enterprises, the 'third sector' and 'third way' – shows that New Labour and the new politics more generally, may be beginning to do so. Excellent work has been done recently by outside commentators who have discovered co-operation and mutuality, particularly in its newer forms. Demos and the Institute for Public Policy Research have each promoted such work. Inside the movement, the Plunkett Foundation, the United Kingdom Co-operative Council, the Co-operative Party, and Co-operative Futures have all published actively, in order to promote CMEs as public policy as well as private practice. 'The new mutualism' has joined the new politics.

A third way that constitutes a *different* way of doing things, a different way of making relations more social, may be beginning to emerge. Terms such as 'the third way' can serve to evade. Political leaders are tempted to have it all ways. They state opposites – for example, the private and the public, the competitive and the co-operative – and do not see them as dynamic contradictions capable of becoming a 'new substance'. Opposites may be used to construct sets of social relations different from the *either* and the *or*, but informed by both: new forms of organisation. This is why CMEs remain so fundamental. They have never been easily classified as private or as public; they are challenges to the categories themselves. They were brought into being to challenge those categories. They were never intended to 'fit in'. Hence their affinities with the new politics.

A gigantic theatre of associated life?

It is part of the problem rather than of the solution to focus on numbers. But that there are still forty-six retail co-operative societies with around 4600 outlets, an annual turnover of £5.2 billion in groceries (6 per cent market share) and £8.5 billion in retail as a whole (market share 4 per cent) needs negotiating at least by any Labour government. New Labour has recognised this by agreeing to set up a Co-operative Commission to report on ways forward for the movement to the Co-op Congress of May 2001. Nine million members may constitute something of a network. The same, of course, is true of the seven million members of 233 trades unions – organising one in three of those at work; and of the 214,000 members of relatively new forms such as credit unions, in more than 500 unions with an annual turnover of £105.8 million; and of the approximately 1500 producer or workers' co-operatives that were trading in 1999; and of the 650 branches of the Workers Education Association that worked with 116,000 students during 1999 (Leadbeater and Christie, 1999).

It is these old, old enterprises, rooted in Protestant Nonconformity, and further back than that in 'the medieval world' (Tawney, 1938) which justify the narrative of Britain put forward as part of a 'rebranding' exercise by Mark Leonard of Demos in 1998, as 'the silent revolutionary, constantly inventing new forms of organisation and new ways of running society'. Constituting society through societies, Nonconformist, commercial, co-operative, friendly, recreational, educational, and political was a large-scale, popular activity in Britain from the late eighteenth century until at least the early 1950s. Such productive activity is not easily captured in a comfortable phrase like 'the voluntary sector'.

The period around 1870 to 1914 was a zenith for such activity. During that time CMEs had grown large, and acquired great ambition. Their presence worried not only the state, but also their private competitors. During that period, there was a counter-attack on them, private as well as public. The late 1940s and early 1950s provided another kind of climax. Their role became more prescribed, partly as a result of state favours, and partly as a result of organisational degeneration. They became very large organisations, but less co-operative and mutual. Goals had been displaced by growth. It is the consequences of this period which were being played out in privatisation and atrophy during the last years of the twentieth century. A 'sector' existed, but it was largely without hegemonic (or small 'p') political ambition, and largely sealed off from other 'sectors', public and private. One of the interesting things about the phrase 'the voluntary sector' as used since that time is that it generally leaves out friendly societies, co-operatives, clubs, educational associations, even trade unions. 'Voluntary action' was preferred to 'voluntary organisation' until the late 1950s. The idea of 'sectors' came to prominence during the late 1940s. This was at a time of agreements to partition, or to limit ambition of many kinds in the interests of what came to be known as 'Western democracy'. Obvious examples from the late 1940s and early 1950s were the conflicts over nationalisation, and the consequent demarcation between the 'private' and the 'public' 'sectors'; or the disputes over central Europe in general and Berlin in particular, and the consequent demarcation between opposing national and ideological 'sectors' or zones. Sectors were intended as lines that could not be crossed. No such limits had applied to the ambition of old, old labour as the silent revolutionary, constantly inventing new forms of organisation and new ways of running *society*, not a sector thereof. 'We have resolved,' as a nineteenth-century trade unionist wrote, 'to constitute the society for which we work.'

Creative affinities, new and old

CMEs constitute a rich and now reviving resource, for four reasons. First, there has been a search in the new politics for forms of enterprise and association that are *neither old style private, nor old style public*. CMEs are such forms. They are public in so far as they have open membership. Open membership is 'membership unlimited' in the sense that it is not limited by privilege, or private law, of the kind that excludes by birth, property, class, race, creed or 'attitude', more generally. Faces fit CMEs by virtue of being human, not by virtue of those to whom they belong, and not by virtue of what belongings those people may have: 'Our humanity is our title deed.' 'Members unlimited' was a phrase of the 1790s, expressing what was then a revolutionary claim towards universality, or social inclusion, of the people by the people for the people, everyone. This was revolutionary because it was a claim to extend and thereby to redefine the 'public'. It was an attempt to extend an emergent 'public sphere' beyond an emergent – and self-defining – 'middle class', in unlimited ways. The question at issue was a revolutionary one: did 'the people' or, as Tom Paine used the term, 'the nation', include everyone, or not?

CMEs are public – public-making – in so far as they grow by means of federation, or co-operation among co-operators, until, in aspiration at least, they become universal. The project was for such forms to become the norm; to set the rules of economy and society; to define, in action, a common- or public, wealth, a state of the union, a new moral world. This was a reshaping or rather, a discontinuous extension, of the 'public', redefining that space at a molten moment, just as it was coming into being. It need no longer be for some self-defining 'middle' class, an enclosure for those who brought the language, and fact, of 'class', in its modern sense, into being. It was not to be confined to a hole in the corner. It was not to be limited by being forever emergent or residual (a 'sector') among dominant, old-style 'private' or old-style 'public' forms. It was not to be patronising, or to need patrons (though dispensing with such has been a long and unfinished struggle).

CMEs are private too, in so far as their value accrues to members, as *mutual* capital. The value belongs to no *one* in particular, and can be alienated by no one in particular. Much older ideas of ownership than emergent private capitalist ones were at stake during the early nineteenth century. The question was: could an older 'moral' economy, which centred multiple (not exclusive) use, human need, and customs in common, be customised and made more deliberate through freely chosen 'member-ship' modes. The value in such enterprises belongs to no *one* in particular. But it does belong to users/members, by virtue of their use and membership. Members/users are the owners. Hence the UK Chancellor of the Exchequer, Nigel Lawson's, puzzlement concerning the Trustee Savings Bank movement. None of his minions could tell him who the owners were, in the sense of enabling him to privatise it, or to sell it in such a way as to put money into the 'public' purse, thus reducing 'private' taxation. In a sense in CMEs, ownership is specific, enclosed, or 'private'. But it is not the same as *individual* private ownership. In trusts, ownership rights are held in trust. In CMEs they are held severally, together, or in common. Ownership as membership, is ownership of more than an individual, alienable entity. Membership is of a society that has continuity across time. Such an idea of ownership is both an historical survival, and a future possibility. It was fought over in the early-modern period of British history, as political economy was struggling to make its way. It was fought over again in battles over 'nationalisation', or public or common, or social ownership (that the language wobbled is significant) versus 'private' ownership.

The language is steadier here; we think we know what it means. 'Privatisation' has sparked new interest in these matters in the early twenty-first century, as co-operatives and mutuals struggle to prevent their assimilation to private capitalist modes. Societies exist by virtue of more than singular decisions. Members are heirs to the capital of former members. They are trustees for the capital of future members. That is in the nature of co-operative and mutual enterprise. Ownership means co-owning a society that has an existence beyond the aggregate of any particular cohort of individual owners. Owners (members) have material responsibilities as well as rights, because of the nature of what it is that they own (are members of). Members belong to what they own, as well as the other way round. They are neither subordinate to what other people own, nor superordinate to what they themselves own. They form part of it. Something not easily described as private or public, in the dominant senses of those terms, has been residual in Britain for two centuries. It may now be emergent once more. It will certainly feature in the deliberations of the Co-operative Commission. Commissioners have undertaken to attempt to codify what co-operative and mutual ownership means in such a way as to make it less vulnerable to private greed from without, and from within.

The second affinity of CMEs is that 'the state' is no longer seen as the sole – or even the main – instrument with which to address policy issues. This has been so in the new politics of the Right since the late 1970s. Ever since then, the state has been problematised. This was also the case in the new politics of the Left, at a theoretical and 'community' level since the 1950s, and at a practical, political level since the late 1990s. At a theoretical level, there was an emergent view of the state among tendencies in the

New Left in the 1970s as a set of (changing) relations of production and thus as amenable to reconstitution through newly constructed relations, of a more communal, even co-operative and mutual kind. Powerful critiques of statist social democracy from the Left prepared the way for related critiques from the Right, some fifteen years later. The political centre also distances itself from the state, defining itself as being placed between public and private, state and market.

CMEs do not and never have seen the state as the main instrument with which to address policy issues. Indeed, for CMEs, 'policy' means their own practice rather than that of some other agent. CMEs tend to go direct, rather than through middlemen, against whom they have always worked. People who only add value to, or subtract value from, the productive process by means of an exclusively financial role (like private shareholders) or by means of an exclusively bureaucratic role (like public functionaries) have not been highly rated by CMEs. They join up policy by means of joined-up practice. Joining-up, in that sense, is what they are and what they do. Joining up is done as directly as can be achieved in a complex economy and society. Hence the affinity of CMEs with new political initiatives that attempt to cut out middle layers which are only bureaucratic or financial.

As democracy itself becomes more direct, aided by information and communications technology, political processes will become more available to direct, unmediated reciprocity. CMEs do not endow the state with a capital letter or a definite article. They are not statist, in that sense. And they are not anti-state, either. Unlike the New Right, they tend not to abstract 'the individual'. To abstract the individual is simply to flip the state/ individual coin: two sides of the same coin, historically inseparable. CMEs prefer to deal in other currency. They see the task as that of remaking the changing set of social relations which constitute states. The *prima facie* affinity is more with the Left than with the new Right, in so far as CMEs never considered that 'the state' could be magicked out of existence by sovereign individuals or by the hidden hand of the market. That dream was always likely to work out in exclusive rather than inclusive ways, for the few rather than for everyone. The affinity, however, is not with Old Labour either, which, at its most extreme, magicked the market out of existence. The affinity is with old, old, or pre-statist labour: a deep resource for New Labour, in the lands of its heart where 'these things' are still remembered, and where The Thing (William Cobbett's characterisation of the state apparatus and 'old corruption') has never been seen as an ally.

A third affinity of CMEs is their independence, a virtue that is now highly prized at most points on the new political spectrum. Independence has also been a keyword for old, old labour's associations and enterprises. The proliferation of unions, co-operative societies, local building societies, place-specific and craft-specific friendly societies, mutual improvement societies and institutes that resisted regional let alone national unions, was a feature of nineteenth-century culture in Britain. Pride in independence in CMEs, however, goes with realising that it is not the same as individualism, or with the 'private' in the dominant, individual sense of that word; it is based on association, or getting together. CMEs think and act in the way they do because of their experience that independence is only available to excluded, less privileged people by means of getting together. Independence, for people without 'private' means, demands organised co-operation, which requires specific forms of association: self-generated, self-managed and self-controlled.

The fourth affinity of CMEs is that they are social or co-operative enterprises. There is a new business agenda that, in aspiration and ethos at least, echoes co-operative and mutual language. Competition and co-operation have been put together, in management books with titles such as *Co-opetition* (Nalebuff and Brandenburger, 1997). Dynamic parts of the European model are analysed as *The Associational Economy* (Morgan and Cooke, 1998). Attaching the label 'social' to businesses has become a marketing tool. 'Trust' is no longer seen as oligopoly, but rather as cost saving. 'Social' businesses range from those with good intentions to those with fully socialised forms. Associates, partners, stakeholders, long-term shared destiny (i.e. supply chain) relationships ... are encouraged within and between tomorrow's companies, and between tomorrow's companies and tomorrow's labour force. Upskilling is seen as functional to business in a way that deskilling once was. Qualities such as 'self-reliance, flexibility and breadth' are cultivated generally, in a way that would have astonished the disciples of F. W. Taylor and Henry Ford.

The social division of labour

Giving material expression to such language has been the project of CMEs. Constitutions and rules, values and principles, identities and ethos, partnerships which are co-owned practically as well as in management-speak have been and remain the daily diet of CMEs. The route from naïve, passive consumer-centredness, to user-centredness to partner, to citizen, to member, to informed, active member, is one that co-operative and mutual enterprises set out to travel every day. Such an ambitious destination is seldom reached. But that is the journey.

One way of summarising these creative affinities is that each of them addresses the question: 'Who does what?' This is a simple way of referring to the social division of labour. How the 'who does what?' question is answered determines how social or anti-social the division of labour actually is at any one time. The value that CMEs add may be measured in terms of the 'social-ness', of the division of labour. A *social* division of labour is one that shares the tasks rather than divides the humans. This is what CMEs make: social, rather than anti-social relations.

Another way of describing degrees of sociality in current, new political, terminology is in terms of degrees of social inclusivity. A social division of labour is an inclusive one, in which 'the many' join and own more of what there is to join and own. At its utopian best, this becomes 'all for one and one for all'. A less social division of labour is an exclusive one, in which only 'the few' can join and own. Samuel Smiles, a nineteenth-century prophet of associated or collective self-help rather than of the individualism that appropriated him during the twentieth century, summarised the urge towards sociality, in his revolutionary (liberal) proposition that 'all men might become what some men are'.

Answering the 'Who does what?' question in detail, within and between enterprises, may also be a way of calibrating *degrees* of co-operation and mutuality. It may be a way of answering the question: 'how co-operative and mutual is any given CME?', or, for that matter, 'How co-operative and mutual is the polity – the society itself, as well as the Societies which constitute it?' In their recent work on mutuality, Leadbeater and Christie (1999) discriminate – or clarify the co-operative and mutual difference – by using a distinction between *ethos* and *form*. Some CMEs may be mutual in legal form, or in their rules, or in their Memorandum and Articles of Association, without being mutual in their ethos. Conversely, some companies or voluntary associations may not be co-operative and mutual in their form, but may be more co-operative and mutual in their ethos than some CMEs.

It may be possible to discriminate more precisely than this, by asking the simple question: 'Who does what?' within any particular CME or group of CMEs. If the division of labour can be analysed in an identical way to the way it can be analysed within any other form of enterprise, then it is probable that the enterprise concerned is not very co-operative and mutual. In other words, if managers manage in exactly the same way as in any other enterprise, and Boards govern in exactly the same way as in any other enterprise, and employees work, and consumers consume, and investors invest, and stakes are disposed in exactly the same way as in any other enterprise, then *where is the co-operative and mutual difference?*

An encouraging feature of the present time is that old, old CMEs are putting this question to themselves. They are reinventing themselves, going back to their own values and principles in order to reassess their associational forms (see Chapter 4). The question 'Who does what?' can never receive a finished answer. If it does, the ways in which work is shared will have ossified into divisions of humans.

Such a question is also being put from many sides in the new politics and the wider society. How 'social' is this society, here and now? How might it be made more so? How can we, and us, replace they and them? This is clearly a question that drives Prime Minister Blair. He finds the unequal distribution of life's chances in education, for instance, morally offensive. These are the important questions:

- How values and principles, co-operative and mutual identities, can be shared with everyone who has a stake in the enterprise.

- How *all* members can upskill themselves into knowledge of and conscious participation in the working of the enterprise.
- How the same people can fill different roles at different times (specialisation being a problem for longer-term, universal human development as well as an opportunity for the short-term development of some humans).
- How shared material ownership and shared 'ownership' of a more metaphorical kind ('ownership' of problems and opportunities, as in modern management-speak) can overlap increasingly.
- How Boards can set goals, executives can choose means, managers can manage, electorates can choose, members can join, etc. in ways which, at their weakest, do not *prevent* co-operation and mutuality, and which, at their strongest, actively promote co-operation and mutuality.
- How everyone's stake can be represented deliberately in the enterprise, by means of creative, social invention.

It would have been surprising, perhaps, to many people in yesterday's CMEs, how many of tomorrow's companies now recognise and share many items on such an agenda. The division of labour as the division of classes of humans, one from another, is no longer so acceptable as it was at the time when CMEs began to defend against it, and to attempt to move beyond it. In the current industrial revolution, it has become *economically* important, in the age of information and communications technology, to find forms that work, precisely, against 'divides': the knowledge divide, the skills divide, the information divide, the digital divide. Such divides are no longer seen only or mainly as being socially offensive. They are seen as being economically wasteful, or unproductive. Social inclusion is seen as being necessary if economic potential in the twenty-first century is to be fully realised. In a nice, almost alchemical, irony, lack of co-operation is now seen as 'uncompetitive'.

References

Beveridge, W. (1948) *Voluntary Action*, London, Allen & Unwin.
Leadbeater, C. and Christie, I. (1999) *To Our Mutual Advantage*, London, Demos.
Hirst, P. (1994) *Associative Democracy*, Cambridge, Polity Press.
—— (2000) 'Can associationalism come back?', circulated paper.
Minkin, L. (1991) *The Contentious Alliance: Trade Unions and the Labour Party*, Edinburgh University Press.
Morgan, K. and Cooke, P. (1998) *The Associational Economy: Firms, Regions, and Innovation*, Oxford University Press.
Nalebuff, B. J. and Brandenburger, A. M. (1997) *Co-opetition*, London, HarperCollins.
Seabrook, J. (1978) *What Went Wrong?* London, Gollancz.
Tawney, R. H. (1938) *Religion and the Rise of Capitalism*, Harmondsworth, Penguin.
Williams, R. (1964) *Second Generation*, London, Chatto & Windus.

—— (1974) *Television: Technology and Cultural Form*, London, Fontana.

—— (1983) *Towards 2000*, London, Chatto & Windus.

Yeo, S. (1987a) 'Three socialisms: statism, collectivism, associationism', in Outhwaite, W. and Mulkay, M. (eds), *Social Theory and Social Criticism, Essays for Tom Bottomore*, Oxford, Basil Blackwell, pp. 83–113.

—— (1987b) 'Notes on three socialisms, mainly in late-nineteenth and early-twentieth century Britain', in Levy, C. (ed.), *Socialism and the Intelligentsia 1880–1914*, London, Routledge, pp. 219–270.

Conclusion: the future of mutuality

Johnston Birchall

Around 200 years ago, there was a great burst of activity as people in Britain responded to the new uncertainties and needs thrown up by the industrial revolution. They invented friendly societies, building societies, co-operatives and other types of association. Around 150 years ago, the same thing happened in Germany, with the invention of co-operative credit banking and agricultural co-operation. In the twentieth century the Scandinavians added co-operative housing, and the Quebecois credit unions. For upwards of two centuries, mutual forms of organisation have flourished in the country of their origin, spread to many other countries and evolved into big businesses. They have been destroyed by Fascist governments, taken over by Communist governments, and co-opted by social democratic governments to help run their welfare states. They have some times been ignored by governments, at other times closely regulated. In developing countries, colonial, and then nationalist, governments have tried to implant them as major tools of development, not with as much success as they had expected.

It is only in the last few decades that mutuals have been under serious attack, from intensified competition and in some cases demutualisation. With these attacks have come a reappraisal of their strengths and weaknesses. Looking backwards, some commentators schooled in the individualist way of thinking have struggled to understand a curious form of organisation that seems to be a quaintly outdated form that, it is assumed, cannot possibly compete with the ubiquitous, and triumphant, joint stock company. Historians are perhaps best placed to see them clearly, as time capsules that, often in an attenuated and diluted form, still carry the promise of earlier values – social solidarity, equity, fellowship and association. Economists have dissected them, and found in some cases – notably in the financial service sector – that they have some in-built advantages and not only can compete with their joint stock competitors but should be encouraged to do so. Some political philosophers have discovered in them a communitarian alternative to the atomistic individual, but have perhaps put too much weight on a heterogeneous collection of organisations that are more mundane than that.

What is clear from the foregoing chapters is that there are several trends going in a bewildering variety of directions. Some sectors – building societies, insurance mutuals – are being destroyed by demutualisation, and will continue to be so unless protected by governments. As protection is unlikely (at least in those countries that are in the Anglo-Saxon tradition), we can look forward to the continued destruction of a form whose value we are only just beginning to appreciate. However, a few large mutuals may remain, making a virtue of their difference and offering genuine member benefits. Whether these can become in reality what they are in principle – genuinely democratic, member-owned businesses – is another question. Second, some sectors are less attractive to demutualisers, but are being eroded by fierce competition – consumer co-ops and credit unions come into this category. Third, there are sectors that, in trying to keep up with the competition, want the best of both worlds. They change their ownership structure in a variety of ways, including demutualisation, in order to be able to raise capital, while trying to keep hold of at least a majority share by members – agricultural co-operatives fall into this category. Then there are those that rely on government policies and devolved service delivery to help them to grow; housing co-ops, leisure service trusts and child care co-ops come to mind. These will prosper as local governments come to realise the benefits of devolved service delivery, and of partnerships that harness the energy and participation of citizens.

These trends are not difficult to spot, because they are on the surface, but at a deeper level something more profound and longer-lasting is happening. There is a growing disillusionment with both free markets and public services, with both excessive competition and the 'compulsory co-operation' of the state. Talk of a 'third way' merely clears the ground for the new mood, and the labelling of a third sector, or social economy, merely identifies some organisations that are neither private nor public, that might point the way towards something new. A lot of work remains to be done to specify the type of organisation that can be efficient and effective on the one hand, and ethically responsible and trustworthy on the other. Some kind of synthesis of the best of public and private is called for, not just in the design of organisations – because theorists agree that this is only one factor – but in the way organisations relate to their stakeholders and the wider community. Existing mutuals are only a rough guide to this and, as Shann Turnbull has argued in his chapter, the newly-invented multi-stakeholder mutual may be a way forward. Existing mutuals are also a poor guide to what a truly stakeholder-controlled organisation would look like. As Birchall and Simmons argued in their chapter, they have a long way to go to restore the sense of involvement that mutuals used to provide when they were small and based in real geographical communities.

What we need are some bold experiments in mutuality that are completely new. The recent announcement by the Kelda Group that it intends to set up a mutual to take over ownership of Yorkshire Water

Services (an English water utility) is a signal that the mutual model may yet be an answer to the intractable struggle between private utility company and state regulator. Much of the detail has to be worked out, but utility co-ops around the world (and particularly in rural USA) show how mutual ownership can be made to work. It would be a wonderful irony if the privatisation of public utilities that occurred in the 1980s in Britain were to be reversed, not by more public ownership but by something that has evolved beyond the public–private antinomy altogether. Another new model is the football supporters' trust, which is becoming popular in many British football clubs. The idea is, where possible, to buy out investors and remutualise clubs that had, at one time, been genuine associations. Where this is not possible, the idea is to form a block vote of supporters who, while being individual shareholders, can collectively influence the way the club is run. We may have to stop thinking of mutuality in 'all or nothing' terms – full ownership and control by one stakeholder interest – and begin to see it as a set of principles and practices that can be moulded to fit many different situations.

In the UK, at the present time there is a gap between the rhetoric of government sympathy for mutuality, and concrete policies and practices. The 'new mutualism' may turn out to be an exercise in political 'spin', a carelessly missed opportunity, or the beginning of a new era which is not just marked by a set of policies but also by a new type of relationship between government and citizens. Liberal pluralists have always put great stress on the value of the intermediate associations of citizens that are placed between the individual and the state. They have been less careful in the type of organisation that they advocate; almost anything will do, whether it is a hierarchical church, an authoritarian sect, an exclusive business association or a credit union, as long as it is in some sense voluntary (see Birchall, 1988b, chs 2–3). In future, they will have to be more specific about the kinds of organisations they wish to see promoted; the mutual sector, in its ideal form if not always its practice, challenges us to specify who will own and control our 'civic society', and for whose benefit.

Mutuality as a field of study

Can we now see a distinct field of study opening up, to which several disciplines might contribute? I think so. We may begin with the three-level definition of mutuality. At the top level, we need political philosophers, historians and sociologists to explore the concept of mutuality as a synonym for fraternity or solidarity. At this level we are concerned with one of the most basic political values that is intimately connected with issues such as political legitimacy, the 'democratic spirit' and citizen participation. When he was writing about equality, Tawney commented in relation to equality and liberty that 'fraternity has hardly been considered at all' (1964, p164). More recently, some political philosophers have begun to consider it, calling it by different names such as 'associative democracy' (Hirst, 1994) or community (Boswell, 1990; Etzioni, 1996). Like Peter Kellner, with whose work we began our introduction, I believe that 'mutuality' is a good term because it has not been used much since the nineteenth century, and is free from the ideological overtones with which other concepts are laden (Kellner, 1998). It also has the virtue of connecting abstract discussions of democracy and community with real organisations that are meant to encapsulate these into their design.

At the sociological level, we are concerned with one of the most basic concepts, that of social order; what it is that holds a society together when other social processes – inequality, relative deprivation, class differentials, ethnic struggles – are pulling it apart. The debate on social order used to be captured by a conventional Left–Right argument about how much conflict could be expected in a capitalist society. Functionalists found more social order than was there, Marxists expected more conflict than was there, but both neglected the everyday processes by which various kinds of order were accomplished. Game theorists have shown how order can build up over time, provided that people engage in repeated exchanges and get to know each other. What they miss, and the 'sociology of habit' provides, is the effect of habits and routines that enable people to get by without constantly having to recalculate their own interests (Birchall, 1988a). In the mutual institutions of the nineteenth century we can see something of what Kropotkin called 'a certain collective sense of justice, growing to become a habit' (Kropotkin, 1914, p58).

As Stephen Yeo has shown in the last chapter of this book, historians also have their part to play in evaluating how the capacity for mutual co-operation has varied over time and place, and how the relationship between social, political and economic institutions changes over time. Through the study of mutuality, we can see how these changes constitute no less than a shift in the character of a whole society. Similarly, Deborah Mabbett's chapter has demonstrated how important it is to recover the 'lost history' of mutual forms of organisation, to find out how and when they lost their distinctive character by being squeezed between two more powerful institutions: the state and the market.

At the middle level of our definition of mutuality, we can see how economists and organisation theorists concerned with state regulation and agency costs can contribute to our understanding of the potential of mutual forms of organisation. Their focus may be on the internal workings of the mutual, or on its impact on how markets work and how such values as competitiveness, a long-term view of investment, and accountability to consumers can be pursued. Drake and Llewellyn's chapter is a model here, as is Jerker Nilsson's path-breaking chapter explaining how the form the organisation takes reflects its business environment. Birchall and Simmons show how mutuals, if they are to prove their superiority to investor-owned organisations, have to work at a strategy for member participation that enables them to become in practice what they are in principle. Shann Turnbull's chapter shows how stakeholding has to be designed into organisations if they are to solve their corporate governance problems.

At the base level there is much work to be done on the history of mutual forms, their current situation, problems of management and control, arguments for and against demutualisation, and on the potential for new forms of mutual to emerge to meet a variety of needs. At this level, the rate of growth of mutual forms in different countries, their degree of market penetration, their contribution to meeting the needs of the economically and socially excluded, and more generally of public-service users, are all issues that are vital to public policy. Johnston Birchall's chapter has shown how a mutual institution such as consumer co-operation can survive and adapt over several generations, surviving political repression, cultural deformation and competitive pressures, but having to reinvent itself and develop a new sense of purpose in the world if it is to survive. This kind of historical analysis is necessary if we are to see how mutuals have reached the situation they are in, and are to find ways of reinventing, or relaunching them so as to avoid demutualisation. The chapters by Race Mathews, and by Olive McCarthy and her colleagues, illustrate another technique used at this level – comparative analysis; by studying successful co-operative systems we can begin to assess the potential for this form under different social and economic conditions, and identify what is holding it back. Public policy is concerned with what works, and there is a need for evaluations of the strengths and weaknesses of mutuals that are used to meet public purposes; David Rodgers' closely argued chapter relating housing co-ops to social exclusion is a model of this type of analysis.

What kind of research questions might profitably form the basis of a mutuality research agenda? Many questions can be raised following on from the work of our contributors. Here are a selection:

- Under the impact of threats of demutualisation, can large-scale mutuals and co-operatives find ways of living up to their principles as member-owned businesses, designing into their structures and practices the maximum feasible member participation? Or are they simply too big?
- Can mutuals find ways of distributing some of the their value to members in order to avoid the temptation to demutualise, but without compromising member ownership? Are the ways different in relation to different types of mutual: farmer co-ops, mutual insurance, building societies, consumer co-ops, and so on?
- How strong are the arguments in favour of legislation to stop demutualisation? What kind of legislation is being proposed, and what does it imply for relations between the mutuals, their member and state regulation? Are there any justifications for governments giving tax incentives to mutuals, or is a 'level playing field' between them and their competitors taken as axiomatic?

- What opportunities are there for the development of new forms of mutual, and for the conversion of investor-owned companies (in particular privatised utilities) into mutuals? Should they follow the example of the new football supporters' trusts in the UK, and aim for group ownership within a conventional firm (Michie, 1999), or perhaps aim for a complete buyout, as has been proposed for water companies (Holtham, 1997)?
- What are the blockages to the devolution of public services to mutuals? Are managers and elected councillors really committed to the kind of devolved management and participatory democracy that mutuality implies?
- In those countries where mutuals are used as part of a state-sponsored system to insure the population against basic risks, and to deliver services, how does the performance of such mutuals compare with that of public-sector providers such as the UK National Health Service? Are they closer to their patients? Are the systems of governance and accountability different and, if so, are they more, or less, effective?

There are other, equally urgent questions. For instance, this book has been confined to issues concerning developed countries, but there is a pressing need to find effective ways of dealing with economic development in developing countries, in particular in stemming the migration of people from rural areas, and in stabilising the informal sector in the new megacities. What is the potential for self-help organisations in economic development, and what is the role of international development aid in releasing this potential (see Parnell, 2000)? What should the relationship be between existing mutuals, such as co-operatives and trade unions, and the informal sector economy (see Birchall, 1999)?

Finally, for mutuality to be established as a field of study, then it is important that it be recognised as such and incorporated into the higher education curriculum. For those wishing to teach it there will be a need for a good textbook, as well as some more specialist texts. As our authors demonstrate in their own writings, there is plenty of good material available, but it is quite specialised. What is needed is a work of synthesis, something that enables students to see the subject as a whole. It is hoped that this book may serve that purpose.

References

Birchall, J. (1988a) 'Time, habit and the fraternal impulse', in Young, M. (ed.), *The Rhythms of Society*, London, Routledge.

——(1988b) *Building Communities: The Co-operative Way*, London, Routledge.

——(1999) *A Co-operative Trade Union Strategy for the Informal Sector*, Geneva, International Labour Office.

Boswell, J. (1990) *Community and the Economy: The Theory of Public Co-operation*, London, Routledge.

Etzioni, A. (1996) *The New Golden Rule: Community and Morality in a Democratic Society*, New York, Basic Books.

Hirst, P. (1994) *Associative Democracy: New Forms of Social and Economic Governance*, Cambridge, Mass., Polity Press.

Holtham, G. (1997) 'The water industry: why it should adopt the mutual society model', *Journal of Co-operative Studies*, 29(3), pp. 3–8.

Kellner, P. (1998) *New Mutualism: The Third Way*, London, Co-operative Party.

Kropotkin, P. (1914) *Mutual Aid: A Factor of Evolution*, Boston, Mass., Extending Horizons.

Michie, J. (1999) *New Mutualism, a Golden Goal?*, London, Co-operative Party.

Parnell, E. (2000) *New Mutualism Helping Self-help: Co-operative Action for International Development*, London, Co-operative Party.

Tawney, R. H. (1964) *Equality*, London, George Allen & Unwin.

Index

References to figures are in **bold** type, and those to tables in *italic*.

agency problems 16, 17, 18; conflict between debt and equity holders 30, 32, 33; market competition, effect of 31, 34

agricultural co-operatives: drawbacks of 149, 150; entrepreneurial *see* entrepreneurial agricultural co-operatives; future of 149, 150, 151; organisational form 134, *135*, 139; traditional *see* traditional agricultural co-operatives; *see also* agriculture sector

agriculture sector: economic changes 133; firms' responses to changes 133; political changes 132; technological changes 133; *see also* agricultural co-operatives

Arizmendiarrieta, Don Jose Maria 160; *see also* Mondragon Co-operative Corporation

asset substitution agency problem 30, 32, 33

associationism 227–8

associative governance 171, *172*

Australia; credit unions 163–7

'boomerang' ownership 195

BOOT schemes 186

building societies: agency problems 18, 32, 34, 36, 37; average annual growth rates 22, 23; benefits of mutuality 38; business strategies 24, 29–30; demutualisation 14, 15; future industry profile 38; inter-generation financial transfers 25; market competition, influence of 29–30; performance 32, 34; pressures for

conversion 24, 25, 37; reducing the attraction of conversion 38; relationship between annual growth rate and required rate of return on assets 20, **20**, 21, 22, *22*, 23; reserves, build-up of 24; risk profiles 33; *see also* financial services mutuals

Canada: credit unions 51–4

CCT 98

co-operative and mutual enterprises (CMEs) 234; independence 238–9; open membership 236; ownership 237; policy issues 237, 238; public 236; remaking the changing set of social relations 238; social enterprises, as 239; value accruing to members 236–7; *see also* mutuals

Co-operative Bank 84, 85

Co-operative Commission 235, 237

Co-operative Party 83

Co-operative Services Inc. (Detroit, US) 156

Co-operative Wholesale Society Ltd (CWS) 84; attempted takeover of 85, 86; control of 86; corporate image 85; future of 88–9; ownership structure 84–5; performance of 85; *see also* consumer co-operatives

collective self-activity 232, 233

collectivism 227

commercial loans 167–8

communication problems: organisational hierarchies 179, 195

compound boards: employee ownership 188; examples of 182;

existence of 182; *see also* stakeholder mutuals

compulsory competitive tendering (CCT) 98

consumer co-operatives 72; democratic control of 74, 80–81; dividends 72, 74, 81–2; ethical and environmental policies 83–4, 85; funds, sources of 87–8; historical development of 73–7, 78, 79; incentives to join 74, 82; influence on government policy 83; Japan 72, 79–84; justification for 89–91; management incentives 88; membership of 72, 92; performance of 87, 92; principles of 74, 87, 89, 90–91, 92; problems with movement 77; prospects for take-over of 91–2; protection against market failures 82–3; 'Rochdale Pioneers' 72, 74; size of the movement 74–5, 234; 'social dividends' 82, 88; targeting of members 220; *see also* Co-operative Wholesale Society Ltd

Consumers' Association 83

control: distributed 193, 194–5; forms of *173*

credit unions: access to 41; aid to mutualist businesses 168; Australia 163–7; Canada 51–4; central bodies, role of 42; co-operation, need for 56; commercial loans 167–8; control of 41; developing countries 54–5; development of 42, 43, *43*, 44, *44*, 54, 57; economic development, role in 155, 167, 168; future action required 167–8; government, relationships with 56–7, 166; Ireland 44–6; membership profiles 45, 47, 50, 57; mutual status of 45, 51, 54; need to differentiate themselves 57–8; need to reinvent and reposition themselves 156, 163; operating values 41, 42, 155; prime focus of 41; regulation and legislation 46, 48, 50, 53, 55, 56; safeguards against demutualisation 57, 166, 167; scale and size of operations 42, 44–5, 47, 49, 52, 54, 235; services provided 45, 48, 50, 52–3, 55; taxation 45–6, 48, 53–4; UK 47–9; US 49–51; volunteerism, level of 58; *see also* Mouvement des Caisses Desjardins

CWS *see* Co-operative Wholesale Society Ltd

demutualisation: deregulation, effect of 34; trend towards 14, 15

deregulation: impact on demutualisation 34

Desjardins, Alphonse 42, 156–7; *see also* Mouvement des Caisses Desjardins

distributed control 193, 194–5; competitive advantages of 194

diversified ownership 193

dividends: consumer co-operatives 72, 74, 81–2; 'social dividends' 82, 88

dominant shareholders 182

economic development: role of credit unions 155, 167, 168

employee ownership: compound boards, need for 188; conditions for success 187–8; tax incentives for 187

entrepreneurial agricultural co-operatives 134, *135*, 136, 137, *138*, 140, 141, 142; benefits 136; business activities 140, 141; business strategies *144*, 148, 149; control 136, 140, 141, 142; efficiency of 147–8; investors 137, 140; management 141, 149; membership 141; ownership 136, 140; problems for 147, 148, 149; profit distribution 140, 141, 142

environmental policies: consumer co-operatives 83, 84, 85

ethical policies consumer co-operatives 83, 84, 85

'exit' option 28–9

expense preference behaviour 17, 30–31, 32, 34

farming *see* agriculture sector

financial services mutuals: agency problems 25, 26, 33, 34; board of directors, role of 28; competition and statism 130; competitive advantage, sources of 19; control over assets 25; demutualisation, trend towards 14, 15; efficiency advantages of 19; growth maximisation objective 29; relational contract structures 26; risk profiles 34, 35, 36; suitability of mutuality 19; *see also* building

societies; credit unions; friendly
societies
friendly societies: administration of
sickness benefits 120, 121;
administrative allowances 121;
government intervention 121;
incentives of 122, 124; moral issues
124–5; need for change of policy
125; pooling 121; recruitment
policies 123; surplus income 120;
voluntary insurance 122; *see also*
industrial offices

Gambia: credit unions 54, 55

Honduras; credit unions 54
housing co-operatives 63, 64; benefits
of 64, 65, 66, 67, 68, 69; challenge
for advocates of 65; democracy,
underpinning and protecting 69;
power of tenants 70–71; skills
development, opportunity for 68, 69;
see also housing sector
housing sector: characteristics of 62;
housing conditions 62–3; landlord/
tenant relationship 63; rights of
tenants 63, 70; *see also* housing co-
operatives
human capital 67

individualistic theories of member
participation 209, **210**, 210–12
individuals: ability to communicate and
process information 180, *180*, 181
industrial democracy 161–2
industrial offices 122–3; administration
of sickness benefits 120, 121;
incentives of 122, 124; moral issues
124; recruitment policies 123;
voluntary products 123; *see also*
friendly societies
insurance: historical development 118;
operating procedure 118; *see also*
friendly societies; industrial offices
Ireland: credit unions 44–6

Japan: consumer co-operatives 72,
79–84; keiretsu *see* keiretsu

keiretsu (Japan): feedback information
178, **178**, 179, 194; organisational
structure 185; problems 185

Kellner, Peter 61–2

Labour Party: organisational form 229,
230; relationship with supporting
associations 230, 231, 232; roots 227;
see also New Labour
leisure services: provision of 100, 101,
102; *see also* new leisure trusts
life assurance companies: conversion to
plc status 15; *see also* Standard Life
lifelong learning 229
local government *see* public services
loyalty cards 3

managers: motivation of 17, 27–8;
see also agency problems
MCC *see* Mondragon Co-operative
Corporation
Member participation in mutuals 204–5;
attitudes towards participation 218,
219, 219; decision-making 205, **206**;
individualistic theories of 209, **210**,
210–12; influences on 206; levels of
206; motivation for participation 206,
207; mutualistic theories of 212, **213**,
213–16, **217**, 217–18; need to
promote 222–3; pre-conditions for
207, **208**, 208–9; strategies for 219,
220, **220**, 221–2, 223
Mondragon Co-operative Corporation
(MCC): activities of 161; business
strategy 162; control 161;
development of 160–61; firms'
organisational structure 183;
industrial democracy 161–2; mutualist
values and principles 161;
organisational structure 161, 162,
184; primary co-operatives 161;
secondary support co-operatives
162–3; size of 161; Social Council
183; worker ownership 162
Mouvement des Caisses Desjardins 156;
commitment to continuous
reinvention 157, 158; creation of
new mutualist and co-operative
businesses 159; development of 157;
mutualist values and principles
159–60; regional and local economic
development 158–9; services
provided 157–8; structure 157, 158
'mutual capital' 236
'mutual dividends' 38

mutual support networks 66
mutualistic theories of member
    participation 212, **213**, 213–16, **217**,
    217–18
mutuality: definitions of 3–4, 245, 246,
    247; field of study 245–7; higher
    education curriculum 248; learning
    about 62; research agenda 247–8; *see
    also* mutuals
mutuals: benchmarking of 16;
    definition of 226–7; democratic
    control 203, 204; distinction between
    ethos and form 240; member apathy
    204; member benefits 203; member
    participation *see* member
    participation in mutuals; *see also* co-
    operative and mutual enterprises;
    mutuality

national health insurance scheme:
    creation of 119; *see also* friendly
    societies; industrial offices
New Labour: associationism, need to
    promote 227–8; CMEs 228–9, 234;
    Co-operative Commission 235, 237;
    commitment towards mutualism 1, 2;
    culture change 228; impatience with
    the past 227; lifelong learning 229;
    requirements for 227–9; social
    exclusion 228; 'third way' 234; *see
    also* Labour Party
new leisure trusts (NLTs) 101;
    accountability 105; conditions
    necessary for 102; control 105–6;
    development of 101, 102, 108, 109;
    employee involvement 104; multi-
    stakeholding, implications of 109,
    110; organisational form 101;
    participation of community 107;
    performance issues 103, 104;
    principles of 103–4; regulation of
    111; relationships between partners
    105, 106, 107

organisational form: business
    environment, effect of 132;
    communication problems 179, 195;
    relationship with business structure
    35, 36
OTCs 186
ownership: forms of *173*, 173
ownership transfer corporations (OTCs)
    186

pension provision: competition,
    consequences of 128; government
    promotion of private pensions 126;
    maladministration 127; mutual
    providers of 127, 128; policy debates
    on 128, 129; stakeholding 130
plc *see* public limited companies
privatisation 186; need for distributed
    control 194, 195
profits: distribution of 195–6
property rights and contracts 17
public limited companies (plcs): agency
    problems 27, 30, 32, 33, 34, 36, 37;
    control of assets 26; delegated
    monitoring 28; managers' motivation
    27–8; relationship between annual
    growth rate and required rate of
    return on assets 20, **20**, 21, 22, *23*,
    23; risk profiles 33
public sector reform 95, 96, 97–9, 109;
    managerial *97*, 108, 109; policy *97*,
    108; structural *97*, 108, 109; *see also*
    public services
public services: agencification of 97;
    co-operatives' provision of 111, 112;
    compulsory competitive tendering
    98; customer strategies 98;
    governmental control 110–11;
    influence of local government on
    other agencies 98–9; participation of
    public in policy-making 99;
    partnerships, opportunities for
    99–100; strategic planning 98; *see
    also* new leisure trusts; public sector
    reform

risk profiles 33, 34, 35, 36
'Rochdale Pioneers' 72, 74

shareholders: dominant 182;
    importance of 172
sickness benefits: administration of 120,
    121; *see also* friendly societies;
    industrial offices
'social capital' 68
'social dividends' 82, 88
social division of labour 239, 240, 241
social exclusion 61, 228; causes of 62;
    strategies to combat 61, 62
'social inclusion' 228, 239–40, 241
social relations 239
Solomon Islands: credit unions 55

stakeholder mutuals: accountability 171;
avoidance of corruption 193;
community representatives 191–2;
competitive advantages of 194;
compound boards 182; control 171,
172, 172, 188, 189, **189**, 190;
creation of 186, 188–9; democracy,
enriching 196; division of power 185,
188, 190; governance 171, *172*;
information flows **189**, 190, 191;
ownership 171, *172*, 186, 193; profit
distribution 195; self-regulation 186,
196; strategic stakeholders 171, 190;
tax incentives for transfers of equity
186–7; watchdog committees 191
stakeholder pensions 130
Standard Life 202, 203
strategic stakeholders 171, 172, 173,
190
supervisory boards: evolution of 183;
membership of 183

tax incentives: transfers of equity 186–7
trade unions 235
traditional agricultural co-operatives
134, *135*, 136, 137, *138*, 139–40;
business activities 140; business

strategy 143, *144*, 145, 147; capital
allocations 143; changes to
organisational form 145; control 139;
management 140; market efficiency
142, 143, 145; ownership 139;
problems for 145, *146*, 147; profit
distribution 139; volume of
production 142–3

unitary control: conflicts of interest 174,
175, 176, 192; corruption of power
174, *175*, 176–7; directors,
independence of 176, 177; lack of
independent feedback information
on performance 177, 178, **178**, 179,
193–4; loss of information 179;
problems of 174, 179–81; self-
evaluation 192
United Kingdom: credit unions 47–9
United States: Co-operative Services
Inc. 156; credit unions 49–51

'voluntary sector' 235

watchdog boards 183, 191
workers' co-operatives 235
Workers Education Association 235